D1084971

HAZLETT

Emotional Insight

Emotional Insight

The Epistemic Role of Emotional Experience

Michael S. Brady

OXFORD
UNIVERSITY PRESS

OXFORD

UNIVERSITY PRESS

Great Clarendon Street, Oxford, OX2 6DP,
United Kingdom

Oxford University Press is a department of the University of Oxford.
It furthers the University's objective of excellence in research, scholarship,
and education by publishing worldwide. Oxford is a registered trade mark of
Oxford University Press in the UK and in certain other countries

© Michael S. Brady 2013

The moral rights of the author have been asserted

First Edition published in 2013

Impression: 2

All rights reserved. No part of this publication may be reproduced, stored in
a retrieval system, or transmitted, in any form or by any means, without the
prior permission in writing of Oxford University Press, or as expressly permitted
by law, by licence, or under terms agreed with the appropriate reprographics
rights organization. Enquiries concerning reproduction outside the scope of the
above should be sent to the Rights Department, Oxford University Press, at the
address above

You must not circulate this work in any other form
and you must impose this same condition on any acquirer

Published in the United States of America by Oxford University Press
198 Madison Avenue, New York, NY 10016, United States of America

British Library Cataloguing in Publication Data
Data available

ISBN 978-0-19-968552-3

As printed and bound by
CPI Group (UK) Ltd, Croydon, CR0 4YY

Links to third party websites are provided by Oxford in good faith and
for information only. Oxford disclaims any responsibility for the materials
contained in any third party website referenced in this work.

For my mother Dorothy, and in memory of my father John

Acknowledgements

This book has been a long time coming. ("Not long enough", some might say.) I started thinking about the issues while on Arts & Humanities Research Council (AHRC) funded research leave at the Research School of Social Sciences (RSSS) in Canberra in 2005; two further periods of research leave, in Geneva in 2009, and Glasgow in 2010, resulted in a basic draft of the manuscript, which has been reworked and revised since then. I thank to the AHRC, the Australian National University, and the Universities of Geneva and Glasgow, for their generosity, hospitality, and support.

Some of the ideas in Chapter 2 first appeared in my paper 'The irrationality of recalcitrant emotions' in *Philosophical Studies*; Chapter 3 is a development of the paper 'Emotions, Perceptions, and Reasons', which first appeared in *Morality and the Emotions*, edited by Carla Bagnoli; and an earlier version of some of the material in Chapter 5 was published as 'Virtue, Emotion, and Attention', in a special edition of *Metaphilosophy* edited by Heather Battaly.

I have many intellectual debts. Parts of the book have been presented, in various forms, to audiences in Antwerp, Belfast, Christchurch, Dubrovnik, Edinburgh, Fullerton, Geneva, Glasgow, Hull, Lancaster, Leeds, Lisbon, Manchester, Osnabrück, Prague, Rijeka, Southampton, Stirling, Uppsala, and Weggis. Thanks to the audiences at each for their questions and comments. Particular thanks are due to the following people, whose conversations, criticisms, feedback, and tolerant listening have made this considerably better than it would have been: Carla Bagnoli, Heather Battaly, Anna Bergqvist, J. Adam Carter, Tim Chappell, Alix Cohen, Amy Coplan, Julien Deonna, Sabine Döring, Fabian Dorsch, Jamie Dow, Miranda Fricker, Daniel Friedrich, Akiko Frishchut, Richard Gregory, Emma Gordon, Allan Hazlett, Sonia Hughes, Kevin Mulligan, Courtney Murphy, Ryan Nichols, Renny O'Shea, Graham Peebles, Glen Pettigrove, Nicholas Southwood, Fabrice Teroni, Cain Todd, and David Wall.

I am extremely lucky to have worked in two philosophy departments—at Stirling and Glasgow—that have managed to combine philosophical excellence and impressive sociability. So I'm especially grateful to colleagues past and present—in particular, David Bain, Ben Colburn, Jennifer Corns, Robert Cowan, Rowan Cruft, Antony Duff, Adrian Haddock, Stephan Leuenberger, Sandra Marshall, Alan Millar, Adam Rieger, Martin Smith, Peter Sullivan, Alan Weir, and Mike Wheeler—for their friendship, intellectual help, and dedicated commitment to socializing over the years.

Many thanks to Peter Momtchiloff at Oxford University Press for his patience and support; to the editorial and production teams at OUP for their hard work; and to the referees of the manuscript, Ronald de Sousa and Adam Morton, for extremely helpful comments and suggestions.

I owe a special debt to the following. Stephen Clark let me transfer to study philosophy when I was a recalcitrant and unhappy first-year undergraduate at Liverpool, on the basis of a correct answer to a logic puzzle and a promise to work hard. I've remembered this kindness, and have tried to keep my promise. Peter Goldie was always inspiring, supportive, and generous with his time and his comments; philosophy is the poorer without him. Duncan Pritchard has provided, time and again, extremely valuable feedback and advice, friendship and support. Extra-special thanks are due to Fiona Macpherson, who has read through (and suffered my blethering about) many iterations of this material, and who has lent her considerable philosophical talent to the daunting task of getting me to make some kind of sense. If she has failed to do so, it's not for want of effort, or any reticence in administering, repeatedly, the intellectual equivalent of a Glasgow kiss. Finally, my greatest debt is to my parents, Dorothy and John, and my sisters, Catherine and Frances, who were always there to provide emotional support and understanding whenever these were needed.

Contents

Introduction

The courtroom drama provides a rich source of examples for thinking about epistemological matters. Consider, for instance, Sidney Lumet's classic 1957 film *12 Angry Men*, in which Henry Fonda's juror manages to convince the other jurors of the defendant's innocence, after all but Fonda were initially willing to deliver a 'guilty' verdict. The drama is organized around a host of epistemological issues concerning prejudice and bias, the reliability of testimony, the significance of disagreement, and the status of experts.[1] But central to the film—as the title indicates—is the presence of emotion in the jury room, and in particular the issue of the effects that emotion can have on deliberation and judgement. One such epistemological effect, as we all know, is deleterious. To illustrate, consider the following exchange between Lee J. Cobb's 3rd Juror, and Fonda's 8th Juror.[2]

3RD JUROR: It's these kids—the way they are nowadays . . . When I was a kid I used to call my father "Sir". That's right . . . "Sir". You ever hear a kid call his father that anymore?

8TH JUROR: Fathers don't seem to think it's important anymore.

3RD JUROR: You got any kids?

8TH JUROR: Two.

3RD JUROR: Yeah, well I've got one. He's twenty. We did everything for that boy and what happened? When he was nine he ran away from a fight. I saw him. I was so embarrassed I almost threw up. So I told him right out. "I'm gonna make a man outta you or I'm going to bust you in half trying". Well, I made a man out of him alright. When he was sixteen we had a battle. He hit me in the face. He's big, y'know. I haven't seen him in two years. Rotten kid. You work your heart out . . .

---

[1] To take another example, consider the trial in *To Kill a Mockingbird*, discussed in Miranda Fricker's book *Epistemic Injustice*, Oxford: Oxford University Press (2007).

[2] *Twelve Angry Men*, original screenplay by Reginald Rose (1954); quotations from (1996) Methuen Drama version.

Cobb's character transmutes his sadness and frustration—and possibly guilt and shame—at his estrangement from his son into anger towards the young defendant, who seems to represent a substitute for the son; as a result, he believes the defendant guilty. Here a particular configuration of emotions has a negative epistemological effect: it is because Cobb's character is emotional in these ways that he believes what he does about the young man on trial. And here the drama illustrates part of our common-sense thinking about emotions, which is that they can lead us astray in our beliefs and in our actions. For it is because the 3rd Juror is emotional that he forms his erroneous belief; and it is because the 3rd Juror has this belief that he votes in the way that he does.

However, the film illustrates another, and more optimistic, view of the epistemic and practical effects of emotion. Consider now the following exchange between Fonda, Ed Begley's 10th Juror, and Jack Warden's 6th Juror:

> 8TH JUROR: According to the testimony, the boy looks guilty. Maybe he is. I sat there in court for three days listening while the evidence built up. Everybody sounded so positive, you know, I . . . I began to get a peculiar feeling about this trial. I mean, nothing is that positive. I have questions I would have liked to ask. Maybe they wouldn't have meant anything. I don't know. But I started to feel that the defence counsel wasn't doing his job. He let too many things go. Little things.
> 10TH JUROR: What little things? Listen, when these fellas don't ask questions, that's because they know the answers already and they figure they'll be hurt.
> 8TH JUROR: Maybe. It's also possible for a lawyer to be just plain stupid, isn't it?
> 6TH JUROR: You sound like you've met my brother-in-law.

As the story progresses, we discover of course that there *is* something dubious about the witnesses and the defence counsel; the 8th Juror's feelings *get things right*. Moreover, his reticence to judge the boy guilty, and his coming to realise that the boy is in fact innocent, are grounded in his *trust* in his feelings about the witnesses, the defence council, and the trial as a whole. In this case, the character's emotions have a positive effect along both epistemic and practical dimensions: Fonda's character believes correctly as a result of his feelings, and the outcome is that an innocent man's life is saved.

This illustration of the positive epistemological effects of emotional experience is not anomalous. For it is a commonplace of everyday thinking that our emotions can get things right in this way, and when they do they can inform us about value. It is, indeed, something of a cliché that in certain circumstances—when buying a new house, or deciding whether to change careers, or pondering the marriage proposal—that one should listen to, and sometimes follow, one's 'heart', understood as meaning one's emotional responses to the property, the career, the proposal. Common-sense thus supports the idea that emotions can play a positive epistemic role: emotions can constitute reasons for our beliefs and judgements, or can provide information about our evaluative situation.

But how are we to understand the positive contribution that emotions can make to our epistemic standing? And what are the conditions in which emotions make such a contribution? My aim in this book is to answer these questions. In doing so I hope to illuminate a central tenet of common-sense thinking, contribute to an ongoing debate in the philosophy of emotion, and illustrate something important about the nature of emotion itself. For as will become apparent, the epistemological story that I end up telling will be grounded in a novel and distinctive account of what emotions are and what emotions do. On this account, emotions help to serve our epistemic needs by capturing our attention, and by facilitating a reassessment or reappraisal of the evaluative information that emotions *themselves* provide. As a result, emotions can promote understanding of and insight into ourselves and our evaluative landscape.

The book will be organized around a critical examination of an increasingly popular theory in the philosophy of emotion, namely the *Perceptual Model*. The focus on the perceptual model is warranted for three reasons. The first is that the perceptual model seems better placed to capture our common-sense views about the epistemic role and value of emotion than other, more traditional theories of emotion. Indeed, we'll see that the perceptual model is an attractive prospect for those who favour 'cognitive' theories *and* for those who favour "feeling" theories, since versions of the perceptual model which promise to avoid traditional problems for these theories can be formulated along both cognitivist and feeling-based lines. The second reason is that the perceptual model is characterizable as *primarily* an account of the epistemic role and value of emotional experience. This is because the central claims of the perceptual model are that emotions can play a positive epistemic role by constituting reasons or evidence for evaluative judgements, and that the conditions in which emotions do so are analogous to the conditions in which sensory perceptual experiences constitute reasons or evidence for empirical beliefs. Moreover, the perceptual model would seem to be the only extant account of emotion that can be regarded as explicitly aimed at answering our two questions. It therefore makes an obvious, and natural, focal point for an investigation into this theme.

The third reason for investigating the perceptual model is that it is mistaken; emotions are not akin to perceptions at the epistemic level. Indeed, I will argue that we can only capture our common-sense thinking about the epistemic value of emotion if we *reject* the perceptual model. But this is not a purely negative thesis, since the reasons why the perceptual model is mistaken will bring to light distinctive and hitherto unexamined ways in which emotions can have epistemic value. In other words, a focus on the perceptual model is warranted because the reasons why this model fails to provide adequate answers to our two questions will help to illuminate the epistemic credentials that emotions in fact possess, and thus help us to answer our questions along rather different lines. I propose, therefore, that the common-sense idea that emotions play a positive epistemic role will be best investigated *via* a critical examination of the model of emotion that is explicitly aimed at explaining this idea, and that such an examination will expand and enhance our understanding of the positive epistemic role that emotions can play. The end result will be a deepened appreciation of the truth to be found in our common-sense thinking about emotion, and of what is right, but mainly of what is wrong, with a recent and important development in the theory of emotion. The details of the specific chapters of the book are as follows.

In Chapter 1, I support the idea that emotions can play a positive epistemic role by showing how the idea emerges from a commonplace or platitude about what emotions do, and from close links between emotion and attention. I then investigate what emotions must be like in order to play this epistemic role. I argue that traditional cognitivist and feeling accounts will struggle to capture common-sense thinking about the epistemology of emotion, but that versions of both cognitive and feeling theories might fare better on this score in so far as they embrace the thought that emotional experience is akin to perceptual experience. As a result, I claim that support for the perceptual model can be generated from an examination of the epistemic viability of rival theories of emotion, and that proponents of these theories have good reason to take the model seriously.

Chapter 2 consists of a detailed examination of the perceptual model. As we'll see, the perceptual model is not a single distinctive theory, but a broad church. I consider versions of the theory that maintain that emotional experiences are literally perceptual experiences, and versions that maintain that the former are merely akin to or analogous to the latter. I argue that non-literal versions are more plausible, and then proceed to investigate in some detail the epistemological thesis that is at the heart of all forms of the perceptual model. I first outline the claim that emotional experience is thought to constitute reason or evidence for evaluative judgement, in much the same way that perceptual experience constitutes reason or evidence for empirical judgement. I then fill in this outline, by presenting the standard "indirect realist" account of the role that *perceptual* experience plays in the justification of empirical belief, and by seeing what the perceptual model of emotion looks like on these lines. Finally, I consider, only to reject, the possibility of adopting a "direct realist" account of the role that emotional experience plays in the justification of evaluative belief.

In Chapter 3, I argue that we have good reason to be sceptical about the perceptual model, as presented in Chapter 2, since there are significant disanalogies between emotional and perceptual experience at the epistemic level. These differences are grounded in differences in the *nature* of emotional and perceptual experiences, and, in particular, in the different relations emotional and perceptual experiences have with attention. The idea that emotions can direct our attention is explained in some detail in the first chapter. But in Chapter 3, I claim that emotion can also capture and *consume* attention, and that this serves an important epistemic goal. In particular, I argue that emotions, through the capture and consumption of attention, can motivate the search for reasons that bear on the accuracy of *their own* initial assessment of some object or event, and thus motivate the rational *reappraisal* or *reassessment* of that object or event. If so, however, this suggests that emotional experiences are not reasons for evaluative judgements at all, since such reasons are constituted by the very considerations that bear on the accuracy of emotions themselves. Emotions are not reasons or evidence for evaluative judgements, but instead they motivate the search for considerations that are. If we hold that sensory perceptual experiences *are* reasons or evidence for empirical judgements, then the epistemic analogy between emotions and reasons, and with it the perceptual model of emotion, collapses.

In Chapter 4, I continue the critical examination of the perceptual model, with a view to putting the epistemic credentials of emotions in a more positive light. A central claim, in this chapter and the next, is that we can give due credit to emotion's positive epistemic influence only if we reject the perceptual model of emotion. I begin by claiming that even though emotions are not genuine reasons for evaluative judgements, they might nevertheless play a positive epistemic role in so far as they can be *proxies* or *substitutes* for such reasons. I then argue that the perceptual model, in thinking that the epistemic yield of emotions mirrors that of perceptions, actually obscures or understates the epistemic importance of emotion. This is because emotion has an epistemic role to play that goes beyond that played by perceptual experience, a role which (as I argue in Chapter 3) is strongly linked to the idea that emotion facilitates its own reappraisal through the capture of attention. I provide more details of this picture here, by maintaining that emotional experience can (thereby) promote evaluative *understanding*, and in doing so serves an epistemic need. This illustrates two things: first, why it is not permissible for us to rest content with the epistemic deliverances of our emotional experiences, in conditions where evaluative understanding is available; and second, why emotional experience has value that is not envisaged by common-sense thinking or philosophical orthodoxy. As such, criticism of the perceptual model, far from debunking the epistemic credentials of emotional experience, actually illuminates the significant epistemic value that emotional experience has.

The proposal that emotions can, through the capture of attention, promote evaluative understanding needs further development and support, however. For it seems obvious that emotional effects on attention can be negative as well as positive, in which case I need to specify or explain the *conditions* in which emotions play the positive and novel epistemic role that I have identified. In the final chapter I attempt to provide such a specification by appealing to the *virtuous* governance of attention. I argue that such governance is itself dependent upon understanding in a number of ways. I then argue that this account of virtue, emotion, and attention allows us to explain what the perceptual model cannot, namely the conditions in which we are *right* to rest content with what our emotional proxies tell us about value. As such, the account I develop in Chapter 5 explains the conditions in which emotions play the distinctive epistemic role that I identify in the previous chapter, *and* also allows us to capture the common-sense thought that in certain conditions at least, we are right to put our trust in the deliverances of our emotions. My account therefore promises to deliver what the perceptual model cannot, namely a plausible way in which we can capture common-sense thinking about emotion's epistemic credentials. But it also illustrates how emotions have epistemic roles and value, in facilitating their own reassessment and in promoting evaluative understanding of our evaluative situation, that go a good deal beyond what common-sense and philosophical orthodoxy have supposed.

Let us proceed, then, to explore how we ought to understand the idea that emotions can make a positive contribution to our epistemic standing, and discover the conditions in which emotions can do so.

1

Towards the Perceptual Model

It is a staple of common-sense thinking about the mind that emotions have significant practical value. Emotions can, for instance, be responsible for setting up goals or ends, as when my shame over my behaviour at the Christmas party moves me to give up drinking. Emotions can enable us to stick to our plans, as when pride at giving up smoking strengthens my resolve so that I don't give in to temptation. Emotions are capable of moving us directly to do something that we have reason to do, as when disgust at the mouldy bread prevents me from eating it. And emotions often have strategic value, as when my angry disposition is responsible for me being left alone to work uninterrupted by colleagues. It is, of course, uncontroversial that emotions can have *disvalue* from the practical stand-point: we all know the negative effects that shame, pride, and anger can have. But this should not blind us to the obvious fact that emotion, when properly regulated and controlled, plays a vital role in our practical lives. Although emotions can lead us astray, it is doubtful whether we could achieve much if anything in the way of successful pursuit of our practical goals and ends without the capacity to experience (when appropriate) fear and anger, pride and joy, shame and guilt, curiosity and love, and the very many other emotional responses that characterize human lives.[1]

This fact suggests and supports another tenet of common-sense thinking, namely that emotions have significant *epistemic* value. Emotions can, that is,

[1] For a recent and influential account of the necessity of emotions for successful deliberation and decision, see Damasio, A. *Descartes' Error*, New York: G. B. Putnam's Sons (1994). Damasio's point isn't, of course, that emotion *guarantees* successful deliberation and decision, but that "certain aspects of the process of emotion and feeling are indispensable for rationality" (p. xxiii). Rational decision-making needs emotion, therefore, even though emotion is often not sufficient for the making of good decisions.

enhance our standing with respect to our beliefs and judgements. This would seem to follow directly from the idea that emotions have practical value, given that practical achievements require or depend upon suitable epistemic states. But it also enjoys support from everyday experience: emotions can make things salient for us, as when my nervousness draws my attention to how many people have come to see the talk, or my anger makes me notice just how loud my fellow passengers are when talking on their mobile phones. Emotions can inform us about value, as when my feeling of happiness on seeing her again tells me how lovable she is, or when my feelings of suspicion let me know that the salesman isn't to be trusted. Emotions can tell us things about ourselves, as when my pride upon hearing about English football hooligans rampaging through a European city informs me that I have dubious nationalistic commitments, or when my disappointment upon being overlooked for the role of Head of Department tells me that I really wanted the job. Again, it is uncontroversial to hold that emotions can and often do make us epistemically worse off: we all know the negative epistemic effects of jealousy, fear, and hope. Still, this should not blind us to the obvious fact that emotion, when properly regulated and controlled, plays a vital role in our epistemic lives. Although emotions can lead us astray epistemically, it is doubtful that we could attain the epistemic positions required for the successful pursuit of our goals, or have the same access to value, or attend to all of the things that we ought to attend to, in the absence of (appropriate) emotion.

The aim of this book is to investigate the idea that emotions enhance our epistemic standing, the ways in which emotions can do so, and the conditions that facilitate these outcomes. In particular, I want to investigate something that is both a central element of common-sense thinking about the epistemic value of emotion, and an issue of importance in moral epistemology, namely the thought that emotions have significant relations with our beliefs about or knowledge of *value*. Now the idea that emotions have epistemic importance is not new; there is, after all, a literature on emotions that have particular epistemic ends: these include "curiosity, intellectual courage, love of truth, wonder, meticulousness, excitement, humility".[2] But my investigation is not restricted to these particular

---

[2] Morton, A. 'Epistemic Emotions', in *The Oxford Handbook of Philosophy of Emotion*, Goldie, P. (ed.), Oxford: Oxford University Press (2010), p. 386. See also Stocker, M. 'Intellectual and other Nonstandard Emotions', in the same volume.

emotions; it has, instead, the goal of examining the epistemic value of emotions in general: that is, of central and paradigm cases of emotion such as fear and anger, joy and pride, jealousy and guilt, love and admiration. The story I will ultimately tell will be applicable to these central cases; but it will also be applicable to the kind of "epistemic" emotions just mentioned. On my view, then, many more emotions will turn out to be epistemic emotions than philosophers of emotion have traditionally thought.

In this chapter, my aim is to first explain how the above thoughts about the epistemic role and value of emotion fall out of a *platitude* about the nature of emotion, and as such are supported by reflection on a commonplace about what emotions are and what emotions do. I will then consider what emotions must be like in order that they can play these roles and have this value. I will argue that such consideration pushes us in the direction of the 'perceptual model' of emotion, so that the model emerges as a plausible attempt to capture our common-sense thinking about the epistemic role and value of emotional experience. This will motivate a detailed examination of the perceptual model in the chapters to follow. As we will see, this examination will reveal that emotion has epistemic value in important and hitherto unacknowledged ways. Let us turn then to one of the few uncontroversial claims we can make about emotions, which will prove as good a starting place as any for our investigation.

1.1 A platitude about emotion

It is a platitude that emotions constitute reactions to objects, events, and states of affairs that are potentially significant or important to us. Thus, as Annette Baier writes: "[w]e all accept the idea that emotions are reactions to matters of apparent importance to us: fear to danger, surprise to the unexpected, outrage to insult, disgust to what will make us sick, envy of the more favoured, gratitude for benefactors, hate for enemies, love for friends, and so on."[3] It is also a commonplace that what is potentially significant or important to us is a matter of what we care or are concerned about. Without such concern, it is puzzling how there could be an

---

[3] Baier, A., 'Feelings that Matter', in *Thinking about Feeling*, Solomon, R. (ed.), Oxford: Oxford University Press (2004), p. 200.

emotional response in the first place. Thus, it is because I love my wife that her welfare is especially significant for me, and this explains why I'm afraid when I hear that driving conditions on her evening commute are hazardous. It is because I'm concerned about my self-image that it is important what my colleagues think of me, which explains why I'm embarrassed at asking a stupid question during the seminar. And it is because I care about my community that the state of the local park matters to me, which explains why I get angry when people dump rubbish there. In the absence of these concerns, it is difficult to understand why I would feel fear, embarrassment, or anger in these cases.[4]

The idea that emotions are reactions to matters of apparent importance or significance, and grounded in our cares and concerns, suggests that emotions involve or motivate a *behavioural response* to such things. This is in line with our experience of emotion: fear often motivates a quick exit, anger a confrontation, disgust a recoil, surprise a leap in the air. And even if emotions don't necessarily motivate action, it is plausible to think that emotions typically involve the subject being *primed* to do something in response to the relevant object or event. I might not actually confront you when angry at your sarcastic remark, but my anger prepares me or readies me for a confrontation. So the practical response involved in an emotional reaction can be plausibly viewed as the mobilization of behavioural resources, which prepares the subject for action in response to the object or event, and which often or perhaps typically results in behaviour. Of course, as was clear from my earlier remarks, this platitude, and the idea that emotions have the role of preparing an appropriate behavioural response to important objects and events, does not imply that the behaviour that emotion motivates (or primes us to enact) will always be appropriate. Perhaps my behavioural response to your sarcasm is disproportionate, as when I punch you; perhaps my attempt to make a quick exit

---

[4] Cares and concerns are standardly understood not as emotional attitudes themselves, but as values or goals that underpin emotional attitudes. Thus, Gerald Clore writes: "[t]he idea is that one has a variety of general goals, standards, and attitudes. These are cognitive prerequisites for emotion because without these structures nothing matters to the person." 'Why Emotions Require Cognition', in *The Nature of Emotion*, Ekman, P. and Davidson, R. (eds), Oxford: Oxford University Press (1994), p. 188. And Richard Lazarus claims that "the bottom cognitive line that must prevail for an emotion to occur is that a goal is judged at stake in the encounter, which is called goal relevance. If there is no goal at stake, and none emerges from the encounter, there is no possibility of an emotion taking place." In Lazarus, R., 'Appraisal: The Long and the Short of it', in Ekman and Davidson (eds) (1994), p. 211.

raises the level of danger as it prompts the animal to attack. Nevertheless, the fact that emotions can motivate the wrong kinds of behaviour in response to potentially important objects and events is obviously compatible with the claim that emotions are in the business of promoting action in order to deal with such objects and events. The claim that the function of emotion is to facilitate an appropriate behavioural response is clearly not undermined by the fact that sometimes emotions move us to do the wrong thing—any more than the claim that the function of perceptual experience is to give us knowledge of the external world is undermined by the fact that our perceptual experiences sometimes lead us astray.[5]

The idea that emotions involve or motivate a behavioural response to important objects and events is a useful starting point for an investigation into the epistemic value of emotions. This is because appropriate behaviour typically requires us to be in a suitable epistemic state, and I want to argue that emotions, when properly controlled and regulated, have significant value in enabling us to attain such states. In other words, I propose that emotions have significant value in so far as they enable a subject to be in the epistemic conditions that are necessary for the appropriate behavioural response to danger, loss, insults, and the like.[6] The account of the epistemic value of emotion that results from this investigation will, however, be rather complex. One reason for this is that appropriate behaviour will require different epistemic states in different circumstances, and part of the story I wish to tell is how emotion has epistemic value in enabling us to be in these different states or conditions. A second reason is that emotion has epistemic value in more "direct" senses that are not so tightly tied to behaviour. A third reason is that the account will combine psychological and normative elements. I want to argue that emotions enhance our epistemic standing both with respect to what we actually care about—that is, to things that are important or significant to us

---

[5] I use "function" here in the weak sense implying something that emotion typically does, rather than the stronger sense of something that emotion has evolved, through a process of natural selection, to do. I make no claims about the biological function of emotion (or indeed perception).

[6] There are interesting cases where successful behaviour requires or is aided by *false* belief: for instance, I might be confident enough to deliver a fluent and successful lecture only if I falsely believe that most of the students like me. I assume, however, that in the majority of cases, successful behaviour requires true belief, so will restrict my focus to these instances.

as we actually are—and enable us to get a better grasp of things which we *ought* to be concerned with—that is, to things that are *genuinely* important or significant. Despite these complications, we can say that the account, in outline, is that emotions have significant epistemic value, under the right conditions, along the following three dimensions:

(i) Emotions can have epistemic value when it comes to the detection of important objects and events, something which is clearly necessary for an appropriate behavioural response *to* such things. One aspect of this is that emotions can improve the speed at which we notice the relevant objects and events in our environment, and in a way that is relatively "cost-free". As a result, emotions can have value in so far as they facilitate a 'fast and frugal' detection of important objects and events. Another aspect of this is that emotion is very often the way in which *the value of* significant things registers with us, such that without emotion the import of many such objects and events would pass us by. So it is not just that emotion *can* have epistemic value when it comes to the detection of important objects and events in the relevant conditions; we can, in addition, make the stronger claim that we would be worse off, from the standpoint of noticing things that we ought to notice, in the absence of emotion.

(ii) Emotions can have epistemic value because they involve an appraisal or assessment of a situation. Such assessment is also needed for appropriate behaviour, since this requires not just that we notice some potentially important object or event and register its import; it also requires an assessment or appraisal of *the way in which* the object or event is important or significant. But the idea that emotions involve evaluations of objects and events suggests that emotions can have epistemic value in a more straightforward, non-behavioural sense. For if emotions involve evaluations, then it seems clear that emotions can, under the right conditions, inform us about, or enable us to have access to, value. Emotions can, in other words, play a role in grounding evaluative judgement or belief, or in generating evaluative knowledge. This is, of course, one of the roles that common-sense thinking assigns to emotions; common-sense has it that fear can tell me about danger, jealousy about infidelity, joy about good things, disappointment about violated expectations, and so on.[7] The idea, therefore, that emotions enable us to respond appropriately to important objects and events suggests that emotions involve assessments or appraisals. And the idea that emotions involve assessments or appraisals suggests that emotions can, in the right conditions, constitute reasons or evidence for evaluative judgement. Emotions can, in other words, help to justify our evaluative judgements and generate evaluative knowledge.[8]

(iii) The thought that emotions can inform us about value indicates a third way in which emotions can play an important epistemic role. For emotions not only involve assessments or appraisals of objects and events; emotions can also motivate a reassessment or reappraisal of the objects and events, and in so doing can promote evaluative *understanding*. This form of assessment is also needed for appropriate behaviour in some circumstances, since appropriate behaviour will sometimes require not just that we correctly believe or know *that* some object has some evaluative property, but also to understand

---

[7] This raises, of course, the large and difficult question of the *nature* of these values. Thankfully, my criticisms of the perceptual model of emotion, and my positive account of the epistemic value that emotion has, don't require me to do anything as ambitious as trying to settle the question of what it is for something to be dangerous, insulting, morally wrong, etc. (This is a good thing, since I don't *have* a way of settling this question.) What the criticisms and positive account do require is that we rule out "dispositionalist" accounts of these values, and adopt something at least as strong as a "rational sentimentalist" view. On the former, dangerousness is a matter of what we are disposed to fear, wrongness a matter of what we are disposed to feel guilty about, at least under certain conditions. On the latter, dangerousness is a matter of what we have *reason* to fear, wrongness a matter of what we have *reason* to feel guilty about. And I think that there are good reasons—as presented and explained by Justin D'Arms and Daniel Jacobson—to favour rational versions of sentimentalism over dispositionalist accounts. (For references and further discussion, see Chapter 3, § 5.) Rational sentimentalism is, it seems, compatible with cognitivist and non-cognitivist accounts, so my views should be acceptable to those in the former camp (like McDowell) and those in the latter (such as Blackburn and Gibbard). In addition, my views should also be compatible with stronger versions of value realism. As a result, although dispositionalists might not find my account acceptable given their views on the nature of value, it seems to me that most other theorists writing on value theory or metaethics ought to find nothing objectionable in the account on *this* issue at least.

[8] Are there systematic differences between emotions with respect to their epistemic value? Might some emotions tend to alert us more reliably to important objects or events, or tend to generate more true beliefs than other emotions? Indeed, might it be the case that there are some emotions that we would, from an epistemic standpoint, be better off without? These are difficult questions. In the final chapter, I consider emotions that might systematically lead us astray, or, following Peter Goldie, "skew the epistemic landscape". But I argue in that chapter that even these emotions can have epistemic value in so far as they are governed or controlled by virtuous habits of attention.

why this is the case. Appropriate behaviour can require, that is, an understanding of one's environment, an insight into the value of the objects and events therein. For example, an appropriate apology requires that one understand why one's behaviour was wrong, and not merely that it was wrong. In addition, emotions can motivate a reassessment or reappraisal of the concerns that underlie our emotional responses, and as such can promote more accurate evaluative knowledge about and understanding of *ourselves*. Again, the idea that emotions can promote evaluative understanding of both kinds indicates that emotions can have epistemic value in a more straightforward or direct sense. This is because we might think that understanding is our ultimate epistemic goal, and as such emotions can have value in so far as they enable us to attain the highest epistemic good. Finally, the fact that emotion has epistemic value on this dimension will have a bearing on the story we tell about the epistemic value of emotion on our other two dimensions. Put simply, the fact that emotions motivate reappraisal and reassessment and thereby facilitate evaluative understanding can enable emotions to more efficiently alert us to things that we ought to notice, and to inform us about value. It is in this way that the normative importance of emotion in motivating reappraisal and reassessment can have a positive impact on the psychological functioning of emotion in alerting us to and appraising things that we actually care about. Emotion, through promoting insight and understanding, enhances our epistemic standing and psychological capacities.[9]

This last point indicates the relation between the value of emotion on one dimension and the value of emotion on others. As such, a *complete* account of the epistemic value of emotion on all three dimensions will only emerge towards the end of the book, when I develop the proposal that emotions promote understanding and specify the conditions in which emotions can do so. For the rest of this chapter, my aim will be to focus on the first two ways in which emotions are thought to have epistemic value, and then

---

[9] As we'll see, emotion, through promoting understanding, can also ground a non-emotional capacity to recognize value, and in this way enhance our non-emotional epistemic abilities.

consider the question of what emotions must be like in order to have value in these ways. As we'll see, this discussion will provide a good deal of support to the perceptual model of emotion. And it is the perceptual model which will be both the focus of investigation in the chapters to follow, and the motivation for my own account of the relation between emotion and understanding.

1.2 Emotion, attention, and salience

Emotions have epistemic value along the first dimension in so far as they enable us to detect potentially important objects and events. There are two elements to this picture: first, emotions have epistemic value in so far as they alert us to the presence of such objects and events quickly and at little mental cost; second, emotions have epistemic value in so far as they alert us to objects and events that we would otherwise have missed. So without emotion, we would often fail to notice things that we ought to notice; and without emotion, the costs of noticing things that we do notice will typically be higher. The idea that emotions have value along this dimension is often cashed out as the thought that emotions help to make important things *salient* for us. And a common way of explaining this is by saying that emotions capture our *attention*.[10] Now the notion of attention—and of the relations between emotion and attention—will be of importance throughout this book, so it will be useful to explain the concept in some detail, both in order to explain and defend the idea that emotions have value along this first dimension, and in order to set the stage for later arguments and discussion.

There has been relatively little philosophical work on attention. Malebranche and Reid are notable historical figures with an interest in the subject;[11] Merleau-Ponty and other representatives of the phenomenological tradition

---

[10] Thus, Elgin writes that, "Emotions are sources of salience. They fix patterns of attention, highlighting certain features of a domain and obscuring others." 'Emotion and Understanding', in *Epistemology and Emotions*, Brun, G., Doğuoğlu, U., and Kuenzle, D. (eds), Farnham: Ashgate Publishing (2008), p. 43.

[11] Malebranche, N., *The Search After Truth*, Columbus, OH: Ohio University Press (1674/1980); Reid, T., *Essays on the Active Powers of the Human Mind*, Brody, B. (ed.), Cambridge, Mass.: MIT Press (1969).

took attention to be philosophically important.[12] More recently, de Sousa, Robinson, Evans, Faucher and Tappolet, and White have all addressed the subject;[13] and there is increased interest in the topic from philosophers of mind and cognitive science, such as Christopher Mole.[14] There is, however, a much more significant literature in psychology and cognitive science on the subject.[15] A good place to start, as with other psychological writings on emotion, is with William James. According to James, "[e]veryone knows what attention is. It is the taking possession by the mind, in clear and vivid form, of one of what seem several simultaneously possible objects or trains of thought. Focalization, concentration, of consciousness are of its essence. It implies withdrawal from some things in order to deal effectively with others."[16]

There are a number of important ideas here which seem central to our notion of what attention is and what attention does. One of these is *selectivity* or choice of some object or idea.[17] Attention involves focusing on some object or idea at the expense of other objects and ideas. But

[12] Merleau-Ponty, M., *Phenomenology of Perception*, trans. Smith, C., London: Routledge (1945/2008).

[13] de Sousa, R., *The Rationality of Emotion*, Cambridge, MA: MIT Press (1987); Robinson, J., 'Startle', *Journal of Philosophy* (1995), 92(2): 53–74; Evans, D., *The Science of Sentiment*, New York: Oxford University Press (2001); Faucher, L. and Tappolet, C., 'Fear and the Focus of Attention', *Consciousness and Emotion* (2002), 3(2): 105–44; White, A. R., *Attention*, Oxford: Basil Blackwell Publishers (1964).

[14] See Mole, C., *Attention is Cognitive Unison*, Oxford: Oxford University Press (2010); and Mole, C., Smithies, D., and Wu, W. (eds), *Attention: Philosophical and Psychological Essays*, Oxford: Oxford University Press (2011).

[15] The following represent some of the major works, but the psychological literature on attention is vast: Matthews, G. and Wells, A., *Attention and Emotion: A Clinical Perspective*, Hove: Lawrence Earlbaum Associates (1994); Derryberry, D. and Tucker, D., 'Motivating the Focus of Attention', in Niedenthal, P. and Kitayama, S. (eds), *The Heart's Eye: Emotional Influences in Perception and Attention*, London: Academic Press (1994), 167–96; Duncan, J., 'Attention', in Wilson, R. and Keil, F. (eds), *The MIT Encyclopedia of Cognitive Sciences*, Cambridge, MA: MIT Press (1999), 39–41; Pashler, H., *The Psychology of Attention*, Cambridge, MA: MIT Press (1998); Matthews, G. and Wells, A., 'The cognitive science of attention and emotion', in Dalgleish, T. and Power, M. (eds), *Handbook of Cognition and Emotion*, Chichester: Wiley (1999); Öhman, A., Flykt, A., and Esteves, F., 'Emotion drives attention: Detecting the snake in the grass', *Journal of Experimental Psychology* (2001), 130(3): 466–78; Posner, M., 'Attention in cognitive science: An overview', in Gazzaniga, M. (ed.), *The Cognitive Neurosciences*, Cambridge, MA: MIT Press, (1995), 615–24; Styles, E. A., *The Psychology of Attention*, New York: Psychology Press (1997); Johnson, A. and Proctor, R., *Attention: Theory and Practice*, London: Sage Publications (2004).

[16] James, W., *The Principles of Psychology*, Cambridge, MA: Harvard University Press (1890/1983), 403–4.

[17] Faucher and Tappolet (2002) note: "The contemporary research tradition on attention has followed James in thinking that selectivity in information processing is the essence of attention", p. 112.

selectivity, even if a central aspect of attention, is not the only notable feature. For James also mentions the "clear and vivid form" that the mind has of the object of attention, which suggests that *clarity* is also a characteristic. This thought about attention is not particular to James, but is, as Johnson and Proctor note, a central theme in the history of thinking about attention.[18] Thus, Malebranche claimed that attention (or attentiveness) essentially involved clarity: "It is . . . necessary to look for means to keep our perceptions from being confused and imperfect. And, because, as anyone knows, there is nothing that makes them clearer and more distinct than attentiveness, we must try to find the means to become more attentive than we are."[19] Similar thoughts can be found in other important early psychological texts. Titchener writes that "[i]t seems to be beyond question that the problem of attention centers in the fact of sensible clearness."[20] Pillsbury holds that "[t]he essence of attention as a conscious process is an increase in the clearness of one idea or a group of ideas at the expense of others."[21] And Wundt maintains that "an increased clearness of ideas" is an "essential constituent" of attention.[22]

Notions of selectivity and clarity are combined in a standard metaphor in the contemporary psychological literature, which likens attention to a spotlight directed towards, and illuminating, part of our environment.[23] The idea of a spotlight captures the sense in which some parts of the environment are selected at the expense of others, and that by being selected or illuminated we get a clearer impression of those aspects. This idea, which will also prove important in later chapters, is unsurprising, if we think that one of the points of attention is precisely to select some object *so that it receives preferential processing*, and as a result is seen more clearly. But it is also useful for our purposes here to note that there are

---

[18]   Johnson and Proctor (2004), ch. 1.

[19]   Malebranche (1674/1980), pp. 411–12.

[20]   Titchener, E. B., *Psychology of Feeling and Attention*, New York: MacMillan/New York: Arno Press (1908/1973), p. 182.

[21]   Pillsbury, W. B., *Attention*, New York: Arno Press (1908/1973).

[22]   Wundt, W., *Lectures on Human and Animal Psychology*, trans. Creighton, J. B. and Titchener, E. B., New York: Macmillan (1907), p. 249.

[23]   See Eriksen, C. W. and Hoffman, J. E., 'The extent of processing of noise elements during selective encoding from visual displays', *Perception and Psychophysics* (1973) 14: 155–60; Eriksen, C. W. and St James, J. D., 'Shifting of attentional focus within and about a visual display', *Perception and Psychophysics* (1986) 40: 225–40: Posner, M. I., 'Orienting of Attention', *Quarterly Journal of Experimental Psychology* (1980) 32: 3–25.

different kinds of attention. James divides attention up in virtue of its objects, which can be sensory or intellectual; in virtue of whether we attend to the object for its own sake or for the sake of some other interest; and in virtue of whether it is "passive, reflex, non-voluntary, effortless" or "active and voluntary".[24] This last distinction is of most interest to us, since it seems that there is significant epistemic value in an attentional shift that is passive, reflexive, non-voluntary, and effortless. One obvious value here is precisely that such shifts are effortless: if our attention is automatically and passively drawn to things that are relevant to our concerns, then we do not need to actively, continually, and consciously scan the environment in order to detect such things. Such voluntary attentiveness is typically very costly from the standpoint of our cognitive resources, and so it will be better, other things being equal, if attentional shifts were non-voluntary. Clark and Watson put this point as follows: "Without an 'automatic' judgement system, all situations would have to be evaluated cognitively for their survival value, which would severely tax resources."[25] It is therefore important for us to have ways of registering or noticing potentially important objects and events that are not (as) costly from the standpoint of cognitive resources. Moreover, the fact that such attentional shifts are automatic and reflexive suggests that there are advantages with respect to the *speed* of response, when compared with attentional shifts that are voluntary and active. Reflexive, automatic shifts of attention would seem to be quicker than conscious, voluntary, and effortful shifts, and there can be obvious practical advantages in a fast response to potential danger and the like.[26]

Granting that there are, other things being equal, advantages to a system that draws our attention to important things in an automatic and reflexive way, why think that *emotion* thereby has epistemic value in governing attention in this way? Why think, that is, that emotion is valuable in so far as *it* shifts our attention, or involves the shift of attention, to objects related to our cares and concerns in a way that is passive, reflexive, non-voluntary, and effortless? We can begin to make this case by first noting relations

---

[24] James (1890), p. 416.

[25] Clark, L. and Watson, D., 'Distinguishing Functional from Dysfunctional Affective Responses', in Ekman and Davidson (eds) (1994), p. 131.

[26] See, for instance, Barrett, L., 'Adaptations to Predators and Prey', in Budd, D. (ed.), *The Handbook of Evolutionary Psychology*, New York: John Wiley & Sons (2005).

between emotion and attention more generally. For it is a commonplace that emotion and attention are closely linked. When I'm in love I'm focused on, attentive to, my beloved, at the expense of other possible objects of attention. When I'm curious my attention is locked into the question or puzzle; when I'm disappointed my mind is turned to the disappointing event; when I'm guilty I focus on what I did wrong. But it is not simply that emotion focuses attention on some object or event. Emotion can make salient ways of dealing with some object or event, or direct attention to coping strategies: fear or shame can make salient ways of escaping the emotional object, guilt can focus attention on suitable reparation for one's behaviour, and so on. Moreover, attention can affect and moderate emotion and mood: if you make me attend to the fact that the attractive barista smiles at everyone in the coffee shop and not just at me, then that will be enough to change my mood from elated to sad; and if I attend to the in-flight movie rather than the fact that I am 35,000 feet above ground, then this calms my anxiety.

But it is also a feature of everyday experience that emotions can draw our attention, quickly and automatically, to potentially significant objects and events. Consider, for instance, how one's attention automatically and reflexively shifts to the source of the loud noise when startled by a firework, or to the spider crawling across the wall when afraid. It is thus a common feature of our lives that emotions have this kind of effect on attention: fear alerts us to danger, startle to loud noises, and so on.[27] The idea that emotions direct our attention to potentially important or significant objects, in a quick, reflexive, automatic way is, moreover, a staple of psychological and (occasionally) philosophical theorizing. A great deal of work in psychology has been generated by Paul Ekman's idea that emotions are "affect programs".[28] Affect programs are "relatively discrete special-purpose mechanisms that are sensitive to some important aspect of human life",[29] and which evolved because they were of adaptive value with respect to various recurring and universal human situations. Affect program responses are short-term, reflexive, and phylogenetically ancient

---

[27] The idea that startle is an emotion might strike some as dubious. For an argument that it is indeed an emotion, see Robinson (1995).

[28] Ekman, P., 'Biological and cultural contributions to body and facial movement', in *The Anthropology of the Body*, Blacking, J. (ed.), London: Academic Press (1977), pp. 38–84.

[29] D'Arms, J. and Jacobson, D., 'The Significance of Recalcitrant Emotion', in *Philosophy and the Emotions*, Hatzimoysis, A. (ed.), Cambridge: Cambridge University Press (2003), p. 138.

reactions to a limited class of perceptual inputs. On this line, fear is an automatic, reflexive response to potential danger, which results from an affect program which has evolved to deal with threats. In philosophy, Aaron Ben-Ze'ev captures the thought as follows: "like burglar alarms going off when an intruder appears, emotions signal that something needs attention."[30] The idea of a burglar alarm—something that alerts us automatically and quickly to the presence of intruders, and which requires no prior cognitive effort on our part—is a helpful metaphor for the kind of reflexive and automatic system that emotions, on this view, are thought to involve.[31]

There is, in addition, considerable psychological and neuroscientific evidence in support of the idea that emotions are responsible for the involuntary, reflexive, and automatic orientation of attention to potentially important objects and events. Faucher and Tappolet cite evidence that subjects experiencing anxiety or phobia tend to have their attention involuntarily oriented to potential threats. In other words, there is evidence that "anxiety is accompanied by an increase in involuntary attention to threat stimuli".[32] For instance, in "homophone spelling tasks", anxious and phobic subjects tended to identify more words as threat-related, and more ambiguous material as threatening, than did control subjects, suggesting that anxiety involves "an increased attentional bias towards threat-related stimuli".[33] Similarly, in "emotional Stroop tasks", anxious subjects take longer to identify the colours of fear-related words and meanings, which "is assumed to reflect the fact that increased attention is given to the content of such words".[34] Comparable results were

---

[30] Ben-Ze'ev, A. *The Subtlety of Emotions*, Cambridge, MA: MIT Press (2000), p. 13.

[31] The question of whether affect program responses are "basic" or "primary" emotions is far too large to discuss here. So I make no claim that the affect program responses of fear, anger, surprise, disgust, happiness, and sadness are the core or fundamental emotions, and that all other emotions are combinations or elaborations of these. (In any case, I'm not sure that happiness itself counts as an emotion . . .) But I do want to say that *paradigm* emotions involve (i) phenomenology, (ii) intentionality, (iii) action-tendency, (iv) bodily change, (v) valence, and (vi) susceptibility to influence by cognitive and conative states. Whether particular emotions are like fear, anger, jealousy, shame, and other central cases will depend upon whether particular emotions have enough of these features to be classed alongside the central kinds.

[32] Faucher and Tappolet (2002), p. 114.

[33] Faucher and Tappolet (2002), p. 115. See also Matthews and Wells (1994).

[34] Faucher and Tappolet (2002), p. 116. See also Matthews and Wells (1994).

obtained in "dot-probe detection tasks", where subjects suffering from anxiety were faster than control subjects in detecting a dot probe that appeared close to a threat-related word.

Since these experiments focus on involuntary and automatic shifts of attention in subjects who are suffering from anxiety disorders such as phobias, however, they are unlikely to show that emotion has epistemic *value* in so far as it puts us in an excellent epistemic position for appropriate behaviour—at least if we doubt that anxious or phobic subjects are more reliable when it comes to identifying and registering genuine threats. So the fact that "people in [fear-related] states appear to experience *involuntary orienting of attention towards congruent stimuli*" does not show that emotion has distinctive value along this dimension.[35] Nevertheless, there is evidence that the emotions of *normal* subjects can draw or shift attention in an automatic and reflexive way to potentially important objects and events, and can thereby have epistemic value.[36] Such evidence is generated by "popout tasks", such as those conducted by Öhman and fellow researchers, who "have studied how frightening stimuli catch attention".[37] Subjects in the experiments are asked to pick out a stimulus from amongst a mass of other stimuli—for instance, one image that is amongst eight similar images. Öhman et al. found that subjects located an emotional object—such as a spider or a snake—more quickly than they located a neutral object. As Faucher and Tappolet put things, "it is as if the spider or snake is 'popping out' from the background, capturing attention automatically".[38] Since normal subjects are generally quicker at identifying emotion-relevant objects, the thought is that it is emotion itself that is responsible for this automatic orientation or capture of attention.[39] The fact that

---

[35] Faucher and Tappolet (2002), p. 120.

[36] Here I assume that there are in general reliable links in normal subjects between fear and potential danger, links that are lacking in phobic subjects. It might be difficult, after all, to think of a way of distinguishing normal from phobic subjects that is unrelated to questions of reliability. So I'll assume that reliability makes the difference in these cases.

[37] Faucher and Tappolet (2002), p. 119. See also Öhman, Flykt, and Esteves (2001).

[38] Faucher and Tappolet (2002), p. 119.

[39] This does not imply that emotion involves the constant scanning of the environment for such objects; it is not as if we have a standing state of fear in which we more quickly locate threats, for instance. The thought, rather, is that there is constant, automatic, pre-emotional and pre-attentional *monitoring* of the environment for potentially important stimuli—such as stimuli associated with spiders or snakes—and that there is an automatic and reflexive shift of

emotional stimuli "pop out" from backgrounds and capture attention therefore suggests that emotion has positive epistemic value in so far as it involves the reflexive and automatic shifting of attention to important or significant objects and events.[40]

However, even if this is correct and emotion *can* have value along these lines, this does not by itself imply that we would be epistemically worse off along this dimension without emotion. For we might think that objects, events, and coping strategies can be salient for us in the absence of emotion or mood. Consider, to illustrate, our capacity to recognize things, such as vocalizations as words in a language, or that the chess pieces display a bad pawn structure, or that this is a Dartford rather than a Sedge Warbler. This capacity—to attend to the salient, discriminating features of such things and ignore irrelevancies—is something that can operate in a reflexive, automatic, and non-emotional manner.[41] And perhaps, for all that I have said, it is the case that things are *usually* salient for us through the operation of such non-emotional recognitional capacities. As a result, the claim that we would be worse off when it comes to detecting important objects and events in the absence of emotion has not been adequately supported.

I think, nevertheless, that a case can be made for this claim. For although things might be salient for us in the absence of emotion, as the existence and operation of recognitional abilities indicates, emotions are nevertheless of central importance for making *the value of* objects and events salient for

---

attention, and corresponding mobilization of bodily resources, once emotional stimuli are detected. See, for instance, Öhman, A., 'Fear and Anxiety: Evolutionary, Cognitive, and Clinical Perspectives', in Lewis, M. and Haviland, J. (eds), *Handbook of Emotions*, 2nd edition, New York: Guildford (2000): "threat stimuli must be detected wherever they occur in the perceptual field, independently of the current direction of attention... Many perceptual channels can be automatically and simultaneously monitored for potential threat. When stimulus events implying threat are located by the automatic system, attention is drawn to the stimulus...", p. 578. As James suggests, these automatic and reflexive attentional and behavioural changes are the result of instinct; see James (1890), pp. 416–17. Or as Faucher and Tappolet (2002) note, "the fact that some stimulus tends to attract attention is partly the result of some internal, possibly innate disposition of the subject", p. 112.

[40] Faucher and Tappolet (2002) write that, "[q]uite generally, it seems plausible that a short-lived emotion of fear involves... an involuntary shifting of attention towards its intentional object... This is particularly obvious in the case of fear directed at a real object. When experiencing the fear of a bear charging us, for instance, one's attention, be it visual or auditory, involuntarily shifts towards the bear and this shift co-occurs most of the time with overt movements of the sensory organs and the body," pp. 127–8.

[41] I would like to thank an anonymous reader of the MS for raising this point, and for pushing me to clarify my views on this issue.

us, such that without emotion many important or significant objects would pass us by. To see this, note that emotion is typically involved in the (quick and reflexive) registration of objects or events as *mattering* in the way that demands a response. Perhaps the differences between the Dartford and Sedge Warbler are salient to me in my current situation, because I recognize this as a Dartford rather than a Sedge Warbler; but unless these differences engage me emotionally, perhaps as the object of surprise or curiosity, it is doubtful that in normal circumstances what is salient is thereby registered *as important* by me. By the same token, it might be apparent or salient to me that the chess pieces display a bad pawn structure; but unless this engages me emotionally, perhaps because I have money riding on the game, it is doubtful that I am thereby alerted or attentive to anything significant. Indeed, the absence of emotion in such cases typically registers the fact that what is (reflexively, automatically) salient is *not* important: if I am unmoved in recognizing that this is a Dartford rather than a Sedge Warbler, or that the chess pieces display a bad pawn structure, then it is usual for me to think that what is salient to me in these circumstances is not important. A lack of emotion therefore tends to *indicate* that the relevant object or event is unrelated to my underlying cares and concerns, and thus lacks the importance or significance that is grounded in such cares and concerns.

Now I am happy to admit that although the absence of emotion is usually a sign that what is salient is not important, this need not be true. For it is possible for us to quickly and reflexively recognize *value* in the absence of emotion. To illustrate, think of how the attention of parents with a toddler are drawn, reflexively and automatically, to potential sources of danger in a house they are visiting—such as the sharp corners on the coffee table, baseboard plug sockets, fragile vases, the pet cat, etc. It is not clear that such reflexive shifts of attention to potential danger need involve fear; indeed, it is more plausible to think that this recognitional capacity is habitual and non-emotional, at least if visiting with the toddler is something that they regularly do.[42] Nevertheless, it is also plausible to think that the *development* of this capacity to recognize value is one that has involved, to a large degree, emotional engagement with potential danger. This is because I hold the parents to possess the recognitional capacity *as a result of*

---

[42] Thanks to Anna Bergqvist—to whom I owe the example—Ben Colburn, and Robert Cowan for discussion on this point.

possessing a form of evaluative understanding; and I'll argue later that this epistemic state is difficult if not impossible to attain without emotional engagement.[43] If so, then emotion will be standardly or essentially involved in the development of the ability to non-emotionally recognize value.

In light of this, we can maintain that emotion has epistemic value in virtue of directing our attention, quickly and efficiently, to objects and events that are of potential significance. On the one hand, emotion alerts us, reflexively and at little cost, to the importance of things that are suitably related to our cares and concerns. On the other hand, and as I'll argue later, emotion is centrally involved in the promotion of evaluative under-standing, and thus grounds our capacity to non-emotionally attend to important things. Without emotion, we would thus be significantly worse off when it comes to the detection of important objects and events, since we would either fail to experience potentially important things *as* mattering to us, or fail to develop the kind of evaluative understanding required to recognize value in a non-emotional way.[44]

1.3 Emotion and evaluation

I explained earlier how emotions register potentially important matters by directing our attention to such things. Emotions such as fear and surprise do this reflexively and automatically, which is beneficial from the stand-point of time of response and cognitive cost. We also saw that this epistemic aspect of emotion is in the service of emotion's practical function of facilitating an appropriate behavioural response: this is because the point of registering or drawing our attention to such objects and events is to enable us to deal appropriately with them. As Nico Frijda claims, "[t]he function of emotions is to signal events that are relevant to the individual's concerns, and to motivate behaviour to deal with those events."[45] But as I argued at the end of the previous section, emotions do more than alert us

---

[43] Think, in support, of how fearful parents are initially around a newborn child, of how *emotionally* aware of potential dangers when the child start to crawl, or then walk, or interest themselves in plug sockets and the tails of cats . . .

[44] Since the argument here depends upon arguments that appear later in the book, the conclusion here should of course be regarded as provisional.

[45] Frijda, N., 'Why Emotions are Functional, Most of the Time', in Ekman and Davidson (eds) (1994), p. 121.

to the presence of objects and events that are relevant to our concerns; they also register such events *as important* to us, and this suggests that emotions have epistemic value along a second dimension. For the thought that emotions register certain objects and events as important is the thought that emotions involve some form of appraisal or evaluation; and such appraisals or evaluations constitute epistemic states having value both in virtue of enabling appropriate behaviour, and in virtue of grounding or justifying evaluative belief or judgement. Emotional evaluations are, in other words, valuable both from the perspective of facilitating the right behavioural response in certain conditions, and from the perspective of providing us with evaluative knowledge. In this section I will explain in more detail the idea that emotions involve some form of appraisal or evaluation, and suggest why this is important from the standpoint of appropriate behaviour, and why, intuitively at least, this allows emotions a role in the justification of evaluative attitudes. In the rest of the chapter I will turn to the important question of the *nature* of the evaluation or appraisal that emotion involves, in order to set the stage for a more thorough investigation of the thought that emotion has epistemic value in giving us access to the evaluative world. As we'll see, this discussion pushes us in the direction of the perceptual model of emotion, the nature and epistemology of which is the topic for Chapter 2. Let us turn, then, to the idea that emotions involve assessment or appraisal of some object or event.

The thought that emotions register or bring to our attention objects and events that are relevant to our cares and concerns implies that emotions are *intentional* mental states or phenomena. Such states are characterized in terms of being 'about' certain things, or in terms of being directed at things that constitute their 'objects'. But the precise nature of this relationship needs careful explanation. In one sense, the object of an emotion such as fear is its 'target': the target of my anger at the Principal's pay rise is *the Principal's pay rise*, which is what my anger is 'about'. Or the object of my shame when I behave inappropriately at the Christmas party, or what my shame is about, is *my behaviour at the Christmas party*. To clarify matters, I'll follow normal usage and refer to such things (the pay rise, my behaviour) as the 'material objects' of emotions. But there is another sense in which emotions are intentional. For my anger at the Principal's pay rise is not simply about the pay rise in the sense of being directed at this. My anger is also about the value (or more correctly, the disvalue) that the pay rise has in these circumstances; and similarly with other emotions. In this sense, then, my anger is about unfairness, my shame about shamefulness, my guilt about wrongness, and so forth. Again following normal usage, I'll refer to such things as the "formal objects" of emotions. So emotions are intentional, not simply in the sense of being about some object or event, but also by being about the particular way in which the object or event is valuable or disvaluable. And this suggests two ways in which emotions can register important objects or events: first, by drawing our attention to objects and events; second, by alerting us to *the way in which* some object or event is important or significant.[46]

We might put this point slightly differently. One way of understanding intentionality or aboutness is in terms of *representation*. Thus, as Tim Crane writes, "[a]n intentional mental state is normally understood . . . as one which is about, or represents, something in the world."[47] If so, we can regard emotions as having a dual representational role: emotions can represent the objects and events that constitute their targets, such as pay rises and behaviour at parties, and emotions can represent *that* such things have certain evaluative properties or features, like the properties of being insulting or being shameful. The first representation has non–evaluative content, we might say, whilst the second has evaluative content. Emotions would therefore seem to involve a representation of some target object or event *and* a representation of the value of that target. Here is how Sabine Döring puts it: "you hate your rivals, grieve over your mother's death, or are afraid of the aggressive-looking woman: your rivals, your mother's death and the aggressive-looking woman are the targets of your hatred, grief and fear respectively."[48] However, "[h]ating your rivals implies that you are seeing them as awful people; grieving over your mother's death

---

[46] Of course, it won't always be easy for us to fix precisely upon the way in which some object or event is significant; our grasp of our evaluative situation might be rather loose. For instance, although my feelings of guilt inform me that I have done something morally wrong, the precise nature or aspect of the wrongness might elude me. Nevertheless, the story I'll tell in later chapters about the epistemic value of emotion is in part a story of how our grasp of the evaluative situation can be improved through emotional effects on attention. If so, then emotions themselves can help us to grasp more precisely the formal object of our emotion.

[47] Crane, T., 'The Problem of Perception', *The Stanford Encyclopedia of Philosophy (Spring 2011 Edition)*, Edward N. Zalta (ed.), <http://plato.stanford.edu/archives/spr2011/entries/perception-problem/>.

[48] Döring, S., 'Explaining Action by Emotion', *The Philosophical Quarterly* (2003), 53(211): p. 221.

implies that you are regarding her death as a sad event; being afraid of the aggressive-looking woman implies that you are thinking of her as dangerous."[49] In other words, in hating your rivals, you represent them as awful; in grieving over your mother's death, you represent this as a sad event; in being afraid of the woman, you represent her as dangerous.[50]

Now we saw earlier the idea that emotions alert us to the import of objects and events, and in so doing seem to involve an appraisal or evaluation of such objects and events. And there are other good reasons to think that emotions are intentional or representational in this way. One is that something like this is needed in order to distinguish emotions from each other. If we are sceptical about the idea that we can differentiate emotions on the basis of how they feel—on the grounds that different emotions, such as anxiety and excitement, can involve feelings of the same bodily and visceral changes—then we need to appeal to some other element in order to distinguish fear, anger, pride, guilt, shame, and the like. However, we cannot appeal to the target in order to achieve this goal, since the same object—your promotion, for instance—can be the target of my joy, indignation, fear, and many other emotions. In order to distinguish these different emotions, we need to appeal to the different ways in which they represent the object—as a cause for celebration (when you are my friend), or an injustice (because I was overlooked despite being better qualified), or a threat (because you've always had it in for me).

---

[49] Döring (2003), p. 221.

[50] Central or paradigm cases of emotion involve straightforward evaluations and are directed at formal objects which are clearly values: think of fear and dangerousness, guilt and wrongness, grief and loss, and so on. But there are other cases of emotion which involve assessment or appraisal that aren't so closely tied to value: surprise, complacency, and indifference come to mind. This is related to the thought that central or paradigm cases of emotion have a "valence", but that not every emotion does. Now one could argue that even these latter emotions involve evaluation in some broad or attenuated sense: indifference suggests a negative appraisal that the object lacks value, complacency suggests a positive evaluation of one's lot in life. Or one could argue that these are not, after all, emotions. There is, however, a third option, which is to focus on central or paradigm cases, and investigate and clarify the common-sense idea that *these* emotions have epistemic value. It can hardly be illegitimate, after all, for an exploration of common-sense thinking on emotion to restrict itself to the very emotional experiences that ground common-sense thinking. The fact, if it is a fact, that non-standard emotions don't seem to be particularly helpful when it comes to acquiring evaluative knowledge shouldn't therefore undermine my account of how standard emotions can have value along this dimension. I'd like to thank Adam Morton for pressing me to be clearer on this point.

A second reason is grounded in the platitude that emotions enable us to deal with important objects and events, by priming us for and motivating an appropriate behavioural response. For it is hardly plausible to suppose that emotions can facilitate an *appropriate* behavioural response to some important object or event if they do not involve an appraisal of the way in which the object or event is important. Unless fear represents something as a threat, for instance, we lack an explanation of why fear makes it appropriate for the subject to run away from, rather than embrace, or congratulate, or make reparations to, the thing in question. So the thought that emotions enable us to deal appropriately with important matters supports the idea that emotions involve an appraisal or representation of the way in which things matter. In order to facilitate appropriate behaviour, therefore, emotions must register the way in which objects or events are taken to be important.

We therefore have good reason to think that emotions involve evaluative appraisals or assessments, or involve a representation of the way in which something is important to us or matters for us. And this suggests that emotions have value as a result of their evaluative aspect or element. One element of this, as we have just seen, is that emotions have value in providing the intentional epistemic states needed for appropriate behavioural responses to danger, insults, and the like. But the fact that emotions involve evaluations or appraisals suggests that emotions can have a more direct epistemic value, in so far as they generate and justify evaluative judgement or belief, and as such inform us about value. It is, for instance, part of our common-sense thinking about emotion that emotion often plays a role in the formation of our evaluative beliefs or judgements. Thus, I believe that I am in danger *because* or *as a result of* being afraid; I believe that he is untrustworthy as a result of feeling mistrust in his presence; I believe that this flat is right for me because of an immediate and positive affective experience when I first look around. The fact that emotion can play this role is easily explicable on the assumption that emotion has evaluative *content*. If fear involves an assessment of danger, then it is easy to explain why fear generates judgements about danger—if, for instance, we think that we are generally inclined to endorse our emotional appraisals. Moreover, if emotion has evaluative content, then it is *prima facie* plausible to suppose that emotions can play a role in the justification of our evaluative judgements or beliefs. Thus, if fear involves an assessment of danger, and my fear reliably co-occurs with dangerous objects and events, then it is plausible to suppose that fear can in certain circumstances indicate or tell us about the dangerousness of our situation. The fact that emotions have evaluative content thus supports the idea that emotions have epistemic importance in providing reason and evidence for, in generating and justifying, our evaluative judgements and beliefs.

The idea that emotions have value in virtue of their causal and justificatory relations with evaluative beliefs and judgements is one of the central issues that I want to investigate in this book. So in the following chapters I will attempt to explicate the idea that emotions can have epistemic worth along this second dimension—that is, in so far as they inform us about value. In order to make progress on this score, however, I must first address the question of what emotions must be like in order to play the epistemic roles that we have previously identified. In particular, I need to consider the *nature* of the evaluative or representational element in emotion, such that emotion can have both causal and justificatory links with our evaluative judgements or beliefs. For it will be difficult to tell a plausible story about how emotions function to inform us about value in virtue of their evaluative or representational element, without a clearer picture of what this evaluative or representational element is. So in the second half of this chapter I will turn to these questions, and consider what our thoughts about the epistemic value of emotion suggest about the nature of emotion itself.

1.4 Theories of emotion

I have argued that emotions can register the presence of important matters through capturing our attention in a reflexive and automatic way. And I have also argued that emotions register *the way in which* objects and events are important: on this view, emotions involve an appraisal or assessment of the objects or events in question. But what is the nature of the evaluative appraisal involved in emotional experience? For without a grasp of this, the story we tell about how emotions inform us about value will be obscure. The best and simplest way of making progress here is to identify the kinds of things that can in general play a representational role, and then investigate which of these is the most plausible candidate to be the representational or intentional element in emotion. (It might turn out, of course, that the intentionality of emotion isn't, ultimately, to be understood in terms of the intentionality of some other element which is a constituent of emotion. Perhaps, instead, the intentionality of emotion is *sui generis*. We will return to this possibility later.)

Now the obvious candidates for representational or intentional mental states are desire and belief. Desires and beliefs are propositional attitudes, and propositional attitudes are representational states par excellence. To have a belief—such as the belief that it is raining in Glasgow—is to have an attitude of acceptance or holding true of the proposition *it is raining in Glasgow*. To have a desire—such as the desire that it rain in Glasgow—is to have an attitude of wanting the proposition *it is raining in Glasgow* to be true. Beliefs and desires are thus representational states because they represent that the world is a particular way in the case of belief, and represent that the world is *to be* a particular way in the case of desire.[51] Let us begin, then, by considering the possibility that it is desire that constitutes the representational element in emotional experience.

1.4.1 Desire theories

We have already seen that emotion involves a motivational aspect as well as an epistemic aspect; for emotion involves the mobilization of behavioural resources which prime us to take appropriate action in response to the matter of importance that emotion registers. Given this, it is plausible to think that emotion involves, as a result of such mobilization, a desire to act in a particular way. If so, however, we might think that desire can do "double duty" by constituting the epistemic aspect of emotion as well. This isn't an outlandish suggestion, since there is a long-standing tradition in metaethics which maintains that desires have evaluative content: that desiring something involves regarding it as valuable or desirable in some way.[52]

---

[51] There are two main reasons for thinking that something is a representational state: (i) it has accuracy or correctness conditions, and (ii) it can help to explain and predict behaviour. See, for instance, Fiona Macpherson's 'Introduction: Individuating the Senses', in *The Senses*, Macpherson, F. (ed.), Oxford: Oxford University Press (2011). It is obvious that attributing beliefs and desires to subjects can help explain and predict behaviour. But it is also clear that belief and desire have accuracy conditions: belief is accurate when the world is as propositional content presents it as being, whilst desire is accurate if it is the case that the world is *to be* a particular way.

[52] See, for instance, G. E. M. Anscombe's *Intention*, Ithaca: Cornell University Press (1963), p. 70ff; and Davidson, D. 'Intending', in *Essays on Actions and Events*, Oxford: Clarendon Press (1980), p. 97, n. 7.

It is, however, unlikely that desire can be the representational or evaluative element in emotion. One reason is that the desires that are involved in emotional experience seem to lack the kind of representational content needed for emotions to be informative about *particular* values. To see this, note that on our common-sense view, fear is supposed to tell us about danger, anger about insult, sorrow about loss, and so on. However, desires with the same content can be present in different emotions, in which case emotions will not be able to tell us different things about the world in virtue of this putative representational element. For example, fear, embarrassment, disgust, and anger can *all* involve the desire *that I escape from this object.* But then the representational element of emotion cannot be desire, if different emotions are to inform us about different values in virtue of their intentional aspects.

One response might be that I have not specified the content of the desire in each emotion with enough care. It might be argued that the desire in the case of fear would be that *I escape the source of danger,* in the case of embarrassment that *I escape the scene of my social faux pas,* and so on, and that such contents can inform us about different values. However, this response seems false. It is more natural to interpret the desire involved in fear as a desire to flee that is *motivated by* an appraisal that one is in danger, given the possibility of explaining one's desire to flee by citing the (putative) fact that one is in danger. Moreover, this possibility is live if we think that an appraisal of danger and a desire to flee can diverge or come apart. And it certainly seems conceptually possible for a subject to emotionally appraise her situation as dangerous and yet not desire to take the appropriate action. We ought not, for both of these reasons, identify the evaluative appraisal involved in emotional experience with desire itself.

But the main reason to think that the intentionality of emotion is not simply a matter of the intentionality of desire is the need to capture our common-sense views about the epistemic value of emotion. As we have seen, part of our common-sense thinking about emotion is that emotion can, under the right conditions, tell us about value: our emotions can, in other words, provide us with information about the evaluative world. If so, then presumably we can be *justified* in our beliefs or judgements about the evaluative world *on the basis of* our emotional experiences. But desire seems ill-fitted to play this epistemic role, given the truism that one ought not to form beliefs or judgements on the basis of desire. It is an epistemic failing, after all, to believe something because it satisfies some desire that one has; believing in this way is a form of wishful thinking. So even if the desire-theorist can avoid the difficulties discussed earlier, their theory is unlikely to provide an adequate account of the epistemic role that we intuitively think our emotional experiences can have. For this reason, we should look elsewhere for our account of emotional intentionality.

1.4.2 Judgementalism

If the representational or intentional element in emotion is not a conative state like desire, then perhaps it is a cognitive state like belief. Indeed, the idea that emotions inform us about the evaluative world because they consist, in part, of evaluative belief or judgement, a position usually termed "judgementalism", has been prominent in the history of the philosophy of emotion and has its defenders today.[53] On this view, fear represents danger in virtue of being partly constituted by a judgement that one is in danger; shame represents shamefulness because it consists, in part, in a judgement that one has done something shameful; and so on for other emotions. Since the content of such evaluative judgements is genuinely distinctive, then different emotions can inform us about different values in virtue of such representational content. For this reason, judgement or belief seems a much better candidate than desire when it comes to identifying the representational element in emotional experience. Moreover, since belief can diverge from desire, then this identification allows for common-sense cases of divergence between emotional appraisal and motivation. In addition, beliefs, unlike desires, can obviously play a justificatory role with regard to other beliefs, in which case the "wishful thinking" worry that undermines the desire model is not germane with respect to judgementalism. Finally, judgementalism offers a simple explanation of the obvious fact that emotional experience and evaluative judgement or belief are very closely linked: that my anger goes together with a judgement that I have been insulted or wronged. Indeed, judgementalism offers an explanation of the equally obvious fact that emotions tend to disappear when the relevant evaluative judgement is changed. Suppose I am angry at you because I believe that I am the target of your insulting jokes, and then

---

[53] Proponents of judgementalism include Solomon, R., *The Passions*, New York: Anchor (1977); Lyons, W., *Emotion*, Cambridge: Cambridge University Press (1980); Marks, J., 'A Theory of Emotions', *Philosophical Studies* (1982), 42(2): 227–42; and Nussbaum, M., *Upheavals of Thought*, Cambridge: Cambridge University Press (2001).

you point out that you were making fun of the character called Mike Brady in *The Brady Bunch* TV series. In this situation I would no longer believe that you are insulting me and as a result my anger would cease. If we think that emotions are partly constituted by evaluative judgements, we have a simple explanation of why emotions cease when the subject's evaluative judgements change.

The fact that judgementalism is an improvement over the desire model does not mean that it is ultimately successful in capturing our common-sense idea that emotions can inform us about value, however. For one thing, there are well-known problems with the judgementalist claim that the intentionality of emotion is the intentionality of judgement.[54] For another, judgementalism is in fact incompatible with one of the central elements in our common-sense take on how emotions play a positive epistemic role. Let us take these objections in turn.

There are *general* objections to the idea that judgementalism is an acceptable account of emotional intentionality, and hence of emotion as such. First, some have argued that young children and non-human animals can have emotional experience without being capable of forming propositional attitudes like judgements or beliefs—on the grounds that young children and non-human animals lack the conceptual sophistication for accepting or endorsing propositions. As John Deigh puts it:

> [J]udgements, like beliefs, are states of mind that imply acceptance or affirmation of propositions. Consequently, to have emotions requires being capable of grasping and affirming propositions. That is to say, one must have acquired a language. Since beasts never acquire a language and babies have yet to acquire one, [judgementalism] cannot account for their emotions.[55]

We might think that this first objection is too strong, on the grounds that it is possible to have propositional attitudes like beliefs without having formulated the relevant propositions in language. Nevertheless, judgementalism is subject to other serious difficulties. A second problem with judgementalism is that emotions can be experienced in response to fiction or to imagination: I might indulge in revenge fantasies and as a result feel angry, or I might be terrified by the masked psychotic in the horror film.

---

[54] For a helpful overview of some central problems with judgementalism, see Griffiths, P., *What Emotions Are*, Chicago: University of Chicago Press (1998), ch. 1.

[55] Deigh, J., 'Concepts of Emotions', in Goldie (ed.) (2010), p. 27.

Since I don't believe that someone has wronged me or that the masked psychotic is real, these emotions don't involve the relevant evaluative beliefs or judgements.

A third problem is that emotions can conflict with our evaluative beliefs or judgements: there can be cases of "recalcitrant" emotion, which persists "despite the agent's making a judgement that is in tension with it... A recalcitrant bout of fear, for example, is one where the agent is afraid of something despite believing that it poses little or no danger."[56] In addition to fear, there are clear cases of recalcitrant anger, guilt, jealousy, and shame. Now judgementalism is committed to making implausible claims about those who experience such emotion. Since subjects who suffer from recalcitrant emotions do not consciously assent to the judgement that is supposedly constitutive of their emotion, judgementalists must maintain that the relevant judgement is unconsciously held. This is criticizable on two counts: first, it imputes too much irrationality to the subject of emotional recalcitrance; second, it violates a principle of logical charity in our ascription of mental states. On the first count, judgementalism implies that someone who suffers from recalcitrant fear, let us say, displays an incoherent evaluative profile with respect to the question of whether some object is dangerous. But as Bennett Helm has written, "conflicts between emotions and judgements do not verge on incoherence, for they are readily intelligible and happen all too often".[57] On the second count, Patricia Greenspan has argued that positing the existence of unconscious evaluative judgements is a "last resort from the standpoint of explanation".[58] This is because we can assume "that the agent is functioning quite rationally in general, so that our ascription of beliefs to him ought to be governed by the principle of 'logical charity'. We need some special reason... for attributing to him an unacknowledged judgement in conflict with those he acknowledges."[59] Since the only reason the judgementalist seems to provide for this attribution stems from their adherence to the judgementalist theory, their explanation of recalcitrant emotions is undermined.[60]

---

[56] D'Arms and Jacobson, (2003), p. 129.

[57] Helm, B., *Emotional Reason*, Cambridge: Cambridge University Press (2001), p. 42.

[58] Greenspan, P., *Emotions and Reasons*, London: Routledge (1988), p. 18.

[59] Greenspan (1988), p. 18.

[60] This argument has been widely accepted. For a dissenting voice in the judgementalist camp, see Nussbaum (2001).

These are amongst the well-known and well-rehearsed reasons why judgementalism in the philosophy of emotion has fallen out of favour. It still has its defenders, but it is fair to say that the burden of proof is on them to show how judgementalism is more plausible than these objections suggest. But there is another reason why we might regard judgementalism as unhelpful, again given our primary task of explaining and understanding the epistemic role that emotions are thought to play. For part of this thinking, as the examples in the *Introduction* and earlier in this chapter suggest, is that emotional experience is often the "input" to which evaluative judgement or belief is the "output". In other words, we often form evaluative judgement on the basis of, or as a result of, emotional experience. If this is the case, then it must be possible for emotion to occur *before* evaluative judgement, such that it can play a causal role in the formation of that doxastic state. This seems to be the most plausible and most natural way to interpret the epistemic state of Henry Fonda's 8th Juror in *12 Angry Men*. Here it is the juror's feeling that there's something peculiar about the trial that comes first, and *then* the juror starts to believe that the defence council wasn't doing a good enough job, that he was missing things, and that, ultimately, he was unreliable or untrustworthy. And certainly, everyday experience suggests that in many cases we first have an emotional response to an object or event—such as a feeling that the lecture is going badly—and *then* endorse this feeling when we form the judgement that the lecture *is* going badly. Think, in this instance, of the phenomenology of coming to realize that the lecture really is going as badly as you (perhaps tentatively) felt it was.

Moreover, the phenomenology of emotional experience supports the idea that we can be emotionally *inclined* towards some evaluative judgement—say, that the lecture is going badly—without endorsing our emotional presentation and thus without accepting that the lecture is going badly. This seems to mirror the phenomenology when we are *practically* inclined towards some behaviour on the basis of a desire—say, a desire to supersize our fast food order—without endorsing our desire to do so and thus without deciding that we will. It is not particularly plausible, in this latter instance, to claim that my desire is *itself* an intention or decision to supersize, rather than something that is typically an input to our intention or decision. By the same token, it is not particularly plausible to hold that feeling is *itself* a judgement or belief, rather than something that is typically an input to judgement or belief. In so far as judgementalism maintains that emotions are constituted by evaluative judgements, however, it will be unable to accommodate the thought that sometimes we form evaluative judgements as a result of endorsing some prior emotional appraisal. If, then, we accept the intuitive picture of emotions as inputs to which evaluative judgements are outputs, and hold that this better represents common-sense thinking about emotion's epistemic role, we have a further reason to be suspicious of the prospects for judgementalism as an account of the intentional or representational element in emotional experience.

1.4.3 Other cognitive theories

Suppose we reject the idea that the representational element in emotion is to be identified with either desire or judgement. Does this mean that we should reject the idea that the intentional element of emotional experience is a (familiar) propositional attitude at all? Perhaps not. There are, after all, propositional attitudes such as *thoughts* or *imaginings* that are representational but which do not involve endorsement or acceptance of the representational content. I might have the thought that I should take up windsurfing, or the thought that I'll change allegiance from Labour to the Scottish National Party at the next election, without endorsing these plans; I might imagine or fantasize about or assume for the sake of argument all kinds of propositions that I don't accept. It could be the case, therefore, that the intentional content of emotion is still a propositional attitude, only an attitude—like thought or imagining, conjecture or supposition—that falls short of belief or judgement.[61]

This suggestion as to the intentional or representational element of emotion can avoid some of the problems that face judgementalism. Suppose we think that judgementalism cannot accommodate the fact that young children and animals have emotions, on the grounds that judgements require the endorsement of propositions, and young children and animals lack the conceptual capacities to endorse anything. This doesn't constitute an objection to our weaker cognitive position, since it is not a condition of this position that the relevant thoughts are endorsed. In addition, weaker cognitivist accounts can allow for emotional responses to fiction, since these might involve simply imagining that some object or

---

[61] See, for instance, Greenspan (1988).

event has some evaluative property or feature. Further, weaker cognitivist accounts can accommodate the existence of recalcitrant emotions, without supposing that the subject of such emotion has an incoherent evaluative profile. Instead, it is perfectly possible to think or imagine that some object has some evaluative property—as when I entertain the possibility that camping in the Scottish Highlands would make for a wonderful summer holiday—without believing that it would be. Finally, a weaker cognitivism is compatible with our common-sense picture of emotions as inputs to evaluative judgements, since it is clearly possible for a subject to first entertain some evaluative thought or imagine some evaluative possibility and *then* endorse such a thought or possibility by forming an evaluative judgement.

Nevertheless, weaker versions of cognitivism are, *as they stand*, problematic. To see this, note first that entertaining thoughts or making assumptions or conjectures or fantasizing about propositions are all things that we actively do: we make assumptions or fantasize in order to serve some goal, such as to test a hypothesis or to amuse ourselves during the speaker's tedious talk. Emotional experience is typically passive, however: there's a big difference between my assuming for the sake of argument that I have done something shameful—perhaps with a view to working out what the appropriate responses might be, should I ever behave in this way—and my actually being ashamed. Whereas the former is intentional activity on my part, the latter is something that happens to me. This difference is important, given, once again, our central aim of examining the epistemic role and value of emotional experience. This is because thoughts or imaginings do not seem capable of constituting inputs for evaluative judgements or beliefs, and hence do not seem capable of informing us about how the evaluative world really is. We might put the point this way: the fact that entertaining some thought is an intentional act suggests that it fails to have the right kind of causal and justificatory relations with evaluative judgement. Typically, entertaining some thought or imagining some situation does not lead me to form the relevant beliefs. But even if it did—if I was inclined towards believing my fantasies or imaginings—such things are surely not *reasons* for me to believe as I do. If I slip into reverie about being asked to be Radio 4's resident philosopher, this attitude fails to justify the belief that I'll be asked. This looks, once again, like wishful thinking, which is a paradigmatic case of an irrational belief-forming process. So appealing to intentional or representational states that fall short of belief does not, by itself, offer a promising way of explaining our common-sense view about the epistemic role and value of emotion.[62]

If weaker cognitivist accounts are to provide a plausible epistemological story, then they must accommodate the idea that the evaluative attitudes involved in emotional experience are both weaker than belief, and the kind of *passive* attitudes that can play a genuinely informative and justificatory role. Emotional appraisals, in other words, must be constituted by evaluative thoughts (or similar) that happen to us or strike us, rather than thoughts (or similar) that we entertain or consider or contemplate or assume or imagine; and they must be constituted by thoughts (or similar) that strike us in such a way that they could be in the business of justifying evaluative judgements we make as a result of being struck in this way. What is important, for our purposes, is that supporters of weaker cognitivist theories are now attempting to meet this challenge by shifting to a *perceptual* model of emotion. That is, supporters of weaker cognitive theories maintain that the relevant kind of cognitive-but-passive attitude is a perceptual one. Thus, as John Deigh writes,

recent defenders of cognitive theories have dropped the standard [i.e., judgementalist] model in favour of a broader account of the evaluative cognition that is essential to emotions . . . Such cognition, they argue, need not be an evaluative judgement of the kind that implies grasping and affirming a proposition. It may, instead, be a perception.[63]

This should come as no surprise. Perceptual experiences are, after all, passive experiences; and perceptual experiences are, after all, paradigms of informative states or attitudes. There is very good reason, therefore, for supporters of weaker cognitive theories to look towards the perceptual

---

[62] It might be argued here that states such as thinking and conjecturing can be involuntary and passive, and can (therefore) provide reasons. A conjecture—such that it is possible that Jones changed clothes after the murder—can simply occur to us or strike us, and can give a reason for another belief—that we should go and check to see whether he dumped the clothes at his flat. This seems correct. But it also seems correct that the conjecture in this case is *itself* a belief—namely the belief that it is possible that Jones changed his clothes. Conjectures, after all, are standardly taken to be beliefs or judgements based upon things like guesswork. Might guesses themselves provide reasons, even though they are typically active rather than passive? It is not so clear that they can. But even if they can, the reason or evidence that emotion (arguably) supplies is not best modelled on reasons provided by guesses. Emotion is (again arguably) a response to evaluative information in our environment; guessing is a last resort when not much in the way of evaluative information is to be found. I'd like to thank Adam Morton for pressing me to be clearer on this point.

[63] Deigh (2010), p. 28.

model as providing the right kind of intentionality for emotional experience. If so, then the perceptual model of emotion seems to emerge as the cognitivist's best hope for capturing the intentionality of emotion.

In the following section we'll see how a similar conclusion about the adoption of the perceptual model is warranted with respect to cognitivism's great rival as a general theory of emotion, namely the feeling theory. If so, then the case in favour of the perceptual model as the most promising way in which to explain the intentionality of emotional experience, and to capture our common-sense view of the epistemic role and value of emotion, will look rather strong.

1.4.4 Feeling theories

Earlier we saw the attempt to make desire do double duty: since desire is plausibly the motivational element in emotional experience, and since some philosophers have thought that desires have evaluative content, the idea was that desire could serve as both representational and motivational. A similar attempt might be made with another element that is widely held to be central to emotional experience, namely *feeling*. According to our platitude, emotions enable us to cope with important or significant matters. We have partly explicated this idea by saying that emotions prepare us for an appropriate behavioural response, by mobilizing bodily resources: thus, fear primes us for "fight or flight" behaviour by instigating visceral, somatosensory, and muscular changes that will enable us to cope with a threatening stimulus. It is plausible to think that the feelings involved in emotional experience are, at least in part, the consciousness of such changes. Indeed, there is a long-standing tradition in the philosophy of emotion that maintains that emotions are nothing but the consciousness of bodily changes. This is the view we have received from William James and Carl Lange. For instance, the basic line of James's paper 'What is an emotion?' is that emotions are perceptions of physiological changes and disturbances, which occur after we perceive a suitable object in our environment. He writes: "My thesis . . . is that the bodily changes follow directly the *perception* of the exciting fact, and that our feeling of the same changes as they occur *is* the emotion."[64] On this account, emotional

---

[64] James, W., 'What is an emotion?', *Mind* (1884), 9: p. 189. For Lange's view, which he developed independently from James, see Lange, C., *Ueber Gemuthsbewegungen*, Leipzig: Theodor Thomas (1888).

experience is triggered by some environmental event which we perceive, which leads to a physiological change, and is then experienced by the subject; it is this consciousness of the bodily change that constitutes the emotion.[65] Might we claim, then, that consciousness of bodily changes can have intentional or representational content, and as such play the epistemic role of informing us about value?

As with judgementalism, there are *general* problems with the claim that the intentionality of emotion can be captured by bodily feelings, and a more particular problem with the thought that feeling theories (of this stripe, at least) can explain how emotions play a positive epistemic role. Let us take these objections in turn.

We earlier saw that one reason to resist identifying the representational element in emotion with desire is that desire lacks the kind of representational content to inform us about *particular* values. The same desire can be present, after all, in radically different emotions. A similar charge can be raised against the James–Lange theory. As Walter Cannon argued, the same visceral changes—such as increased heart rate, increase of blood sugar, inhibition of digestive activity, sweating, discharge of adrenalin, widening of pupils, and the like—occur in different emotional states such as fear and rage, and also in non-emotional states such as fever, exposure to cold, and asphyxia. As he writes, "[t]he responses of the viscera seem too uniform to offer a satisfactory means of distinguishing emotions which are very different in subjective quality."[66]

A second well-known criticism of feeling theories is that some emotions seem to lack feelings of bodily changes. It might be true to say that "I love her" or "I am happy in my job" or "I am furious about the ongoing, illegal war", without it being true that I am experiencing feelings of bodily

---

[65] A weaker interpretation of the James–Lange theory is available. This does not maintain that feelings of bodily changes are all that there is to emotion; instead, it holds that awareness of bodily changes is all that there is to the affective experience of emotion. On this latter view, an emotion itself can partly consist in things other than an awareness of bodily change. However, the difference between these interpretations doesn't, it seems to me, make a difference to the arguments in this section.

[66] In Cannon, W., *Bodily Changes in Pain, Hunger, Fear and Rage*, New York: Appleton (1929), p. 352. See also Errol Bedford's claim, in support of Cannon's point, that the feeling theory is inadequate at the psychological level, as "it presupposes a richness and clarity in the 'inner life' of feeling that it does not possess. What evidence is there for the existence of a multitude of feelings corresponding to the extensive and subtle linguistic differentiation of our vocabulary for discussing emotions?" In Bedford, E.,'Emotions', *Proceedings of the Aristotelian Society* (1957), 57: p. 282.

changes typically associated with love or happiness or fury. Long-standing emotions of this kind thus pose a problem for an account that identifies emotions with feelings. One response, on behalf of the James–Lange theory, to this criticism is to hold that long-standing emotions are *dispositions* to feel the relevant bodily changes, and that unless I sometimes *feel* fury when thinking about the illegal war, it's simply not true to say that I am furious about the war.[67] This response has its costs, however, since cognitivist opponents of the feeling theory can make the same move and thus avoid arguments which purport to show that cognitions such as thoughts or beliefs are not essential to emotional experience. For the cognitivist can equally say that emotions are essentially *dispositions* to think the relevant thoughts or form the relevant beliefs, and so need not be worried by evidence which indicates the possibility of emotional experience without cognition.[68]

But perhaps the most important criticism of the James–Lange theory, at least for our purposes, is that bodily feelings seem to lack the right kind of intentional or representational content, and as such are ill-fitted to inform us about the value of objects and events in the external world. Bodily changes are not, in other words, "about" the external world and its objects. For instance, the ache in my stomach can inform me (if it can inform me of anything at all) that something's amiss in my digestive system; and the pounding headache can represent (if it can represent anything at all) that something's not quite right in the old brain. As such, consciousness of bodily changes can tell me about bodily stuff that is going on. But headaches, digestive disorders, back twinges, and aching limbs do not, on the face of it, seem capable of representing or informing me about things *beyond* my body. Consciousness of bodily changes therefore seems ill-fitted to be the intentional or representational element in emotional experience, since it is poorly placed to play the epistemic role that common-sense says that our emotions play.[69]

---

[67] For this line, see Prinz, J., 'Embodied Emotions', in Solomon, R. (ed.), *Thinking About Feeling: Contemporary Philosophers on Emotions*, Oxford: Oxford University Press (2004b).

[68] A different version of the same charge—that some emotions lack feelings of bodily changes—was made by Cannon, who noted that animals still experience emotions even when connections between the brain and viscera have been destroyed. If so, then emotions cannot be feelings of visceral changes. See Cannon (1929).

[69] The idea that feelings cannot capture the intentionality of emotion was made prominent in work by Bedford and Anthony Kenny. See Bedford (1957), and Kenny, A., *Action, Emotion and the Will*, London: Routledge (1963).

The challenge for feeling theories is, therefore, to explain how feelings can be intentional or representational in the right kind of way. And what is important for our purposes is that, as with weaker cognitive theories, supporters of feeling theories are trying to meet this challenge by adopting some form of perceptual model of emotion. On the one hand, contemporary defenders of the James–Lange theory, such as Jesse Prinz, argue that feelings of *bodily* changes can represent and hence inform us about value because such feelings are a form of perceptual experience, and because perceptual experience is standardly taken to represent and hence inform us about things in the external world. On the other hand, some theorists appeal to a category of feelings neglected by James and Lange, and argue that these feelings are akin to perceptual experiences at the representational level. On this account, the representational element in emotional experience is a form of "psychic" or "intellectual" feeling, such as the feeling of satisfaction one gets after completing a particularly taxing crossword puzzle, or the feeling of puzzlement one experiences when pondering why *she* is going out with *him*. This is the approach adopted by Robert C. Roberts, who maintains that emotional feelings are a kind of "evaluative construal", and that this is a form of (or at least akin to) perceptual experience.[70] What unites these different camps is the idea that feelings can be suitably representational or intentional if we regard them as a form of (or akin to) perceptual experience. If so, then the perceptual model of emotion has started to emerge as the feeling theorist's best hope for capturing the intentionality of emotion, and in a way which avoids the traditional problems that the theory faces on this score. As such, contemporary developments in feeling theories of emotion also push us in the direction of the perceptual model.

1.5 Conclusions

The discussion in the previous section suggests that we have good reason to investigate the possibility that the perceptual model of emotion best

---

[70] See Roberts, R., *Emotions: An Essay in Aid of Moral Psychology*, Cambridge: Cambridge University Press (2003). Roberts's view is more sophisticated and complicated than this suggests, and it would be remiss to call him a card-carrying feeling theorist. Nevertheless, he introduces the kind of thing an emotional construal is by appealing to psychic or intellectual feelings, and so his perceptual theory has affinities with feeling accounts to this extent. We'll see the views of Prinz and Roberts in more detail in Chapter 2.

captures our common-sense thoughts about the epistemic role and value of emotion. We have seen, in support, that a platitude about emotion suggests that emotional experience has both an epistemic and a practical dimension; that the epistemic element involves the direction of attention onto potentially important matters and an evaluative appraisal of those matters; and that extant accounts of emotional intentionality provide *prima facie* support for the idea that emotions are akin to perceptions of value. At least, we have seen that philosophers of emotion, from both cognitive and feeling camps, have reason to take the perceptual model seriously, in so far as this model promises to provide ways in which each can avoid significant objections. In other words, the perceptual model can be employed by theorists in cognitive and feeling camps to argue in favour of their respective accounts: the cognitivist can appeal to perception in order to capture the sense in which emotional appraisal is a passive, and thereby epistemically respectable, affair; and the feeling theorist can argue that emotions, as perceptions, can have the right kind of intentional or representational content.

In light of all this, it appears that the perceptual theory emerges, quite naturally, from an examination of the common-sense thoughts and platitudes about emotions that we considered at the beginning of this chapter, and from a consideration of whether existing theories of emotion are up to the task of accommodating such thoughts and platitudes. The time is therefore right to examine the perceptual model in detail, and to consider the epistemological story that perceptual theorists wish to tell, to see whether the optimism about this relative newcomer in the philosophy of emotion is warranted.

2

The Perceptual Model

At the end of the previous chapter we introduced the idea that the intentional element in emotion is a matter of *perception*. In this chapter I propose to investigate the "perceptual model" of emotion in detail. At the heart of the model is the claim that emotions and perceptions are similar along a number of dimensions, and in §1 I outline the ways in which emotions and perceptions are thought to be alike. What is particularly important, for our purposes, is that one of these dimensions is *epistemic*. For supporters of the perceptual model hold that emotions play a role in the justification of evaluative judgement or belief that mirrors the role played by sensory perceptions in the justification of empirical judgement or belief. Indeed, some supporters maintain that to accept the perceptual model *just is* to be committed to this epistemological claim.[1]

Given our aim of investigating the epistemic role and value of emotional experience, and given the fact that the perceptual model would seem to constitute the most developed account of such a role and value to date, then it clearly makes sense for us to examine the perceptual model's epistemological claim in detail. In order to do this, I'll address two questions, the answers to which will prove important for the epistemological story that the perceptual theorist wishes to tell. The first, which constitutes the topic of §2, is whether we should understand emotions as literally perceptions, or as only analogous to perceptions. The second, to be examined in §3, concerns the account that the perceptual theorist wishes to give about how *sensory* perceptions justify empirical judgements, and hence the story that the perceptual model will adopt or deploy in

---

[1] See, for instance, Sabine Döring's paper 'Conflict without Contradiction', in Brun, G., Doğuoğlu, U., and Kuenzle, D. (eds), *Epistemology and Emotions*, Farnham: Ashgate Publishing (2008), where she states that "in the rationalization of other states and actions the emotions play the non-inferential role of perception, and in that sense, so I claim, they *are* perceptions", p. 85.

order to explain how emotions justify evaluative judgements. This will set the scene for an investigation, in the chapters to follow, of the plausibility of the explanation the perceptual model gives of the common-sense idea that emotions can inform us about value.[2]

2.1 Similarities between emotional and perceptual experience

The perceptual model maintains that the intentional or representational element of emotion is a perception of value.[3] On this account, fear involves a perception of something as dangerous, anger involves a perception of something as insulting, joy involves a perception of something as wonderful, shame involves a perception of something as shameful, and so on for other emotions. However, we need to be careful about terminology here. This is because perception is *factive*: if I perceive that the milk has gone off, then it is true that the milk has gone off. This is similar to other factive states like remembering: if I remember that she unplugged the fridge last night, then it is true that she unplugged the fridge last night.[4]

---

[2] Some might worry about the use of 'justification' here. William Alston, for instance, has argued that there isn't any one thing that people mean by justification these days. See Alston, W., *Beyond 'Justification': Dimensions of Epistemic Evaluation*, Ithaca, NY: Cornell University Press (2005). As Alston notes, some think of justification along deontological lines, others in terms of reliability, others in terms of proper function. However, the predominant view remains that there is nothing wrong with the concept and that we should therefore refrain from being pluralists about justification. I'll proceed on the assumption that the latter path is correct, partly on the basis that it remains the standard view, and partly because it seems to be the view of those who support the perceptual model.

[3] Supporters of perceptual models of the emotions include Elgin, C. *Considered Judgement*, Princeton: Princeton University Press (1996), Ch. 5; Elgin, C., 'Emotion and Understanding', in Brun, Doğuoğlu, and Kuenzle (2008); Döring, S. 'Explaining Action by Emotion', *The Philosophical Quarterly* (2003), 53(211): 214–30; Döring (2008); Johnston, M. 'The Authority of Affect', *Philosophy and Phenomenological Research* (2001), 63: 181–214; de Sousa, R., *The Rationality of Emotion*, Cambridge, MA: MIT Press (1987); Prinz, J., *Gut Reactions*, New York: Oxford University Press (2004a); Roberts, R.C., *Emotions*, Cambridge: Cambridge University Press (2003); Tappolet, C., *Emotions et valeurs*, Paris: Presses universitaires de France (2000); Tappolet, C., 'The Irrationality of Emotions', in *Philosophical Perspectives on Irrationality*, Weinstock, D. (ed.), Oxford: Oxford University Press (forthcoming); Zagzebski, L., *Divine Motivation Theory*, Cambridge: Cambridge University Press (2004); and Deonna, J., 'Emotion, Perception and Perspective', *Dialectica* (2006), 60(1): 24–49.

[4] See McBrayer, J., 'A limited defense of moral perception', *Philosophical Studies* (2009), 149(3): 305–20.

Clearly, supporters of the perceptual model do not wish to maintain that emotions are perceptions, given that the latter are factive—for then emotions would give us infallible access to the evaluative world. Rather, the claim is that emotional *experience* is, or is analogous to, perceptual *experience*.[5] Perceptual experience is not factive, since one can have a perceptual experience as of something, such as a six-foot white rabbit, when no such creature exists. So we should rephrase the earlier claim, and hold that according to the perceptual model fear involves a perceptual experience as of something dangerous, joy involves a perceptual experience as of something wonderful, and shame involves a perceptual experience as of something shameful.

We saw in the first chapter that the perceptual model appears attractive to both the cognitivist and feeling theory camps, as representing a promising way to capture the intentionality of emotional experience whilst avoiding traditional objections that have been raised against the respective theories. We can garner further support for the perceptual model by considering a number of important ways in which emotional responses are similar to sensory perceptual experiences, taken to be the paradigm of perceptual experiences.[6]

First, both emotional experience and sensory perceptual experiences possess phenomenal properties: there is something that it is like to have an experience of fear—fear *feels* a certain way—just as there is something that it is like to have a visual experience of redness—redness *looks* a certain way.[7] Second, both are typically "passive": emotional experience, like sensory perceptual experience, is something that happens to us automatically, rather than something that we voluntarily do.[8] In this way both sorts of experience can typically be regarded as reactions or responses to properties, objects, and events in one's environment; indeed, both emotional and sensory perceptual experiences are typically caused by features of one's

---

[5] A different way of putting this would be to say that emotion is like perception as a capacity; for perception as a capacity is not infallible.

[6] See de Sousa (1987), Ch. 6.

[7] If we think that there can be unconscious emotional and perceptual experiences, this claim should be qualified: perhaps we could say that paradigmatic emotional and perceptual experiences possess phenomenal properties.

[8] Again, there are exceptions: I can choose to see an ambiguous figure in one way rather than the other; and I can work myself in to a state of rage or anxiety. Robert Solomon emphasized the idea that emotions are more like actions than we think. See Solomon, R., 'The Rationality of the Emotions', *Southwestern Journal of Philosophy* (1977), 8: 105–14.

environment. Third, on standard views both sorts of experience have representational content—they present the world as being a certain way, and thus have correctness conditions. My anger represents that I've been wronged in some way, and is correct if and only if I have been wronged in that way. By the same token, my visual experience represents that there's a teapot in front of me, and is correct if and only if there is a teapot in front of me. So emotional and sensory perceptual experiences can be accurate or inaccurate responses to the objects and events in one's environment. Fourth, both emotional experience and sensory perceptual experience can diverge or come apart from one's beliefs or judgements about the relevant objects and events. Perceptual experiences diverge from one's beliefs about the external world in the case of known visual illusions such as the Hering illusion; in this illusion we have a perceptual experience of two lines being bent, but know that the lines are in fact straight. And emotional experiences, as we have seen, diverge from the relevant evaluative beliefs in the case of "recalcitrant" emotions, such as the guilt people sometimes experience despite believing that they have done nothing wrong.

There is, however, a further point of similarity, and one which is of central importance given our aims in this book. For emotional experience is held to be akin to perceptual experience at the *epistemological* level. Consider, to illustrate, Catherine Elgin's work. Elgin maintains that it is in virtue of its epistemic role and value that emotional experience can be viewed as akin to perceptual experience. She writes: "[e]motional deliverances are representations conveyed through emotional channels. A representation of frogs as dangerous that presents itself via fear of frogs is a deliverance of that fear."[9] Elgin is concerned to give proper credit to emotion's epistemological credentials, and in doing so will argue against the "standard view", according to which emotional experiences "are at best epistemically inert", and at worst deleterious when it comes to attaining evaluative belief or knowledge. Elgin claims that emotional experiences are like our other "cognitive commitments" such as beliefs and perceptual experiences in that they have a degree of "initial tenability".[10] This suggests

---

[9] Elgin (2008), p. 33.

[10] Elgin (2008), pp. 33–4. And: "The very fact that [emotions] present themselves as indicators of how things stand gives them some degree of initial tenability", p. 40.

that emotional experiences are defeasible reasons for evaluative judgements: my fear of the oncoming storm is a defeasible reason for me to judge that the storm will be dangerous. It is uncontroversial to suppose that *perceptual* experiences are defeasible reasons for empirical judgements. Elgin writes:

> Perception is both triggered by and indicative of aspects of the environment. Perceptual systems evolved and endure because their deliverances promote fitness. Being able to see, or hear, or smell a predator, like feeling instinctively afraid of it, enhances an animal's prospects of evading it. Perception manifestly affords epistemic access to useful information about the environment.[11]

And it is, after all, natural for us to appeal to our perceptual experiences in order to explain *why* we believe what we do, and in order to *justify* our believing as we do. As John McDowell writes, "[S]uppose one asks an ordinary subject why she holds some observational belief, say that an object within her field of view is square. An unsurprising reply might be 'Because it looks that way'."[12] Here the subject cites her perceptual experience to explain and to justify her empirical belief.[13]

Now Elgin rightly admits that perceptual mistakes are possible, which is why she thinks that perceptual experiences only provide defeasible reasons. But she holds that "something's looking blue is ordinarily evidence that it is blue". By the same token, "[i]f the analogy holds, emotional deliverances are indicators, but not always accurate indicators, of aspects of their objects. Just as my experiencing something as blue is evidence, but not conclusive evidence, that it is blue, my being frightened of something is evidence, but not conclusive evidence, that it is dangerous."[14] Elgin concludes that "although our emotions are not utterly reliable indicators of the presence of such properties, we can often tell which emotional reactions reflect the presence of emotional response-dependent

---

[11] Elgin (2008), p. 36.

[12] McDowell, J., *Mind and World*, Cambridge, MA: Harvard University Press (1994), p. 165.

[13] As we'll see, the idea that perceptual experiences are defeasible reasons for beliefs is not one that McDowell himself wants to endorse. This is because the state of something's "looking a certain way" can be interpreted in two ways, one of which is compatible with Elgin's idea that perceptual experiences are defeasible reasons, and one of which is not. Whilst it is fair to say that Elgin's position is the standard one in philosophy of perception, McDowell's account might provide a version of the perceptual model which allows the account to avoid certain objections. I'll have more to say on this point later in the chapter.

[14] Elgin (2008), p. 37.

properties. So under certain recognizable circumstances, an emotional reaction affords epistemic access to such properties."[15] Elgin maintains, then, that emotional experience, like perceptual experience, can constitute evidence for the relevant judgements or beliefs. Emotions can disclose or carry information about value, in much the same way that sensory perceptual experiences disclose or carry information about our non-evaluative environment.

The idea that emotional experiences can be evidence or reason for evaluative judgements, or can disclose or be indicators of value, is a common element across the spectrum of perceptual theories. De Sousa, Deonna, Döring, Johnston, Prinz, Roberts, and Tappolet all hold some version of this thesis. For instance, Döring writes: "An emotion... resembles a sense-perception in having an intentional content that is representational. As a consequence, an emotion can justify a belief. Like a perception, it can do so by its representational content...justifying the content of that belief."[16] And Christine Tappolet states:

If we accept the claim that emotions have contents of this sort [i.e., they present the world as being in a certain way], then it becomes natural to claim that emotions are like sensory perceptions in that they allow us to be aware of certain features of the world, namely values. They do so, at least, under favourable circumstances, that is, when nothing interferes with them.[17]

The idea that emotions play a similar epistemic role to that played by perceptual experiences is not just confined to those seeking to promote the perceptual model in the philosophy of emotion. An analogy between the epistemic role of perceptual and *evaluative* experiences is also drawn, in metaethics, by Graham Oddie. Oddie maintains that in normal circumstances, "the visual experience of a bright red rose—that is to say, the rose's appearing bright red to me—gives me a reason to believe that the rose really is bright red".[18] He now proposes that

[i]f there are genuine experiences of value, they could stand to values as ordinary perceptual experiences stand to the objects of perceptual experience. An experience of the goodness of P, say, would be the state of *P's seeming (appearing, presenting itself as) good*, where this seeming is an experiential, non-doxastic take on the value

[15] Elgin (2008), pp. 40–1.   [16] Döring (2003), p. 215.
[17] Tappolet (forthcoming), p. 7 in MS.
[18] Oddie, G., *Value, Reality, and Desire*, Oxford: Oxford University Press (2005), p. 40.

of P. If there is such a state as the experience of the goodness of P, then, by analogy with the perceptual case, it would give me a reason to believe that P is good.[19]

So Oddie thinks that experiences of value in general constitute defeasible reasons for evaluative beliefs, in much the same way that perceptual experiences constitute defeasible reasons for empirical beliefs.

Oddie differs from supporters of the perceptual model of emotions because he thinks that the relevant experiences of value are *desires* rather than emotions. But it seems that emotions are much more plausible candidates than desires for states in which something seems good to us *in a particular* or *determinate way*. If, therefore, Oddie is to capture the very wide range of evaluative experiences we undergo, then perhaps he too ought to accept that it is emotion rather than desire which plays the representational role in evaluative experience.

Finally, similar ideas can be found in the psychological literature. For instance, Gerald Clore and Karen Gaspar suggest "that beliefs are adjusted to be compatible with internal evidence in the form of feelings, just as they are adjusted to be compatible with external evidence from perceptual experience...Evidence from the sensations of feeling may be treated like sensory evidence from the external environment."[20] The idea that emotional and perceptual experience are similar along an epistemic dimension is thus a given for perceptual theorists of emotion, and also held in disciplines outwith the philosophy of emotion.

So the epistemological claim just discussed is central to—indeed, perhaps definitional of—the perceptual model of emotion. But in order to assess the plausibility of this claim—and with it, the cogency of the perceptual model of emotion—we need to get clearer on the precise nature of the epistemological story that the perceptual theorist wishes to tell. In particular, we need to get answers to two questions: (1) Is emotional experience *literally* a form of perceptual experience? This question is important, since a positive answer might suggest that emotions are *indispensible* for the acquisition of certain kinds of evaluative information. On this view, emotions present or disclose information that couldn't be presented or disclosed in some other manner or by some other means. This, after all, seems true of *sensory* perceptual experience with respect to

[19] Oddie (2005) p. 40.
[20] Clore, G. and Gaspar, K. 'Some Affective Influences on Belief', in *Emotions and Beliefs*, Frijda, N., Manstead, A., and Bem, S. (eds), Cambridge: Cambridge University Press (2000), p. 25.

colours: information about the nature of redness can only be disclosed, we might think, *via* visual experience.[21] (2) How does perceptual experience tell us about the world outside? In particular, how does perceptual experience play a justificatory role with respect to evaluative judgements or beliefs? Since the perceptual model claims that emotional experience either is a form of perceptual experience or is analogous to perceptual experience at the epistemic level, then the epistemic story we tell about how perceptual experience can justify judgements and beliefs is clearly relevant to the story the perceptual theorist will tell about the epistemic role and value of emotional experience. In the following sections I'll take up these questions in turn.

2.2 Literal vs non-literal versions of the perceptual model

The phenomenology, automaticity, and independence from belief of emotional and perceptual experiences strongly suggest that such experiences are at least analogous. But can we say more than this? Can we say, for instance, that emotional experiences are *literally* perceptual experiences as of value? The issue, as I understand it, turns on the question of whether it is the feeling or affective element in emotional experience that plays the representational role; of whether, that is, our feelings are *the way in which* evaluative information is presented or disclosed to us. A positive answer to this question supports the view that emotions are literally perceptual experiences; a negative answer suggests that there is merely an analogy between emotional and perceptual experience at the epistemic level. Let

---

[21] Then again, we might recall the Aristotelian distinction between "proper sensibles", which are objects or properties that can be accessed by only one sense—as colour is accessed by vision—and "common sensibles", which are objects and properties accessible by more than one sense. If value properties are common sensibles, then even if emotional experiences are literally perceptual experiences it won't follow that emotions are indispensable for access to value; for we might have non-emotional ways of accessing values as well. Still, as we'll see, in the absence of a plausible sensory candidate for the disclosure of evaluative information other than affect or feeling, we might think that value is a proper sensible if it is a sensible at all. As such, I'll retain the connection between thinking of emotional experiences as literal perceptual experiences and thinking of them as indispensable for accessing value. This doesn't mean, of course, that I ultimately want to endorse a literal version of the model. Thanks to Fiona Macpherson for pushing me to be clearer on this point.

us turn, therefore, to the question of the precise relation—identity or analogy—that exists between emotional and perceptual experience.

2.2.1 Literal versions of the perceptual model

Literal versions of the perceptual model maintain that emotional experiences *are* perceptual experiences. In order for this to be illuminating, we need some account of what perceptual experience is. A helpful starting point is to hold that perceptual experiences are conscious mental states that result from the operation of a perceptual system or modality. We might then hold, following Jesse Prinz, that a perceptual system or modality is a "dedicated input system", and define this as "a mental system that has the function of receiving information from the body or the world via some priority class of transducers and internal representations".[22] Prinz continues: "Vision, audition, and olfaction are dedicated input systems. They each have their own neural pathways and proprietary representations. If emotions are literally perceptual, they must reside in such a system."[23] So do emotions reside in a dedicated input system?

One possibility is that emotions reside in one of the traditional sensory perceptual systems. We can, however, doubt that emotional experience is a form of visual, auditory, tactile, olfactory, or gustatory experience.[24] For one thing, emotional experiences have a phenomenology which is different from that associated with sight, hearing, etc. As Demian Whiting puts it,

What it is like to undergo fear or anger . . . is nothing like what it is to have a visual experience of any sort. Neither is undergoing fear or anger anything like having any other type of sensory experience, including auditory or tactile experiences.

---

[22] Prinz, (2004a), p. 222. We might put this point slightly differently: talk of 'modality' is thought to capture the *way in which* something is represented, or, as David Chalmers puts it, the *manner of representation*. He writes: "There are many different manners of representation. For example, one can represent a content perceptually, and one can represent a content doxastically (in belief): these correspond to different manners of representation. At a more fine-grained level, one can represent a content visually or auditorily", Chalmers, D., 'The Representational Character of Experience', in Leiter, B. (ed.), *The Future for Philosophy*, Oxford: Clarendon Press (2004), p. 155. Our question might be understood as the question of whether representing a content emotionally is genuinely a matter of representing that content perceptually.

[23] Prinz (2004a), p. 222.

[24] Whiting, D., 'Are emotions perceptual experiences of value?', *Ratio* (2012), 25(1): 93–107.

Crucially . . . emotions manifest a *feeling* quality that is palpably lacking in the case of sensory experience.[25]

For another, we can have emotional experiences which don't involve the senses at all—as when we remember the insults shouted by the gang of teenagers and feel angry as a result. If emotional experiences are literally perceptual experiences, therefore, they must reside in a different dedicated input system, or result from the operation of a different kind of perceptual modality.

A more plausible possibility, given the phenomenology of emotional experience, is that emotions reside in the dedicated input system that generates *affect* or *feeling*. On this view, emotional experience is a form of perceptual experience that involves the affective presentation of evaluative content, and where such a presentation results from the operation of a system that has its own "neural pathways and proprietary representations". Feeling is thus the "manner of presentation" of evaluative information. The basic idea, again as Whiting phrases things, is that "when we undergo emotion we represent evaluative properties to ourselves by means of *feeling*".[26] When we are afraid, it is our feeling of fear that represents the dangerousness of our situation; when we are angry, our feeling of anger is the way in which some wrong is presented to us; when we are joyful, our feeling of joy is the way in which something wonderful is presented to us; and so on for other emotions. This idea has been developed, in varying degrees of strength, by Jesse Prinz, Mark Johnston, and Sabine Döring, amongst others. I'll briefly outline their views, in order to give a flavour of the kind of perceptual model that they propose, before doing something similar with the rival non-literal model.

As we saw in the previous chapter, the central problem with the James–Lange account of emotion is that feelings of bodily change seem to lack the right kind of representational content. For example, my feeling of nausea when I wake up in the middle of the night is not, by itself, about any evaluative feature of the world beyond my body. So feelings of bodily changes seem ill-fitted to be the intentional or representational element in emotional experience. This would seem to pose a significant problem for those who claim that feeling constitutes a perceptual modality, on the assumption that perceptual experiences *do* have representational content.

---

[25] Whiting (2012), p. 96.   [26] Whiting (2012), p. 96.

However, in a number of recent works Jesse Prinz has argued that emotions are perceptions of changes in the somatosensory system, and that such feelings *can* represent 'core relational themes' such as danger, loss, contamination, insult, and the like. If so, the central obstacle to the feeling theory of emotion, namely that bodily feelings lack intentional or representational content, can be overcome. Let us consider his view in more detail.

In 'Embodied Emotions' and *Gut Reactions*, Prinz appeals to a particular account of mental representation in order to show how feelings can have intentional content.[27] This theory is due to Dretske and Fodor. The basic idea is that "a mental state gets its intentional content in virtue of being reliably caused (or having the function of being reliably caused) by something".[28] On this view, intentional content is determined by causal relations. In more detail, and as we saw in the previous chapter: representations are thought to be mental states that carry information, and that can be mistakenly applied. Something carries information if it reliably co-occurs with that thing. For example: smoke can carry information about fire, rings inside a tree carry information about the age of the tree. But states must also have the *function* of carrying information in order to be genuine representations. They must have been "set in place"—for instance, by evolution or by socialization or by some other form of learning—for that purpose. On this view, pain might represent bodily damage, because it reliably co-occurs with bodily damage and was set up, by evolution, for this reason.

Prinz argues that emotions are perceptual experiences of bodily changes. He writes:

The James–Lange theory identifies emotions with feelings of bodily changes. The bodily changes in question are . . . perturbations in visceral organs and adjustments in skeletal muscles. This is clearly a perceptual theory. Emotions are states in the somatosensory system. The embodied appraisal theory that I have been defending descends from the writings of James and Lange. It qualifies as perceptual for exactly the same reasons. Emotions are states within systems that are dedicated to detecting bodily changes.[29]

---

[27] Prinz (2004a); and Prinz, J., 'Embodied Emotions', in Solomon, R. (ed.), *Thinking about Feeling: Contemporary Philosophers on Emotions*, Oxford: Oxford University Press (2004b).

[28] Prinz (2004b), p. 55.

[29] Prinz (2004a), p. 224.

But as perceptual experiences of bodily changes, emotional experiences are caused by those changes. Moreover, since bodily changes can be reliably caused by things outside of the body—such as dangers, insults, loved ones, etc.—then it is possible that emotions can represent such things. For it is plausible to think that emotions like fear and disgust were "set up" by evolution to be "set off" by dangerous and contaminated things. He writes: "Consider fear. It seems quite likely that we are wired to undergo a characteristic perceived . . . bodily change under a variety of threatening conditions. A similar bodily pattern is triggered when the auditory system detects a loud sudden noise, or when the visual system detects a looming object." As a result, "the perception of that bodily state represents danger, because it is under the reliable causal control of danger-ousness".[30] If so, then feelings of bodily changes count as genuine percep-tions, since they result from a dedicated input mechanism, and can have representational content. There is no need for emotions to involve states such as judgement or belief to be the bearers of the evaluative content that is characteristic of emotional experience.

Mark Johnston is another proponent of the perceptual model who maintains that feeling or affect is *the way in which* certain values are presented or disclosed to us, and who thinks that feeling or affect consti-tutes a genuine and distinctive way of seeing the world.[31] Because of this, Johnston thinks that without "affective engagement" with the world we would be blind to or ignorant of the relevant values. The thought is that the world appears to us affectively in a certain way in emotional experi-ence, and this is not to be captured by some other mode or manner of representation. The analogy here, of course, is with the necessity of visual experiences for the disclosure of aspects of our environment such as colours. Without visual experience of redness, for instance, we would lack access to what redness is: the way some red object appears to us in visual perceptual experience cannot be captured by some other mode or manner of representation.[32]

---

[30] Prinz (2004b), p. 55.

[31] Johnston (2001).

[32] Perhaps I need to qualify this as follows: the way the world appears to us in emotional experience cannot *as a matter of fact* be captured by some other mode or manner of representa-tion. Perhaps some such mode *could* nevertheless come into existence. Something similar applies to our access to colours: perhaps a sense other than vision could come into existence and detect colours. Thanks to Fiona Macpherson for discussion of this point.

Johnston makes his case for the necessity of affective engagement by focusing on a particular class of values, which include "the beautiful, the charming, the erotic . . . the banal, the sublime, the horrific and the plain old appealing and the repellent".[33] Johnston thinks that "[i]f one has never been moved or *affected* by the determinate ways in which things are beautiful or charming or erotic or banal or sublime or appealing, then one is ignorant of the relevant determinate values."[34] Similarly, he points out that we can only think and judge about cherry red if we have had sensory experience of cherry red. The idea that we need affective engagement is "most vivid", states Johnston, "in cases in which one can only effectively convey to another the considerations in favor of, say, a style, a song or a friend's manner by having the other sense it, in part by feeling as one does".[35] So Johnston thinks that "affect is . . . the disclosure or sensory presentation of the appealing".[36] Moreover, Johnston suggests that the opposition to the idea that "affectivity [is] a refinement of sensing" stems from a "mentalistic account of ordinary sensing" that we have reason to reject. He wants us to accept, instead, that "the senses are forms of openness to things in the environment, more precisely to things of various kinds, qualified thus and so and standing in a variety of relations to the sensing subject and to each other".[37]

A similar account of the necessity of affective engagement in the disclosure of value is proposed in a number of papers by Sabine Döring.[38] Döring argues for the conclusion that emotions are "affective

---

[33] Johnston (2001), p. 182.

[34] Johnston (2001), p. 183.

[35] Johnston (2001), p. 183, n. 2. Prior to this quoted passage, Johnston writes: " . . . the sensuous values . . . can often only be disclosed perceptually."

[36] Johnston (2001), p. 189.

[37] Johnston (2001), p. 206. It is not entirely clear whether Johnston really does support the idea that emotions are literally perceptions. For he makes it clear that he is concerned with *affective* rather than *emotional* engagement with the world, and holds that affective episodes are distinct from emotions; the latter, Johnston claims, "typically arise after one is drawn to or repelled by something" (p. 182). However, as Ralph Wedgwood suggests in 'Sensing Values?', *Philosophy and Phenomenological Research* (2001), 63: p. 215, n. 1, many paradigmatic cases of emotion seem to consist, at least in part, of being drawn to or repelled by something, in which case the distinction between affective and emotional engagement is not sharp. If so, it is not clear why Johnston's claims about affective engagement couldn't also apply to emotional engagement.

[38] See Döring (2003); Döring, S., 'Seeing What to Do: Affective Perception and Rational Motivation', *Dialectica* (2007) 61(3): 363–94; and Döring (2008).

perceptions", and maintains that "emotional intentionality is felt or affect-ive intentionality".[39] Things are slightly complicated here because Döring thinks that emotions *are* affective perceptions that are nevertheless analo-gous to *sensory* perceptions. We might say: on her view emotions are literally perceptions but not literally sensory perceptions. Now according to Döring, the kinds of feelings involved in emotion are not (simply) the physiological responses and changes that James, Lange, and Prinz focus on. Instead, following Peter Goldie, she thinks that emotions (also) involve "feeling towards" objects and events.[40] Feeling towards is, on Goldie's account, a matter of "thinking of with feeling", and is not reducible to bodily feeling plus a non-emotional evaluative thought. Instead, Goldie thinks that

emotional feelings are inextricably intertwined with the world-directed aspect of emotion, so that an adequate account of an emotion's intentionality, of its direct-edness towards the world outside of the body, will at the same time capture an important aspect of its phenomenology. Intentionality and phenomenology are inextricably linked.[41]

Because of this, the content presented to us in an emotional experience of danger is different from the content of our non-emotional thoughts about danger. Since feelings make this difference, then it is feelings themselves that are the relevant intentional or representational element in emotional experience.

To illustrate, Goldie provides (after Michael Stocker) the example of someone who prior to falling on ice had only "an intellectual appreciation" of the danger, but who after the accident could think about the dangers of ice in an emotional way. Goldie thinks that after the accident there is a difference in both attitude and content, from "intellectual appreciation of" to "feeling fear towards" the danger. That is, after such an accident our

---

[39] Döring (2008), p. 97.

[40] See Goldie, P., *The Emotions*, Oxford: Oxford University Press (2000), esp. ch. 2. The parenthetical remarks indicate that, for Goldie, emotional experience involves both bodily feelings and feelings towards: "our entire mind and body is engaged in the emotional experience, and all the feelings are 'united in consciousness' in being directed towards its object: united 'body and soul', 'heart and mind'. For example, sexual desire is felt with the whole being—body and soul—*for* the one we desire", p. 55.

[41] Goldie, P., 'Emotions, Feelings and Intentionality', *Phenomenology and the Cognitive Sciences* (2002), 1(3): p. 242.

way of thinking of these very same dangers is different. When we think of something as being dangerous, we might just think of it as meriting fear, and we can do that without actually feeling fear towards it. Then, when we come to think of it *with fear*, the dangerousness of the object, and the determinate features towards which the thought is directed, is grasped in a different way. That is to say, the content of the thought is different; one's way of thinking of it is completely new. It is not just the old way of thinking of it, plus some new element. Rather, it is more like coming to see a hidden shape in a drawing, or coming to see the shape of the face on the visible surface of the moon; one's way of seeing is completely new.[42]

Döring also rejects the idea that the emotional presentation of some evaluative content can be identical with a non-emotional presentation of the same content, plus a feeling of bodily change.[43] Certain evaluative content can only be presented in emotional experience, in much the same way that certain non-evaluative content (e.g. about colours) can only be presented in visual experience. So for Döring, "an emotion's intentionality is best understood by analogy with [sensory] perception. This is at least so if it is agreed that a perception also possesses both phenomenology and intentionality, and that its intentional content is also part of its conscious, subjective character."[44]

Each of these versions of the perceptual model maintains that emotions involve the affective disclosure of evaluative information. Each maintains that it is feeling or affect that is doing the representational work in emotional experience. And Johnston and Döring are explicit in claiming that certain values can *only* be disclosed through feeling or affect. Feeling or affect is thus the vehicle for evaluative information that could not be conveyed in a non-affective manner or by non-affective means, at least for creatures like us. On these views, then, emotional experiences are

---

[42] Goldie (2002), p. 243. For Goldie, then, the phenomenology of emotional experience changes the way of thinking about the emotional event, in much the same way as the phenomenology of colour experience can change the way of thinking about an object only previously 'theoretically' understood to be a particular colour.

[43] She writes: "Emotions are evaluations, but evaluations of a special kind... On no account can they be reduced to mere evaluations". In Döring (2007), p. 373. I understand *mere* evaluation here as non-emotional or purely intellectual evaluation.

[44] Döring (2007), p. 376. To reiterate, although she talks here of an "analogy with perception", what she really means is an analogy with *sensory* perception. Her commitment to the idea that emotional experience involves affective perception, and her identification of feeling towards as the intentional element in emotional experience, suggest she holds that emotional experiences *are* literally perceptual experiences, on a broader understanding of "perceptual".

perceptual experiences in a literal sense. Moreover, they illustrate the way in which emotional experiences—as feelings—have a distinctive epistemic value, given that they are indispensible for the disclosure of certain kinds of evaluative knowledge. The truth of a literal version of the perceptual model therefore suggests that our feelings, far from being hindrances to our practices of forming evaluative judgements, are essential to this.

2.2.2 Non-literal versions of the perceptual model

Non-literal versions of the perceptual model can be characterized by the rejection of the claim that it is feeling or affect that does the representational work in emotional experience, although they need not deny that feeling or affect is typically or perhaps even always present when value is disclosed emotionally. That is, whereas literal versions of the perceptual model maintain that certain values can only be known or disclosed through feeling or affect, in much the same way that colours can only be known or disclosed through visual experience, non-literal versions of the model will deny this, and hold that the same values could be disclosed in the absence of feeling or affect—although not in the absence of emotion as such.[45] If so, then feeling or affect is not the manner or mode of presentation of evaluative information. Nevertheless, supporters of non-literal versions of the perceptual model will insist that there remain a number of similarities between emotional and perceptual experience, which warrants talk of the former being analogous to the latter. And in particular, emotional experience can still constitute reason or evidence for evaluative judgement, in a similar way to that in which perceptual experience constitutes reason or evidence for empirical judgement. Both experiences can, that is, still suffice to justify the relevant judgements, so the shift from a literal to a non-literal model doesn't undermine the main epistemological claim that the perceptual theorist wishes to make; or so the non-literal theorist will argue. Let us consider, to illustrate, two prominent versions of this form of perceptual theory.

In *The Rationality of Emotion*, Ronald de Sousa writes that "emotions are best regarded as a kind of perception, the objects of which are what I call

---

[45] See Döring (2008), p. 93 for this contrast between what she calls the "constitutive" and "facilitative" views. The former is adopted by what I am terming literal perceptual theorists, while non-literal theorists are happy to endorse the latter.

axiological properties".[46] Nevertheless, he backs away from the claim that this should be taken literally, writing later:

[h]ow far can we push the idea that emotions are a kind of perception? The thesis I am driving at is this. The ways in which emotions are subjective do not sufficiently undermine the analogy of perception to exclude a significant claim to objectivity. Emotions can indeed be viewed as providing genuine information. But the analogy is not so close as to warrant the assimilation of emotions to perception, any more than to beliefs or desires.[47]

Although de Sousa thinks that emotions are like perceptual experiences in a number of important ways, he denies that affective phenomenology is essential to emotion, holding instead that emotions do not need to be conscious.[48] If we think that unconscious emotions nevertheless have intentional content, then the intentionality of emotion is not grounded in feeling or affect. Emotions are not therefore literally perceptual experiences.[49]

For de Sousa, emotions are instead "species of determinate patterns of salience among objects of attention, lines of inquiry, and inferential strategies".[50] This point about attention will be familiar to us from Chapter 1: emotions control salience or what we attend to; they make us aware of certain features of our environment rather than others; and for de Sousa they lead us to focus on particular inferences and motivate some inquiries rather than others. Indeed, as we also saw in Chapter 1, the fact that emotions control salience indicates one way in which they can be epistemically valuable: for emotions can draw our attention to evaluative features of our world that we might otherwise have missed.[51] Now

---

[46] de Sousa (1987), p. 45.

[47] de Sousa (1987), p. 149.

[48] de Sousa (1987), pp. 149–50. In support of this, note that perceptual *experiences* are, almost by definition, taken to be conscious states, although many people accept that there can be forms of unconscious *perception*.

[49] de Sousa raises additional points of disanalogy between emotions and perceptual experiences in Chapter 6 of the book. He notes that sensory experiences are "decreasingly sensitive" to a subject's physiological condition, her "experiential history" and present doxastic state, and "social and ideological factors". However, "emotions are typically susceptible" to all of these things, which makes them rather more "subjective" than perceptual experiences, pp. 152–3.

[50] de Sousa (1987), p. 196.

[51] As we'll see later, and as de Sousa's remarks about lines of inquiry and inferential strategies suggest, emotions can draw our attention to things other than values—as when fear draws our attention to escape strategies, for instance.

because attention and salience are involved in perception, emotions have, as Prinz points out, "a perceptual flavour".[52] But in so far as emotions involve the mobilization of attentional, inferential, and interpretive resources, they seem rather more cognitive than affective phenomena, and so rather more cognitive than perceptual in a literal sense. For this reason, de Sousa's account is best seen as a non-literal version of the perceptual model.[53]

Robert C. Roberts is another philosopher who supports a non-literal version of the perceptual model, although one that has considerable affinities with literal accounts that appeal to psychic or intellectual feelings, and in particular to what he calls "feelings of construed condition", such as "feeling confident, awkward, ambitious, incompetent, ripped off, excluded".[54] Emotions, on Roberts's view, are "concern-based construals". Now it is difficult to explain, with any precision, what a construal is, although Roberts provides some helpful examples. Thus, I might construe a duck–rabbit figure as a duck at one time and as a rabbit at another; I might see a face in terms of another, as when I see my father's face reflected in my own; I can have the impression that the person behind me in the queue is standing too close; I can think of a chimpanzee in human terms; and so on.[55] These examples suggest that construals can involve a number of different elements gathered from perception, imagination, conception, and thought. Thus, construals "have an immediacy reminiscent of sense perception. They are impressions, ways things appear to the subject . . . they are experiences."[56] But they are not identical with sense perceptions: to see my father's face reflected in mine isn't literally to have a visual sensation of its being that way. Moreover, to think of a chimpanzee in human terms owes as much to imagination and conceptual thought as it does to perception, and to this extent construals resemble de Sousa's

---

[52] Prinz (2004a), p. 223.

[53] Prinz (2004a), pp. 222–3. Prinz argues that on de Sousa's account, "[e]motions are interpretations of things without being explicit judgements . . . [And] many nonperceptual states have this character too. A child might 'see' her stuffed animals as living things. A mugger may 'look at' passersby as victims when deciding whom to assault. An artist may view a model as Venus or Adonis. These are forms of perception only in a nonliteral sense", p. 223.

[54] Roberts (2003), p. 66. Such feelings, for Roberts, are intentional, since they are about oneself; they involve thinking of or construing oneself in a certain way. But they are not identical with emotions, for reasons that will become clear.

[55] For similar examples, see Roberts (2003), pp. 70–4.

[56] Roberts (2003), p. 75.

account of emotions as involving "interpretation without explicit judgement". For Roberts, then, construals are "a hard-to-specify structure of percept, concept, image, and thought". Although hard-to-specify, this should not make them mysterious; for they share this feature with "most of our experiences, as well as most of our unconscious states of mind".[57]

Roberts holds that emotions are *concern-based* construals: that is, and in line with our discussion in the previous chapter, construals that are based upon or grounded in some underlying care or concern. However, despite introducing construals *via* talk of feelings of construed condition, Roberts does not qualify as a literal perceptual theorist. This is because he distinguishes feelings of construed condition from emotions, on the grounds that the former, but not the latter, are "essentially feelings".[58] Roberts thus denies that feelings are necessary for emotional experience, and as a result it cannot be feeling that plays the requisite representational role in emotion.[59] If so, emotions do not appear to be literal perceptual experiences. Nevertheless, in maintaining that there are clear resemblances between emotional experience and perceptual experience, in that they are impressions, ways things appear to someone, and possessed of an immediacy, Roberts qualifies as accepting a non-literal version of the theory.

2.2.3 Which version of the perceptual model should we prefer?

The central claim of the perceptual model is an epistemological claim, namely that emotional experience constitutes reason or evidence for evaluative judgement in a similar way to the way in which perceptual experience constitutes reason or evidence for empirical judgement. The question of whether we should prefer literal or non-literal versions of the perceptual model is the question of how similar the epistemological stories we tell will be. On the former account, the phenomenology of emotional experience—its feeling or affective element—itself discloses information about the evaluative world. On the latter account, the feeling or affective element in emotion, although paradigmatic of emotion or typically present when value is disclosed, is not itself that which represents danger, contamination, loss, beauty, and the like. According to non-literal versions

---

[57] Roberts (2003), p. 77.   [58] Roberts (2003), p. 68.
[59] Roberts (2003) writes: "Emotions are paradigmatically felt, but emotions may occur independently of the corresponding feeling", p. 60.

of the perceptual model, the relevant information is relayed by non-affective means.

Which version of the model should we prefer? This is a difficult question to answer; but I think that there is *some* reason to prefer non-literal versions of the model. I'll present three arguments in favour of non-literal versions shortly. Before doing this, however, we should note that the evidence typically adduced in favour of literal versions is in fact compatible with non-literal versions, and so the case in favour of the former might not be as strong as its supporters suppose. Recall Johnston's claim that "[i]f one has never been moved or *affected* by the determinate ways in which things are beautiful or charming or erotic or banal or sublime or appealing, then one is ignorant of the relevant determinate values."[60] The thought is that we need to be affectively engaged with certain values in order to think and judge about them—just as we need to have visual experience of colours in order to have a proper grasp of colour concepts and make proper colour judgements. However, it might be true that one will be ignorant of the relevant values unless one has been moved or affected in the relevant ways, without its being true that it is the feeling or affect that is disclosing the values. This is because feeling or affect can be so ubiquitous with respect to emotional experiences of the attractive and repellent that we never get evaluative information about such things via emotional experience without *also* having the relevant feelings. But it does not follow from the *coincidence* of evaluative information and feeling or affect that the feeling or affect constitutes the mode of presentation of the information. Consider a parallel argument: perhaps a particular action-tendency is ubiquitous with regard to a particular emotion, such as the fight-or-flight tendency in fear. If so, then one will never get information about dangerous things via fear without also experiencing the tendency to fight or flee. But it would be a mistake to conclude that it is the action-tendency that therefore does the representational work. The non-literal theorist can happily admit, then, that emotional experience involves feeling or affect—and perhaps, with respect to those emotions surrounding the appealing and repellent, *always* involves feeling or affect—whilst maintaining that it is some non-affective element that does the representational work. Since both of our models are compatible with the claim that

---

[60] Johnston (2001), p. 183.

we don't get certain kinds of evaluative information from emotional experience in the absence of feeling or affect, we need other arguments to decide between them.

Let us turn now to arguments in favour of non-literal versions. The first reiterates the main claim against feeling theories of emotion adduced by de Sousa and Roberts. Recall that de Sousa and Roberts both claim that we can <u>have emotional experience in the absence of feeling</u>—when, for example, our emotions are unconscious. If we can have unconscious emotions such as envy or guilt or love that are nevertheless intentional and evaluative—representing objects and events as things to be envied, or as moral wrongs, or as lovable—then we should deny that it is feeling or affect which constitutes the intentional or representational element in emotional experience, at least if we doubt that there can be unconscious feelings. And it seems *prima facie* plausible to suppose that there <u>are uncon-</u> <u>scious emotions</u>. I might, for instance, be envious of the fact that you are a regular guest on Radio 4, and yet be unaware of my envy because I lack the relevant feelings—whether these are bodily feelings or the kind of psychic feelings that Goldie and Döring appeal to in developing the account of feeling towards. The claim that I am envious seems to follow from the fact that positing unconscious emotions sometimes provides the best explanation of behaviour: in this case, of my tendency to be more disparaging about the BBC, or about that particular radio programme, since you started appearing on it. This is telling, given our general aim of investigating the epistemology of emotional experience, since the best explanation of my behaviour in such a case will involve a negative evaluation of the situation where you have some good (i.e. you appear on the programme) and I don't, which is (roughly) the evaluative profile involved in envy. If so, then unconscious emotions must be capable of providing us with evaluative information, and feeling or affect cannot be the manner or mode of presentation of this information.

 Now Goldie responds to this criticism by drawing a distinction between unreflective and reflective consciousness; the former involves being emotionally engaged with the world whilst the latter involves awareness of one's emotional engagement, e.g. "being aware that I feel afraid; being aware that I feel afraid of the oncoming vehicle", and so forth. So to say that a subject S feels an emotion E is ambiguous between claiming that S "has those feelings which are part of his being unreflectively emotionally engaged with the world" and his being "reflectively aware of having certain [emotional] feelings".[61] The idea of unconscious emotions, for Goldie, then turns out to be the idea of feelings of which we remain reflectively unaware. But this move, even if it convinces with respect to *some* cases—cases where, were we to reflect, we would admit to having the relevant feelings—is unconvincing in a case of "disavowed envy"—such as a version of the previous example where I do not admit to having feelings of envy about your job on the radio even after reflection. Goldie needs to rule out the possibility of such cases; but it is difficult to see how he can do so.

A second argument holds that it is not just the possibility of unconscious, disavowed emotions that casts doubt upon literal versions of the perceptual model. We might think that the existence of long-term emotions does as well. Consider, to illustrate, long-standing emotions such as love or pride. All should agree that one can be in love with or be proud of someone, without necessarily feeling love or pride at some particular time. We talk of couples being in love for decades, of parents being proud of all that their children have achieved, without thinking that this implies the persistence of feelings throughout these periods. Instead, the connection with feeling or affect is (at least according to proponents of the feeling account, such as Prinz) *dispositional*: in order for someone to be in love with another, they must at least be disposed to have the relevant feelings on occasion. But even if this is true, it raises the question of whether the person's long-standing emotion can disclose value to her at times when she *doesn't* experience the relevant feelings. Can a wife's love for her husband inform her that her husband is lovable, in those instances where she is not feeling love? It strikes me that the answer here is "yes", since other elements of emotional experience—such as captured attention and inclination to appropriate behaviour—seem perfectly capable of playing the informational role here. She might, after all, realize that she still loves him because she can't stop thinking about how lovable he is, or because she finds herself inclined to phone him at all hours, despite not feeling love or affection at any of these times. In such situations, evaluative information is emotionally conveyed or disclosed, and in an experience that is conscious and avowed—the subject is, after all, aware of her attentional focus and behavioural

---

[61] Goldie (2000), p. 64.

inclinations, and aware of what these mean with respect to her continu-ing love for that person—but not conveyed or disclosed by affect or feeling. As such, both unconscious and long-term emotions can inform us about value, but without relying upon feeling or affect to do so.

At this point the defender of literal versions of the perceptual model might insist that it is only occurrent, conscious emotional experiences that are literally perceptual experiences—in which case citing unconscious or long-standing emotions is beside the point. Moreover, the perceptual theorist will continue, if we do focus on occurrent, conscious emotional experiences we can see that there is, as Goldie and Döring are at pains to point out, a difference in attitude *and content* between non-emotional and emotional evaluations, in which case feeling or affect will convey evalu-ative information that is not (and cannot be) conveyed by some non-affective element. Recall Goldie's distinction between an intellectual apprehension of danger, and feeling fear towards a dangerous thing. For Goldie, the former involves the (mere) thought that something merits danger, whereas with the latter, "the dangerousness of the object, and the determinate features towards which the thought is directed, is grasped in a different way. That is to say, the content of the thought is different; one's way of thinking of it is completely new".[62] But it is not at all obvious—and this is the third argument against the literal interpretation—that the con-tent in such cases *is* different. Suppose we assume that thinking of some-thing as dangerous is thinking of it as meriting fear.[63] If so, then a full or adequate grasp of the concept "dangerous" would seem to require that the subject thinks of it as meriting an emotional response with a typical or paradigmatic affective component; and this would seem to require that the subject has *had* the relevant affect or feeling. Even the non-literal theorist should agree that a complete grasp of the relevant evaluative concept requires an acquaintance with the feeling or affect typically (or paradig-matically) involved in the emotional response. If so, then even a mere intellectual thought about danger will be a thought about something meriting a state with an affective or feeling element.

---

[62] Goldie (2002), p. 243.

[63] This is not an implausible assumption. Sentimentalists will regard this as an analysis of concepts such as "dangerous". But even if we are not sentimentalists, we might regard it as necessarily true that dangerous things merit fear. For more on a "rational sentimentalist" account of value, see Chapter 3.

Given this, we can doubt that thinking of some object as dangerous *with fear* is indeed a way of thinking about it that is "completely new". For to think of the object as dangerous *with fear* would seem to be a matter of thinking of it as meriting the state with the affective or feeling aspect that one is currently experiencing. As such, the difference between an intellectual apprehension of danger, and feeling fear towards that thing, would seem to be a difference between the thought that something merits a state with a feeling that one is not presently experiencing but nevertheless has experienced in the past, and the thought that something merits a state with the feeling that one is presently experiencing. But it is difficult to see how this difference between the experiences constitutes a difference in representational *evaluative* content. It is difficult to see, in other words, how the presence of the relevant feeling or affect conveys different evaluative information *about the dangerousness of the object*. Rather, when we feel fear towards the object, we are informed about, or rather reminded, what feeling fear is like.[64]

To see this more clearly, compare the content of feeling fear towards some object, and hence thinking with fear of that object as dangerous, at time t_1; and the content of non-emotionally thinking of the object as dangerous when one's feeling of fear has dissipated, at time t_2. The content in the first case is that the object merits a state with *this* affective or feeling element; the content in the second case is that the object merits a state with the affective or feeling element that has just dissipated. But I find it hard to understand how the first represents a "completely new" way of thinking about danger, when contrasted with the second. And I find it hard to understand, therefore, how the evaluative content of emotional experience in the first case differs from the evaluative content of the non-emotional experience in the second. All that has happened is that one's relation to the relevant affect or feeling has changed: in the first case the feeling is presently experienced, in the second the feeling is remembered. How can this mark a genuine difference in what is disclosed about the evaluative realm beyond one's body? As such, the central claim that the literal perceptual theorist makes about the necessity of affective

---

[64] The claim that there is a difference in content between non-emotional thought and feeling towards is plausible, if at all, in those cases where the subject hasn't had experience of the relevant feelings. But then we might think that the subject fails to grasp the relevant concept, and as such is not in the business of thinking genuinely evaluative thoughts.

presentation of evaluative information appears to be undermined: the same information can be presented non-emotionally, for instance when one has non-emotional thoughts about danger once one's feelings have dissipated.

These considerations suggest that the most plausible form of the perceptual model will be non-literal. Further support for this conclusion will be presented in the following chapters, where we will consider how evaluative information can be disclosed in a non-affective way. As we'll see, however, such a picture can be used to generate objections to the idea that emotional experience is even *akin* to perceptual experience at the epistemic level. Given that objections to weaker, non-literal versions of the model will be equally objections to stronger, literal versions, we might therefore think that the question of which kind of perceptual theory we should adopt will become moot. But this is to get ahead of ourselves. Let us turn now to our second question, and consider in more detail how sensory perceptual experience is thought to play a justificatory role with respect to empirical judgements or beliefs. As we'll see, the perceptual theorist will claim that a similar account can be told about the role of emotional experience with respect to evaluative judgements or beliefs.

2.3 Emotional experiences as reasons to believe

We have seen that according to the perceptual model, emotional and perceptual experiences are analogous in a number of important ways. One such way is epistemological: according to the perceptual model, emotional experience plays a role in the justification of evaluative belief that mirrors the role played by sensory perceptual experience in the justification of empirical belief. In particular, we saw the claim made by supporters of the perceptual model that emotional experience constitutes reason or evidence for evaluative belief, in much the same way that sensory perceptual experience constitutes reason or evidence for empirical belief. In order, then, to clarify the perceptual model's claims about the epistemology of emotional experience, we need to say something about how sensory perceptual experiences constitute reasons or evidence for empirical propositions. Here we encounter a rather large problem. While pretty much everyone agrees that perceptual experiences are central to—indeed, enjoy a privileged position with respect to—the justification of empirical belief and the promotion of empirical knowledge, it is, to put it mildly, an issue of some debate as to exactly *how* the relevant experiences do so.

One complication is generated by a distinction between "mediate" and "immediate" justification. A belief is mediately justified if part of the justification for that belief comes from other things you justifiably believe. A belief is immediately justified if it is justified but not on the basis of other beliefs. Some of our perceptual beliefs are mediately justified—as when I believe something partly on the basis of perceptual experience and partly on the basis of background beliefs, memories, and the like. For instance, suppose I believe that the car in the outside lane is moving too fast for me to safely overtake the car in front. Certainly my perceptual experience plays a role in my coming to form this belief or make this judgement; plausibly, it plays a role by generating a succession of perceptual beliefs about relative positions of the cars as time passes. But my background beliefs and inferential capacities and memories also play a clear justificatory role here. Compare this with a case where I look ahead and immediately form the belief that there is a car in front. The justification for this belief, plausibly, would seem to depend not upon any background or other beliefs that I have, but solely upon the content of my perceptual experience and perhaps some external factor such as reliability. In what follows I'll be concerned with immediate rather than mediate justification, since proponents of the perceptual model maintain that emotions are themselves, and in the absence of further beliefs, reasons or evidence for evaluative judgements.

A second complication is the long-standing dispute between "indirect" and "direct" realists about perceptual justification and knowledge. Indirect realists maintain that our knowledge of the external world is indirect: in perceptual experience we are aware of some "intermediary" sense impression, on the basis of which we believe that things are thus-and-so. Direct realists, on the other hand, maintain that in (veridical) perceptual experience we directly experience some object or event: the object or event is, in a literal sense, *part of* veridical perceptual experience.[65]

Indirect realists think that their account gains support from the phenomenon of sensory hallucination; for hallucination can involve a perceptual experience that is indistinguishable from veridical perceptual

---

[65] Despite the terminology of "intermediary" sense impressions, indirect realism isn't to be thought of as providing an account of mediate justification. For indirect realism clearly need not hold that anything other than the sense impression is necessary for justification.

experience, in which case hallucinatory and veridical perceptual experiences seem to share a "common experiential factor", some aspect of experience that is common to the veridical case in which there really are insects crawling all over one's skin and the hallucinatory case in which there are not. What we are directly aware of in perceptual experience just is this common factor, rather than the object or event that the common factor represents. Indirect realists will think that cases of illusion provide similar support for their approach. Direct realists think that their account gains support from the phenomenology of perceptual experience, and because it is better placed to deal with the sceptic. This is because it seems that we experience objects and events directly in perceptual experience, rather than indirectly *via* an intermediate element: when I look out of the window I directly perceive the schoolchildren pelting my colleague with snowballs, rather than an impression or sense-datum that represents this state of affairs. In addition, the direct realist will maintain that their account is not hostage to sceptical fortune. For according to the indirect realist, all we are ever aware of is an impression or representation or sense-datum, an intermediary between ourselves and the world. This raises the obvious question about whether the world is in fact how we take it to be in our experiences. How can we know, if all we ever have access to is how things appear, that reality matches up with appearance? If, on the other hand, we are directly in contact with reality in perceptual experience, then the gap between appearance and reality appears to be closed and sceptical worries recede.[66]

The question of which approach we should take to the issue of immediate perceptual justification and perceptual knowledge is far too large to be considered here. A question we *can* answer here is which general approach supporters of perceptual models of emotion favour; and here (too) there seems strong if not universal endorsement of an indirect realist picture. For instance, Döring, Elgin, and Tappolet talk of emotions as mirroring perceptual experiences in having content that is representational, and it is in virtue of this feature that both can play an evidential or rationalizing role.[67] Moreover, Elgin, Oddie, and Tappolet suggest that

---

[66] For a helpful overview of these issues, see Pritchard, D., *What is This Thing Called Knowledge?*, Oxford: Routledge (2006), ch. 7: 'Perception'.

[67] The term "representational" is used with caution at this point, given that there are thorny and ongoing disputes in the philosophy of perception about the relation between representationalism and direct and indirect realism. It might be thought that a view of perceptual experience as representational sits more easily with indirect realism, given that

emotional experiences are, like perceptual experiences, defeasible reasons even when a subject has evaluative knowledge. But direct realism, at least of the kind proposed by John McDowell, maintains that perceptual experiences are *indefeasible* reasons when a subject has empirical knowledge; indeed, it is this feature which is central to allaying sceptical fears.[68] As a result, the idea that emotional experiences enjoy only an initial tenability sits more happily with indirect realism. Finally, proponents of perceptual models of emotion, as we'll shortly see, favour some version of a causal account, where what gives the perceptual experience its evidential force or status is the right kind of causal relationships between the evaluative features or properties, the emotional experience, and the evaluative judgement. But the idea that it is causal relations between the world, experience, and subject which make an epistemic difference is central to indirect realism: the idea, after all, of a causal relation between the world and experience of that world suggests that world and experience are two separate things, and not—as the direct realist supposes for veridical experiences—part of the same experience. Here too the supporter of the perceptual theory of emotion seems to adopt indirect realism.

Let us agree, then, that existing versions of the perceptual model of emotion favour an epistemological account that is indirectly realist and causal. This gives us warrant to look at such an account in more detail.[69]

this term suggests an intermediary between the world and ourselves. But many direct realists regard themselves as representationalists as well, holding that when veridical perceptual experience involves the subject being in a state that represents, they are nevertheless aware of worldly objects rather than any representation. One of the important issues in philosophy of perception is whether it is possible to hold the combination of these views, or whether representationalists are forced to be indirect realists. As such, I don't want to imply here that Döring, Elgin, and Tappolet are, in virtue of talking about representational states, *automatically* indirect realists. They seem, nevertheless, to be indirect realists about emotional and perceptual experience. Thanks to Fiona Macpherson for helpful discussion of this issue.

[68] See Haddock, A. and Macpherson, F., 'Introduction: Varieties of Disjunctivism', in *Disjunctivism: Perception, Action and Knowledge*, Haddock, A. and Macpherson, F. (eds), Oxford: Oxford University Press (2008).

[69] To make things explicit: I'm focusing on this account of perceptual justification because this is the account that seems favoured by the perceptual model of emotion. And although I think that the account here has a measure of independent plausibility, I'm justified in focusing on it here because my main aim is to explore and clarify the epistemological commitments of the perceptual model. If you find versions of indirect realism implausible, then that is another reason you might have for being suspicious of versions of the perceptual model that make use of this picture of justification. And the question of whether a plausible version of the perceptual model can be based upon a direct realist account of perceptual experience will be discussed later in the chapter.

Now with sensory perceptual experience, the basic picture for this kind of indirect realism is that a subject S is immediately perceptually justified in some empirical belief, for example that the cricket ball has just broken the window, provided that (i) she forms this belief on the basis of a perceptual experience with the right kind of content, namely an experience as of the ball breaking the window, and (ii) experiences of this type are reliably causally connected with facts of that type, such that in normal circumstances such experiences will be caused by such facts.[70] This basic account can be clarified in a number of ways.

First, the account combines elements of internalism and externalism. It is internalist, in so far as it proposes that an "internal" state of the subject— namely a perceptual experience—is the "ground" of the belief. It is externalist, in so far as there is no requirement that the subject form her belief as a result of an additional belief about the reliable connection, or an awareness of the adequacy of this ground. This is why it is an account of immediate rather than mediate justification.[71] Despite the lack of any such additional belief, the subject nevertheless has a default right to believe what her senses tell her.[72] To put it another way: in standard cases of justified perceptual belief, the subject is *entitled* to believe what she does about the external world on the basis of her perceptual experience *without argument*.[73] Of course, the default and entitlement can be overridden,

---

[70] As noted, I'm concerned here to look at accounts of perceptual justification that seem most conducive to the claims that supporters of the perceptual model of emotion want to make. And for the latter, the causal condition is important. But of course some accounts of perceptual justification—for instance, the "perceptual dogmatism" favoured by James Pryor and Michael Huemer, amongst others—hold that perceptual seemings of all kinds constitute *prima facie* reasons for belief, and thus do not insist upon a reliable causal connection between seemings (of this kind) and the relevant facts. See Huemer, M. *Skepticism and the Veil of Perception*, Lanham, MD: Rowman & Littlefield (2001); Pryor, J, 'The Skeptic and the Dogmatist', *Noûs* (2000), 34: 517–49. I'll assume, for the purposes of explaining the perceptual model of emotion, that perceptual dogmatism is false. Whether there could be a plausible version of the perceptual model that appeals to perceptual dogmatism is an interesting question, but one that I'll leave to supporters of that model to work out.

[71] This combination of internalism and externalism—where a belief, in order to be justified, must be based upon adequate grounds—is familiar from William Alston's work. See Alston, W., 'An Internalist Externalism', *Synthese* (1988), 74: 265–83. Thanks to Robert Cowan for urging me to be clearer on the elements of internalism and externalism in the standard picture of perceptual knowledge.

[72] See Hopkins, R., 'How to be a Pessimist about Aesthetic Testimony', *Journal of Philosophy* (2011) 108(3): 138–57.

[73] See Cuneo, T., 'Signs of Value: Reid on the Evidential Role of Feelings in Moral Judgement', *British Journal for the History of Philosophy* (2006) 41(1): 69–91. Cuneo writes:

when circumstances are not favourable; but this does not show that when conditions are favourable, the subject must have some experience of or belief about their favourability from which she infers that the world is thus-and-so.[74]

Second, the reasons provided by perceptual experiences are defeasible: the experiences in question can, in normal circumstances, constitute reason or evidence, even though this can be overturned or undermined if new, "defeating" evidence comes to light. Thus, in normal circumstances my perceptual experience as of a sheep in the field is a reason for me to believe that there is a sheep in the field, even though in this instance the animal is a sheepdog wearing a woolly coat. Were this information to become available to me, I would no longer have reason to believe that there is a sheep in the field. Perceptual experiences do not, in other words, typically *guarantee* the truth of some judgement; they are not *conclusive* reasons for perceptual judgements.

Third, there are two causal links in this story, one between the external objects and the perceptual experiences, and one between the experiences and the relevant beliefs. Given, however, that perceptual experiences have very strong connections with beliefs, such that it is very rare that we do not form a belief when we have a relevant experience, the causal link that is really doing the justificatory work is between the external object and the experience. That, after all, is the reliable connection that makes it the case that perceptual experience is a defeasible reason for empirical belief, at least according to those who are not perceptual dogmatists. Overall, then, the standard epistemological account for perceptual justification requires perceptual experiences to have the right kind of content, and the right kind of causal relationships with both facts and beliefs, in order to justify.

"When an agent forms the immediately entitled belief that, say, the table he is touching is hard, his belief is not evidentially based on the belief that his perceptual faculties are reliable. If anything, the proposition *that the particular deliverances of his perceptual faculties are the product of a reliable belief forming process* is something that this agent takes for granted in his everyday activities, but does not explicitly or occurrently believe", p. 89 (italics mine).

[74] One good reason to favour a non-inferentialist and partly externalist account of perceptual justification is that such an account does not "over-intellectualize" the epistemology of perceptual experience, and so allows that young children and animals can have knowledge *via* perception even though they are not possessed of anything like a belief about, or sophisticated understanding of, the reliability of their perceptual experiences.

Supporters of the perceptual model of emotion will maintain that we can tell a similar story with respect to emotional experience and the immediate justification of evaluative judgement. So consider the following example from Terence Cuneo, who endorses something like the perceptual model of emotion. Cuneo asks us to imagine this case:

you walk into a crowded party of associates and friends in a large reception room. As you make your way toward a more quiet area, you're pulled aside by a colleague and introduced to one of his associates. You engage in some light conversation. After several minutes, however, you find yourself feeling very uneasy about this fellow for reasons that are not at all clear to you—it might be his voice, his excessive smoothness in conversation, the sort of distracted attention he gives you or his mildly dismissive remarks about the work of someone you do not know. In any event, you find yourself forming the judgement that this man is untrustworthy. You politely excuse yourself, convinced that your uneasiness and subsequent moral judgement are not unfounded.[75]

Cuneo notes that in this instance, the emotional experience constitutes the "input" to which the evaluative judgement is the "output". The feeling plays "a special sort of role in generating the value judgements in question. It is consequent upon your feeling uneasy about the acquaintance at the party that you form the judgement that he is not to be trusted".[76] So on this account, as with the perceptual account, emotional experience can sometimes occur *prior to* and can *cause* evaluative judgement: we sometimes form evaluative judgements on the basis of, or because we have, some emotional experience. If this is correct, then (as we saw in the previous chapter) we have reason to reject the judgementalist idea that emotional experience is (partly) constituted by evaluative judgement—for obviously, emotional experience could not occur prior to such judgement.

But it is not simply the case that emotional experience can cause or generate evaluative judgement. Emotions can play a rationalizing or justificatory role as well. This is because emotions are not (typically) arbitrary or random responses to important or significant objects and events in our environment.[77] At least sometimes, our emotional responses can be reliably correlated with such objects and events, and in these

---

[75] Cuneo (2006), p. 69.   [76] Cuneo (2006), p. 69.

[77] If we think that there are good evolutionary reasons for fear to be reliably correlated with dangerous things, then the reliable connection will not be a mere fluke. See previous remarks by Elgin in §1, and by Prinz in §2, for the thought that fear was "set up" by evolution to be "set off" by danger.

circumstances our emotional experiences can, as Cuneo puts it, "function as *signs* or indicators of evaluative features".[78] Our feelings, when reliably linked with value, "are evidence of value".[79] The epistemic role and value of emotional experience thus depends upon the existence of reliable causal links between emotional experience and the occurrence of the "core relational themes" of danger, insult, contamination, loss, shamefulness, wrongness, and the like. Emotions, when reliably correlated with such things, can be sources of information about the evaluative world; and when such emotional experiences generate the relevant evaluative beliefs, we have good reason to believe what we do about that world. As a result, the perceptual theorist about emotion can maintain that *emotional* experiences can have the right kind of content, and the right kind of causal relationships with both evaluative facts and beliefs, to constitute evidence for evaluative beliefs.

Most perceptual theorists of emotion also maintain that the relevant justificatory story combines both internalist and externalist elements, which is why it constitutes an account of immediate rather than mediate justification.[80] That is, supporters of the perceptual model of emotion typically favour a similar non-inferentialist, partly externalist account and maintain that emotions can play a positive role in justifying our evaluative beliefs because, in circumstances when emotions are reliably correlated with value, we have a default right or entitlement to form evaluative

---

[78] Cuneo (2006), pp. 69–70.

[79] Cuneo (2006), p. 70. Although we can become aware of the reliability of our emotions in certain circumstances, Cuneo doesn't think that such an awareness plays a justificatory role in the formation of our belief. Recall note 73.

[80] Elgin is a dissenting voice here. She holds that "the epistemic yield of emotions... depends not on taking their deliverances at face value, but on a sophisticated understanding of when and to what extent they are trustworthy", Elgin (2008) p. 37. It is this sophisticated understanding or awareness that enables our emotional experiences to play a positive epistemic role with respect to evaluative belief. Since this account requires that the subject have an understanding of the conditions in which her emotional experiences are reliably correlated with value, then it seems like a more thorough-going internalist account of epistemic justification. This is, nevertheless, compatible with Elgin's claim that emotional and perceptual experiences play analogous epistemic roles, since she thinks that a similar account of justification applies in the perceptual realm. For Elgin, warrant for perceptual judgements also depends upon a sophisticated understanding of the circumstances in which our perceptual experience is trustworthy. However, and for reasons explained, I think that the analogy with perceptual experience is better captured if we prefer accounts which are hybrids of both internalist and externalist elements, and so I'll not focus on Elgin's internalist proposal in the remainder of this chapter.

beliefs on the basis of such experiences.[81] Just as we put our trust in our senses, and are entitled to do so in conditions when sensory experiences are reliably correlated with external reality, so too we put our trust in our feelings, and are entitled to do so when such feelings are reliably linked-up with values. There is no internalist requirement here that the subject has, in addition to the suitably "internal" emotional experience, a further belief about the reliable connection between feeling and value, or an awareness of the adequacy of the emotional experience that grounds the belief.[82]

Consider, to illustrate, the epistemological story told by Döring. She writes:

a judgement made rational by the representational content of the subject's emotion is not a matter of an inference from the occurrence of the emotion. When you are gripped with fear facing a furious gorilla that escaped from his cage in the zoo, fortunately, your judging, and regarding as true, that the gorilla is dangerous does not need to wait for inferential means. Instead, you immediately rely on your emotion. Your judgement that the gorilla is dangerous is non-inferentially justified by your taking your fear's content at face value.[83]

In normal circumstances, taking one's experience at face value is the "default mode" for both perceptual and emotional experience:

In the default mode we operate so as to rely on the representational content of our emotions . . . This is again similar to the case of sensory perception. In the default mode it does not occur to us to ask whether the lighting conditions are really such as to justify the perception of a ripe tomato's redness.[84]

Moreover, when our emotional and perceptual experiences are as a matter of fact reliably correlated with the relevant objects, we are right to take our emotional and perceptual experience in this way. This means that "the

---

[81] I am assuming here that the reliable connection generates the default right or entitlement in the case of emotional experience. For without this, why would we be entitled to trust the deliverances of our emotions?

[82] Cuneo (2006) writes: "I take it to be fairly uncontroversial that cases such as I have just described form a part of our shared experience. To stick with just the moral case, I assume that in some situations, we are prompted to form moral judgements by virtue of having feelings of various kinds—feelings of aversion, disgust, repulsion, uneasiness, distress, guilt, attraction, pleasure, relief, delight and the like, toward various things. I take it to be fairly uncontroversial that in some cases we trust the judgements that are the upshot of feelings of this sort; we take them to be reliable responses to value. I assume also that in some cases we are *entitled* to trust them as such; we commit no epistemic impropriety in so trusting them", p. 70.

[83] Döring (2008) p. 89.   [84] Döring (2008), p. 99.

occurrence of an emotion to a thinker can, in suitable circumstances, entitle him to judge, and possibly to know, its content simply by taking its representational content at face value".[85] Nothing more than this is required, on Döring's account, for the justification of the relevant judgements by the emotional and perceptual experiences. In particular, we do not need to construct an inductive argument, or arrive at the relevant judgement *via* any understanding that in these conditions our emotional or perceptual experiences are reliable. Instead, "[h]aving a representational content suffices for the emotions and perception to play their rationalizing role, especially so as we regard the content of emotion and of perception as true 'by default'."[86]

The overall picture, then, is that emotional experiences can both generate and immediately justify evaluative beliefs. Such experiences perform this role when we trust their evaluative contents; and we are right to trust such contents just in case the emotional experiences are reliably correlated with the relevant values and there are no defeaters to our belief. In the following section, we'll shift from a consideration of which particular indirect realist account the perceptual theorist does (or should) favour, and consider whether there can be a direct realist account of emotional justification. Although none of our perceptual theorists appears to adopt direct realism, it might be important to see what such an account looks like, especially if a direct realism about emotional experience can be seen to possess advantages similar to those that supporters of direct realism about perceptual experience claim for their account.

2.4 A direct realist epistemology for emotion?

We saw earlier that indirect realism is the most widely held account of perceptual justification, but not the only such option. Indeed, an increasing number of philosophers are attracted by some form of direct realism about perceptual experience and perceptual justification.[87] On a direct

---

[85] Döring (2008), p. 93.

[86] Döring (2008), p. 98. As mentioned, the fact that we regard both kinds of experience as true 'by default' is consistent with thinking that they are only defeasible reasons, given that the default can be overridden.

[87] See, for instance, Brewer, W. *Perception and Reason*, Oxford: Oxford University Press (2000); Huemer (2001); Martin, M. G. F., 'The Transparency of Experience', *Mind and Language* (2002), 17: 376–425; McDowell (1994); Pryor (2000); Snowdon, P. F., 'Perception,

realist account, in veridical cases of perceptual experience we are directly aware of external reality, rather than such experience involving an intermediary that is caused by external reality and which is, subsequently, the cause of our empirical belief. Here, the perceptual experience involves or has as a constituent the external object or property; in our perceptual experiences external reality is *disclosed* or *made manifest* to us. As such, perceptual experiences, at least when veridical, are not simply "in the head", but encompass or enclose the object perceived and the causal relationship between the object and ourselves.

As noted earlier, one of the main motivations for direct realism is epistemological. For as John McDowell and other direct realists have argued, common factor theories generate an epistemological problem.[88] If my perceptual experience is the same in both veridical and hallucinatory perceptual experiences, then how is it possible for me to know about the external world on the basis of such experience? Doesn't this make the conditions for knowledge something that is unavailable to me? McDowell suggests that knowledge cannot rest in this way on things beyond our ken. He writes:

> The root idea is that one's epistemic standing on some question cannot intelligibly be constituted, even in part, by matters blankly external to how it is with one subjectively. For how could such matters be other than beyond one's ken? And how could matters beyond one's ken make any difference to one's epistemic standing?[89]

Vision and Causation', *Proceedings of the Aristotelian Society* (1980), 81: 175–92. For a view that is sceptical about whether direct realism can provide a distinctive and plausible account of perceptual justification, see Bonjour, L., 'In Search of Direct Realism', *Philosophy and Phenomenological Research* (2004), 69: 349–67.

[88] In what follows I'm going to focus on McDowell's direct realism. Of the direct realists cited here, McDowell seems the most interested in the epistemological benefits to be gained from direct realism, and so provides a clearer picture of how the story of perceptual justification will go along direct realist lines. His account therefore provides a useful model for how a direct realist account of emotional justification will look. As noted earlier, there are perhaps other possibilities for a perceptual model of emotion along direct realist lines, based upon (e.g.) the "dogmatist" views of Huemer and others. It is not clear to me, however, that such versions—should they be developed—would fare any better than McDowell's model when it comes to avoiding the objections that follow.

[89] McDowell, J., 'Criteria, Defeasibility and Knowledge', in Dancy, J. (ed.), *Perceptual Knowledge*, Oxford: Oxford University Press (1982), p. 215.

McDowell's own proposal is that we jettison the idea that perceptual experiences are defeasible reasons for some belief that p, and which contribute to knowledge only when p is in fact the case. Instead, McDowell wants to maintain that perceptual experiences contribute to justification only when they are cases of "seeing that" something is the case. Seeing that is experiential, in that when S sees that p then it appears to S as if p; it is factive, in that if one sees that p then p is the case; and it is epistemic, in that it constitutes an indefeasible or conclusive reason for S to believe that p.[90] In cases where we see that p, the fact that p is made available to us or manifest to us; and *because* the fact is made available to us or manifest to us, it can function as a justificatory reason for the belief that p. In other words: it is because seeing that p involves the relevant state of the world that this perceptual experience constitutes a reason or evidence for our empirical belief. Any mental state short of this, McDowell suggests, will fail to play the requisite evidential role.

A direct realist account of the justificatory role of emotional experience would therefore maintain, first, that there is no common factor in "good" and "bad" cases of emotional experience; it is not true that emotional experiences gain epistemic status and value because of any *causal* links with value, therefore. Instead, in good cases of emotional experience the evaluative world is disclosed or made manifest to us, and it is in virtue of *this* that emotional experiences can play a justificatory role with respect to evaluative belief. Again, by analogy with the perceptual case, a direct realist account will maintain that emotional experiences will contribute to justification only when they are cases of "feeling that" something is the case. "Feeling that" will mirror "seeing that" in the relevant ways: it will be experiential, so when S feels that p then it appears to S as if p is the case evaluatively; it is factive, in that if S feels that p then p *is* the case evaluatively; and it is epistemic, in that feeling that p constitutes an indefeasible or conclusive reason for S to hold the evaluative belief that p. Moreover, it is *because* the evaluative world is made available or disclosed to us in cases where we feel that something is the case that our emotional experiences can play a justificatory role with respect to evaluative beliefs. Our emotional experiences allow us to directly access the evaluative world; and as a result, such experiences constitute indefeasible or conclusive reasons for evaluative judgements.

---

[90] See Haddock and Macpherson (2008), p. 5.

Whatever plausibility attaches to direct realist accounts of perceptual knowledge, an analogous account of evaluative knowledge appears, on the face of it, to be a good deal less plausible. For one thing, direct realism about emotional experience appears to lack the kind of phenomenological support that the analogous position about perceptual experience can claim. As direct realists maintain, perceptual experience seems to put us into direct contact with external reality: the phenomenology of perceptual experiences is "transparent", in that what we seem to see in such experiences are simply objects and their properties, rather than any intermediary. Because of this, there is little evidence from phenomenology of a mental intermediary between the external world and our empirical judgements. However, the phenomenology of emotional experience does not suggest that we are thereby in direct contact with evaluative reality. Mikko Salmela writes:

Unlike perceptions, emotions are often relatively opaque, as de Sousa has remarked. When you try to describe your visual experience, you end up depicting what you see, whereas the emotional case is the reverse: an attempt to describe an emotional experience may succeed only in portraying the subject's own state of mind/body—angry, sad, happy, excited, and so on—even if the emotion relates to some object in the world. A key difference between emotion and perception is that this kind of opacity is normal in the emotional case, whereas it is rare in the perceptual domain.[91]

A second reason is that direct realism is supposed to capture why perceptual experience enjoys a *privileged* epistemological status when it comes to empirical beliefs, when compared with indirect evidence provided by testimony, let's say.[92] As we'll see in the chapters to follow, however, it is difficult to make the same claim about emotional experience, which seems epistemically inferior to other sorts of reasons or evidence for evaluative beliefs. If so, then a supposed advantage of a direct realist account of perceptual experience will not transfer to emotional

---

[91] Salmela, M., 'Can emotion be modelled on perception?', *Dialectica* (2011), 65(1): p. 25. This might be most plausible when the material and formal objects of emotions are unknown or themselves opaque. But in other circumstances we might think that a description of our feelings—of joy, say—would end up describing what we are joyful about and why. Nevertheless, our description of the feeling isn't *thereby* a description of the value, and if so, Salmela's point about the opacity of the feeling holds. Feelings are simply not transparent in the way that perceptual experiences are.

[92] See Pritchard (2006), p. 79.

experience, on the assumption that emotional experience lacks a privileged epistemological status.

Finally, and relatedly, if we have access to non-emotional reasons and evidence for evaluative beliefs, and do not have to rely solely upon our emotional experience to provide evidence of value, then we might think that McDowell's complaint that indirect realism generates sceptical worries is less pressing in the case of evaluative knowledge. For access to non-emotional reasons and evidence for evaluative beliefs is access to considerations that have a bearing on the epistemic status of our emotional experiences, in which case the factors that make some emotional experience a defeasible reason are not, in one important sense, beyond our ken. So the motivation to adopt a direct realism in order to avoid sceptical worries is not as pressing in the emotional–evaluative realm as it is in the perceptual–empirical realm. As such, it is difficult to see a strong case to adopt a direct realist account of emotional experience.

2.5 Conclusions

In this chapter I proposed that the perceptual model of emotion can be characterized by its acceptance of a core epistemological claim: that emotional experiences can, in suitable circumstances, generate and justify our evaluative judgements. In other words, emotional experiences can constitute reasons or evidence for evaluative judgements, in much the same way that perceptual experiences can constitute reasons or evidence for judgements about the external, non-evaluative world. In order to investigate this claim, I considered two questions: Are emotions literally perceptions? And what story should we tell of how perceptual experiences justify empirical beliefs? To address the first question, I examined literal and non-literal versions of the model, and gave some reason to prefer the latter. I then addressed the second question, describing two ways in which the core epistemological claim can be developed, by analogy with indirect and direct realist accounts of perceptual justification. And I have suggested that perceptual theorists of emotion both accept, and ought to accept, the indirect realist option. In the following chapter I will argue that despite the claims made by its many supporters, we have good reason to reject the epistemological analogy between emotional and perceptual experience, and with it the core or central claim of the perceptual model as such.

3

Against the Perceptual Model

In the previous chapter I looked at the perceptual model of emotion in detail. In the process I examined literal and non-literal versions of the model, identified the epistemic claim that I take to be the common element in different versions of the theory, and considered the epistemological story that supporters of the model tell. According to the model, emotional experiences can, in suitable circumstances, generate and justify our evaluative judgements. In this way they mirror perceptual experiences, since these can, again in the right conditions, constitute reasons or evidence for judgements about the external, non-evaluative world. As such, the perceptual theory seems to be in a good position to illuminate our common-sense thought that emotions can tell us about the evaluative world: the perceptual theory, more than its rivals, seems well-placed to do justice to the epistemological role that people, pre-theoretically, think that emotional experience has.

In this chapter I'll raise serious doubts about the perceptual model's epistemic claim and—at least for versions which identify the model *with* the epistemic claim—about the perceptual model itself. I'll argue that there are significant differences between emotions and perceptual experiences at the epistemic level, and moreover that this follows from an important aspect of emotional experience that supporters of the perceptual model have typically ignored. As we'll see, it is the *nature* of emotion and emotional experience that puts pressure on the perceptual theory. The result, as I'll explain in the chapters to come, will be an account of the epistemic role and value of emotional experience that is rather more complex than the perceptual theory—and indeed traditional common-sense thinking—acknowledges.

3.1 An argument against the "default" view

In the previous chapter we saw Mark Johnston's claim that "affective engagement" with the world is necessary if we are to have access to or knowledge of the determinate ways in which certain people, objects, or events are appealing or repelling. The thought is that the affective element of emotional experience presents the evaluative world to us in a certain way, and this is not to be captured by some other mode or manner of representation. An important part of Johnston's picture is that affect or feeling has a certain kind of "authority" over us. He writes:

[I]t is because affect can be the *disclosure* of the appeal of other things and other people that it can have authority in the matter of what we should desire or do. By "the authority of affect" I mean not to refer to its sheer effectiveness as a source of desire or action, but rather to the fact that the presence of the affect can make the desire or action especially intelligible to the agent himself. It can make the desire or act seem apt or fitting in a way that silences any demand for justification.[1]

This expresses, or clarifies, a central aspect of our analogy, for Johnston continues:

In this way affect is akin to perceptual experience considered more generally. Perceptual experience makes certain immediate perceptual beliefs about the perceived scene seem apt or fitting in a way that silences any demand for justification for those beliefs. If the same beliefs were to immediately arise in the absence of perceptual experience then they would then lack a certain intelligibility from the inside.[2]

Although Johnston talks about affect making desire or action intelligible to the agent, I assume that, given the analogy with perceptual experience, he also thinks that affect makes evaluative *belief* or *judgement* intelligible to the agent. Indeed, this would have to follow if we think that desire and action are often consequent upon evaluative belief, so that the belief is the intermediary element between affect and intentional behaviour. If so, then Johnston can be understood as holding that emotional and perceptual experiences are *sufficient* reasons for evaluative belief or judgement. A reason counts as sufficient in so far as it is good enough to justify some action or belief by itself; a sufficient reason makes action or belief *permissible* for the subject, we might say.[3] But sufficient reasons do not make believing obligatory, in the sense of believing being something that you must do given the evidence. Nor do sufficient reasons entail the correctness of some action or the truth of some belief; they thus fall short of conclusive reasons—reasons which are "such as to eliminate the possibility of

[1] Johnston, M., 'The Authority of Affect', *Philosophy and Phenomenological Research* (2001), 63(1) p. 189.

[2] Johnston (2001), p. 189.

[3] See Schroeder, M., 'What makes reasons sufficient?', MS.

mistake", as Dretske puts things.[4] So reasons can be defeasible, as the perceptual model maintains, and still be sufficient; and reasons will be sufficient to justify belief in conditions in which there are no defeaters. Döring is equally explicit about this aspect of the justificatory story. She writes that:

[W]e treat our emotions as normally reliable cognitive sub-systems. We take for granted that the cognitive function is fulfilled under normal or standard conditions, and it does not normally occur to us to ask whether the conditions under which we experience the world are standard conditions. It is in this sense that we regard their representational content as true by default. In the default mode we operate so as to rely on the representational content of our emotions. For example when we normally encounter a furious gorilla that escaped from his cage in the zoo, we do not normally wonder whether the conditions are really such as to justify fear. This is again similar to the case of sensory perception. In the default mode it does not occur to us to ask whether the lighting conditions are really such as to justify the perception of a ripe tomato's redness.[5]

For Döring, the representational content of emotional and perceptual experience "is regarded as true by default".[6] So on this view, the demand for justification is also silenced: this is just what it is to take our emotional or perceptual experience for granted, or to regard the representational content as true by default. Emotional experience, like perceptual experience, is thus regarded as a sufficient reason for the relevant belief: my fear, under normal conditions and in the absence of defeaters, suffices for me to be justified in believing that I am in danger, in the same way that my perceptual experience as of a grey squirrel on the garden fence, under normal conditions and in the absence of defeaters, suffices for me to be justified in believing that there is a grey squirrel on the garden fence. Or, to put the point in different terms, in normal circumstances we are permitted to form evaluative beliefs on the basis of our emotional experiences, just as we are permitted to form non-evaluative beliefs on the basis of our perceptual experience; we "commit no epistemic impropriety" in trusting our experiences in each case.[7]

It is my aim in this chapter to demonstrate how Johnston, Döring, Cuneo, and other supporters of the perceptual model significantly overstate

---

[4] Dretske, F., 'Conclusive Reasons', *Australasian Journal of Philosophy* (1971), 49(1): 1–22. Thanks to the referees for pushing me to be clearer on the distinction between sufficient, obligatory, and conclusive reasons.

[5] Döring, 'Conflict without Contradiction', in Brun, G., Doğuoğlu, U., and Kuenzle, D. (eds), *Epistemology and Emotions*, Farnham: Ashgate Publishing (2008), p. 99.

[6] Döring (2008), p. 99.　　[7] Cuneo (2006), p. 70.

the epistemic value of emotional experience in normal circumstances, and that this puts considerable pressure on the claim that emotions are akin to perceptions at the epistemic level. The first part of this demonstration is to point out that while (sensory) perceptual experience does, in normal circumstances, indeed constitute a sufficient reason for non-evaluative judgements or beliefs, we have good reason to doubt that emotional experience has a similar kind of epistemic strength or value. This suggests that emotions don't tell us about the evaluative world in the same way that perceptual experiences tell us about the non-evaluative world. This will set the scene for the second part of the demonstration later on in the chapter, where I argue that emotional experiences fail to constitute reason or evidence of *any* kind for evaluative judgements.[8]

To illustrate the first point, consider my perceptual experience as of a red car parked on the pavement outside my flat. In normal circumstances, and in the absence of epistemic defeaters (e.g. that my eyesight is poor, that I am given to hallucinations), it is plausible to suppose that my perceptual experience constitutes very good evidence for—indeed, constitutes a sufficient reason for—my perceptual belief. At least, I would find it very strange if, after citing the fact that I have a visual experience as of a red car outside my flat, I was then asked for, or felt the need to discover, *further* reasons or evidence for this belief. I might, for one thing, be puzzled as to what more I could do to justify the belief in this instance. If perceptual evidence won't suffice, why should additional evidence, in the form of remembering a red car being there yesterday, or testimony from my partner who also claims to see what looks like a red car? We might put the point slightly differently: in such conditions, and absent epistemic defeaters, we are surely *permitted* to form beliefs on the basis of our perceptual experience. This strongly suggests, as the perceptual theorists about emotion maintain, that perceptual experience are sufficient reasons for beliefs about external objects and events.

In contrast, however, we often feel the need to discover reasons or evidence in support of our emotional experience in normal circumstances, and hence in the absence of defeaters. Consider one's experience of fear, upon hearing a noise downstairs as one is trying to get to sleep. Let us

---

[8] Some of the arguments in this chapter appear, in an earlier and shortened form, in Brady, M. S., 'Emotion, Perception and Reason', in Bagnoli, C. (ed.), *Morality and the Emotions*, Oxford: Oxford University Press (2011).

stipulate that circumstances are normal: our hearing is good, we have not been taking hallucinogenic drugs, etc. In this situation, we are *typically* motivated to seek out and discover *additional* reasons or evidence. In particular, we are motivated to seek out and discover considerations that have a bearing on whether our initial emotional "take" on the situation, namely that we are in danger, is accurate. We strain our ears to hear other anomalous noises, or rack our brains trying to think of possible non-threatening causes for the noise. We do not, in other words, think that the demand for justification is silenced, or take the representational content of our emotional experience as true by default. It would be a strange and paranoid person indeed who took each and every such feeling of fear as a sufficient reason to believe that he was in danger.[9]

Or, to take a different example, suppose that I feel guilty about my behaviour the morning after a party at a colleague's house. Here too it is unlikely that in normal conditions I think that my feeling silences any demand for justification, or that I take the representational content of this emotion for granted. It is not the case, in other words, that I regard my emotional experience as *by itself* constituting a sufficient reason for me to believe that I did something wrong at the party. Rather, in such conditions I am typically motivated or inclined to seek and discover reasons or evidence that bear on the question of whether I am *right* to feel guilty, reasons which confirm or disconfirm my emotional sense that I behaved badly. This suggests that in cases like these—which seem to be obvious cases of emotional responses in normal conditions—we typically do *not* rest content with our emotional appraisal. We do not, that is, take our emotional responses at face value, or think that they are true by default. Instead, we *feel the need* for justification to be pressing: we are motivated to seek out facts or considerations which bear on the correctness of our emotional response. Moreover, the fact that we are motivated to discover reasons in normal conditions explains the unfortunate but common practice of "rationalization", whereby people are moved to invent reasons or interpret evidence to fit their emotional hypotheses. Thus, the jealous wife

---

[9] This does not mean that there are no cases where emotions silence the demand for justification; as I'll explain, emotions might silence the demand for justification with respect to certain values associated with *taste*. In addition, there might be cases where an emotional response "settles the issue" of competing reasons for some judgement or action. But even if there are such cases—a question I'll return to in Chapter 5—they will, it seems, be rare, and hardly the default option.

might be moved to fabricate reasons or evidence that fit her emotional construal of her husband's behaviour as unfaithful, or might interpret innocent behaviour on his part as evidence that he is having an affair. So the urge to discover reasons that bear on emotional accuracy is often so strong that when individuals cannot discover genuine reasons, they are inclined to invent them. Nothing like this, we can confidently assume, happens with visual or auditory or tactile experiences, at least in so far as we have those experiences under normal conditions.

This is not simply a point about psychology when it comes to forming evaluative beliefs; instead, the fact that we are typically moved to seek and discover reasons that have a bearing on our emotional situation has normative import too. For it reflects the fact that in normal circumstances it would usually be *impermissible* for us to take our emotional experiences at face value or to think that the need for justification is silenced. This is because it would seem wrong or improper for us to form evaluative judgements *solely* on the basis of our emotional experiences—which indicates that emotional experiences fall short of being sufficient reasons. Consider, to illustrate, a modified version of Cuneo's example from the previous chapter. Suppose that I am chair of a hiring committee for a recently advertised job in my department. After a few minutes of an interview with one of the candidates, I start to feel uneasy and form, as a result, the judgement that the candidate is untrustworthy and would therefore make a bad colleague. Does my feeling in this case suffice to justify my judgement? Surely not. To see this, note that certain behaviour in this case—such as advising the committee to reject the candidate's application—is clearly unjustified, and is unjustified simply because it results from an unjustified evaluative judgement. Or suppose, to change the example, that you believe that a certain house is the one you should buy, simply on the basis of your positive affective response when you walk in to the hallway. Does your feeling in this case function as a sufficient reason for your evaluative belief—so that you would be justified in your evaluative belief solely on the basis of our positive emotional response? Again, I think that this is highly unlikely; I'd imagine that buying the house *solely* on the basis of your judgement would be a crazy thing to do, which reflects the fact that the judgement is not one that you have sufficient reason for. It seems to me, therefore, that the fact that we feel motivated to search for reasons or evidence in relation to our emotional feeling or construal is more than a merely psychological point; it reflects, instead, the normative fact that emotional experience isn't, in normal circumstances, a sufficient reason for evaluative belief.[10]

This suggests, at the very least, that there is a difference in the epistemic *strength* of perceptual and emotional experience. In normal conditions and absent defeaters, perceptual experience does indeed silence the demand for justification, and so we are right to take our perceptual experience at face value. In normal circumstances and in the absence of defeaters, we are rationally permitted to form beliefs and judgements about external objects and events on the basis of perceptual experience, and so perceptual experience really does constitute sufficient reason for these doxastic states. By contrast, emotional experience does not silence the demand for justification, even granted normal conditions and the absence of defeaters. We do not, at least normally, take our emotional experience at face value, or think that our emotional experience discharges our justificatory burden with respect to our evaluative judgements and beliefs; and we are right to regard emotional experience in this negative way.[11] The foregoing points are, of course, compatible with the claims that *sometimes* our sensory perceptual experience does not constitute a sufficient reason for non-evaluative judgements, and that sometimes an emotional experience can silence the demand for justification. Think, to illustrate the former, of a case where my eyesight is working normally and lighting conditions etc. are perfect, and yet a great deal rests upon whether or not things are as we take them to be in perceptual experience. Suppose that the front door of the laboratory fridge looks as if it is closed properly; but given that the fridge contains lab

---

[10] To my mind, this reflects another aspect of common-sense thinking about emotion, and one which initially appears to conflict with the common-sense idea that emotion can inform us about value. For in all of these examples, the right thing to say seems to be that emotional experience alone does not inform us about value, *even if there are reliable causal links between the experience and the value in place*. That is, I'm not justified in rejecting a candidate's application on the basis of the feelings she inspires, even if my feelings are reliably correlated with untrustworthiness in situations like this. But then I'm not justified in believing or judging that she is untrustworthy, on the assumption that a justified evaluative judgement *could* justify the appropriate action. This conclusion reflects, it seems to me, an element of common-sense mistrust about emotional experience, even in conditions where emotion is not leading us astray. There is something intuitively wrong or illicit about relying upon or resting content with our emotions, even when they do not have deleterious epistemic effects. I'll return to this issue again in the following chapters, and explain how common-sense thinking about the epistemic yield of emotions is not in fact conflicted; both of our common-sense views can be true.

[11] These claims about the demand for justification in normal conditions might strike some as controversial. I'll have more to say in defence of these claims in the next chapter.

work vital for my biology PhD thesis which will be destroyed should the fridge door be left open, perhaps I am only justified in believing that the door is closed properly once I go over and physically check. Or, to illustrate the latter, consider a case where my feeling of disgust when smelling the venison shank on my plate gives me a sufficient reason to believe that it is unappetising; here it would be strange if there was a demand for reasons in addition to the fact that I'm disgusted by the smell. Nevertheless, I maintain that in normal cases perceptual experience silences the demand for justification whereas emotional experience does not: it is at the very least rare for feelings of guilt, anger, fear, joy, jealousy, etc. to suffice, by themselves, for the justification of the relevant evaluative judgements. Instead, we typically seek out reasons or evidence that bear on the accuracy of such feelings. The guilty man normally searches for evidence of his wrongdoing, the angry woman usually seeks out considerations that justify her rage, and so forth. If so, then Johnston and Döring, Cuneo and Oddie, and other perceptual theorists, are mistaken in thinking that the *same* justificatory story can be told with respect to perceptual and emotional experience; the strength of the reasons provided by these respective experiences is usually very different.

In the following section I'll support this case by arguing that it is often the emotions *themselves* that motivate us to search for reasons, by modifications of our attention. The difference in epistemic role and status between emotional and perceptual experience thus follows from an account of the nature of emotion, and of how our emotional systems differ from our perceptual ones.

3.2 Emotion and attention revisited

In the first chapter, we saw that there is considerable evidence that emotion and attention are closely linked. One such link is that emotions direct and focus our attention onto objects and events that are potentially significant for us. Recall the quote from Ben-Ze'ev: "like burglar alarms going off when an intruder appears, emotions signal that something needs attention."[12] Thus, fear quickly and reflexively directs and focuses a subject's attention onto a potential threat, and mobilizes a subject's behavioural resources to enable her to react appropriately: namely to fight or flee.

---

[12] Ben-Ze'ev, A., *The Subtlety of Emotions*, Cambridge, MA: MIT Press (2000), p. 13.

Emotions, on this view, and as we saw in the previous chapter, resemble what Paul Ekman has termed "affect program responses", which are special mechanisms that have evolved to enable humans to deal with certain universal situations. Such program responses are short-term, reflexive, and automatic responses to a limited class of stimuli. Anger, on this view, is a fast, automatic, and reflexive response which results from a particular discrete affect program, and which has adaptive value in enabling us to deal appropriately when we have been wronged or insulted by others. Similar things can be said for the other basic or natural emotions. Importantly, affect program responses can occur in the absence of higher cognitive processing, and thus without prior evaluative thought or belief.[13] Indeed, affect program emotional systems are thought to have evolved to function independently of cognitive processing, since, quite apart from the cognitive costs of higher-level, conscious thinking, there are evolutionary advantages in having systems which bypass cognition in order to produce a very quick response when the subject is in potentially important situations. Although affect program responses do not involve evaluative thoughts, they can nevertheless still be understood as constituting appraisals. D'Arms and Jacobson write that the pattern of facial, autonomic, and affective changes which constitute an affect program response to a potentially significant object or event "can be functionally understood as constituting a kind of appraisal of the circumstances. There may be no better way of articulating that appraisal than by saying that it involves construing oneself to be in imminent danger."[14]

Suppose that this is right, and that some emotions, in some circumstances, are akin to affect program responses. Emotions, on this view, are a combination of (non-cognitive) appraisal and behavioural priming or preparation. These emotional experiences result from a system that has developed in order to serve a particular need, namely the need for a system that produces fast, reflexive appraisals of and behavioural responses to potentially important or significant events. And central to the operation of this system is the direction and focusing of attention onto the relevant objects or events.

[13] For this general line, see LeDoux, J., *The Emotional Brain*, New York: Simon & Schuster (1996).

[14] D'Arms, J. and Jacobson, D., 'The Significance of Recalcitrant Emotion' in Hatzimoysis, A. (ed), *Philosophy and the Emotions*, Cambridge: Cambridge University Press (2003), p. 139.

However, emotions such as fear and shame do not just automatically and reflexively direct and focus attention; one of the other things that emotions tend to do is to *capture* and *consume* attention. To say that attention is captured and consumed by emotional objects and events is to say that such objects and events hold sway over us, often making it difficult for us to disengage our attention and shift focus elsewhere. Emotions such as fear and anger stay with us; they are not simply short-term reflexive interruptions to our mental life, but often persist and dominate that life so that we remain focused on and attentive to danger, infidelity, and slights. Think again, to illustrate, about what it is like when one is awoken, in the dead of night, by a noise downstairs and as a result becomes afraid. In normal circumstances one's fear is *not* over very quickly; rather, one remains in a fearful state as one listens attentively for further noises, tries to think of possible non-threatening explanations, rehearses strategies for dealing with the potential danger, considers possible escape routes, and so on. These are the cognitive accompaniments to something else that persists, namely the mobilization of one's bodily resources which constitutes one's being primed or prepared to fight or flee. Or think, to recall a different example, of the jealous woman whose emotional state persists as she thinks about her partner's behaviour at the office party, and tries to recall other occasions where he was so pleased to see *that* person, or remembers times when he was unexpectedly and inexplicably late home from the office, and so forth. Here too the emotion is not a short-term, reflexive response to potential infidelity; instead, it seems to be part of the nature of jealousy to persist beyond the initial triggering event and to consume the jealous person's attention. Similar points can be made about anger, resentment, sadness, shame, guilt, love, and many other emotions.[15]

We have seen that the focusing of attention in emotional experience can enable us to quickly and efficiently notice things that are important for us to notice; indeed, we might think that this is part of the function of

---

[15] Faucher and Tappolet make this point in terms of the *maintenance* of attention, which is a matter of attention being fixed or "held in place". As with directing attention, the maintenance of attention can be either voluntary or involuntary. They write: "we can voluntarily choose to look for four-leaf clovers by shifting our attention on a field or, because we are so innately disposed or because an affective state potentiates a certain class of stimuli, our attention can involuntary turn to certain objects. By the same token, we can maintain our attention on something voluntarily or our attention can be kept focused on something involuntarily." In Faucher, L. and Tappolet, C., 'Fear and the Focus of Attention', *Consciousness and Emotion* (2002), 3(2): p. 113.

emotion, in the sense that this is something useful that emotion does.[16] Might attentional consumption have a similarly valuable role to play in our emotional lives, something that can also be part of the function of emotion? In particular, given our concerns, can attentional consumption be *epistemically* valuable for us? Clearly, the point or value of the persistence of attention does not lie in its alerting us to potentially significant objects and events in our environment; as we have seen, our attention is directed towards and focused on the presence of such objects and events automatically and reflexively, and hence prior to its persistence. Instead, I propose that one of the important things that attentional persistence can do is to enhance our representation of potentially significant objects and events, precisely by enabling us to discover reasons which bear on the accuracy of our initial emotional appraisals.[17] In other words, I propose that the persistence of attention in emotional experience can facilitate, by motivating the search for and discovery of reasons, a judgement as to whether emotional appearance in this instance really does match evaluative reality.[18] On this picture, emotional persistence can enable the subject to determine whether what appears to be dangerous or shameful really is dangerous or shameful, through keeping attention fixed on these questions and promoting critical reflection about them.[19] If this is correct, then

[16] Recall here the caveat from Chapter 1 with regard to the use of "function": the claim that emotion has the function of directing attention is merely meant to convey the thought that this is something useful that emotions generally or typically do. I am not committed to claiming that emotions have evolved to do this, through a process of natural selection, and thus have this function in a stronger sense. Perhaps, for all I have said, the fact that emotions alert us to important things is a helpful by-product of something else that emotions evolved to do.

[17] See Ronald de Sousa: "[P]laying attention to certain things is a *source* of reasons", *The Rationality of Emotions*, Cambridge, MA: MIT Press (1987), p. 196. I claim that this is one of the things that attentional persistence can do, because I think that it can have other roles or functions as well, in particular a monitoring function of keeping the object in view so as to promote the correct behavioural response. But as I'll argue later, the successful achievement of this goal might very well require a determination of the accuracy of the initial emotional response, in which case such a determination might be regarded as a *priority* function of attentional persistence.

[18] See Lee Clark and David Watson, who write that "triggered by environmental events, emotions act as salient internal stimuli that alert the organism to *the need for further information gathering* and action", 'Distinguishing Functional from Dysfunctional Affective Responses', in Ekman, P. and Davidson, R. (eds), *The Nature of Emotion*, Oxford: Oxford University Press (1994), p. 131. (My italics.) On my view, this need is best served through the consumption of attention in emotional experience.

[19] As these examples indicate, the story we tell about how a subject determines the accuracy of her emotional appraisals might turn out to be quite complicated. It shouldn't be thought, for

emotions involve two important links with attention: they can direct and focus attention, thereby alerting us to the presence of potentially important or significant objects in our environment; and they can capture and consume attention, thereby enabling us to determine whether evaluative reality in fact matches emotional appearance.

The idea that emotion can play this role in the formation of evaluative judgement or belief should go some way towards mitigating a worry that some might have about the epistemological story we tell about emotion once we reject the perceptual model. One of the points in favour of the perceptual model is that the epistemological story it presents about how we get justified evaluative belief seems relatively straightforward. For on that view, we have in normal conditions a default entitlement to endorse the content of our emotional experiences. Since this content is evaluative content, and since there can be reliable connections between emotions and values, the perceptual model has a relatively simple explanation of how we can have justified beliefs about danger, loss, achievements, and the like. The worry is that if we reject the perceptual model, we will therefore lack a plausible story to tell about our access to the epistemic realm—perhaps because there would seem to be some mystery as to how we can have access to the values that are closely related to emotions, or as to how we could come to believe that certain things are reasons that bear on the accuracy of our emotional appraisals, independently of emotional experience.

However, the thought that emotions play a role in motivating the search for reasons or evidence that bear on the accuracy of our initial emotional appraisals suggests that such worries are not legitimate. For one thing, access to values—or at least the formation of justified evaluative

instance, that we can always make such a determination by focusing our attention solely and *narrowly* on this particular emotional object or event in these particular circumstances. Instead, the search for reasons that have a bearing on emotional accuracy might involve a subject's memories, as when she compares this emotional reaction with her reactions in other circumstances, or compares the object in this instance with other instances of such putative value. Nevertheless, this is compatible with the idea that emotional consumption focuses attention on and motivates reflection about some emotional object in the *broader* sense, where assessing the accuracy of our initial emotional appraisal of this object provides the *point* of remembering and comparing. After all, it is true that I can be focused on something in a broad sense—for instance, getting to the church on time—even when I am not reflecting on or thinking about this particular goal, but instead am thinking about the fact that the limousine is now ten minutes late, and remembering the traffic report this morning, and wondering where the best place to get a taxi would be. A more complete account about what is involved in our determining whether emotional appearance matches evaluative reality will be provided in the next two chapters.

beliefs—will *not* be independent of emotion, if the emotion is both alerting the subject to the presence of potential value in the environment through a fast and frugal evaluative appraisal, and keeping attention fixed so as to determine whether emotional appearance matches evaluative reality. For another, there is a relatively straightforward story to tell about how we can identify reasons that bear on the accuracy of emotional appraisals; for these will be (for the main part) considerations that raise or decrease the likelihood of the object or event having the evaluative property that the emotional experience presents it as having. And we can usually grasp what sorts of considerations these are in normal conditions because we have a grasp of the core relational theme of the emotion we're experiencing, and—through experience—a grasp of the kinds of things that have a bearing on such a theme. Thus, the core relational theme of fear is "danger", and we usually have a decent awareness, through experience and reflection, of the kinds of things that are relevant our safety in the circumstances in which we find ourselves. Similarly, the core relational theme of pride is achievement or accomplishment by oneself or someone in a suitable relation to oneself, and we can grasp, from a relatively early age, the kinds of things that count as (and don't count as) achievements. Identifying reasons in this way mirrors identifying reasons for action in normal circumstances: we have a goal in mind, such as getting to the pub for last orders, and usually a decent awareness, as a result of experience, of the kinds of things that we can do to make it more likely that this goal is satisfied, such as catching a taxi. Practical reasons are thus considerations that (other things being equal) raise the likelihood of our goal being satisfied.[20]

Lest it be thought that this capacity to identify reasons is, with respect to emotional experience, mysterious or arcane, consider some commonplace or everyday examples: when I am terrified upon hearing sounds downstairs in the middle of the night, the voice of my beloved saying "honey,

---

[20] This is not to deny, of course, that sometimes determining whether our emotions are to be endorsed or rejected is extremely difficult and complex. Quite obviously, debates about the accuracy of some emotion might be hard to settle. But it is to say that in normal circumstances we know the kinds of considerations that have a bearing on the correctness of some emotional appraisal—in the same way that in normal circumstances we know the kinds of considerations that have a bearing on what we ought to do. The fact that debates about the advisability of some action might be complex and difficult to settle should not, after all, cast doubt upon our capacity to identify and recognize practical reasons in normal conditions.

I'm home" is a good reason for me to dismiss my fear; when I awake feeling ashamed about my behaviour the morning after the Christmas party, my memory of regaling the Principal with bawdy limericks is a good reason to endorse my shame; the fact that the stranger at the door has a cockney accent is no reason for me to mistrust him, and so I should not endorse my emotional appraisal of untrustworthiness in this instance; whereas the fact that the home report shows that the flat is structurally sound and the fittings are original are good reasons to think that my positive feelings on first viewing the flat were justified. In such cases normal humans with sufficient experience will be aware of the relevance of these kinds of natural or non-evaluative features to the presence of the evaluative property; and this is because normal humans with sufficient experience will be aware that a beloved's return decreases the likelihood that there are dangerous strangers in the house, the singing of bawdy limericks constitutes the doing of something shameful, the possession of a cockney accent is irrelevant to trustworthiness, and the structural soundness of a flat increases the chances of its being a good flat. As a result, the attempt to determine whether emotional experience matches evaluative reality will not be independent of emotional experience on my view, nor will it involve any arcane or mysterious capacity to "see" or "grasp" the supervenience relations between natural and evaluative properties, beyond the perfectly normal capacity, grounded in reflection and experience, to assess the difference that some natural feature makes to the likely presence of some evaluative property.[21] We need not worry, therefore, that jettisoning the perceptual model leaves us with an epistemological story in which emotional experience has no important role to play; as I'll explain over the course of the next three chapters, that couldn't be farther from the truth.

To return to the main theme: the proposal that emotions involve persistent attentional focus, and that this motivates the search for and discovery of reasons that are relevant to our emotional situation, suggests, interestingly enough, that it is *emotions themselves* that rule out our taking our initial emotional appraisals at face value. In other words, it is our

---

[21] Note that perceptual theorists must themselves accept that we have some capacity to assess the accuracy of our emotional responses, given that they are committed to thinking of emotional experiences as constituting sufficient but *defeasible* reasons for evaluative beliefs. This commitment would be groundless if we were never in a position to judge that there is a mismatch between emotional experience and evaluative reality.

emotions themselves that *raise*, rather than silence, the justificatory question, through keeping our attention focused on the emotional object or event and by moving us to seek out considerations that bear on whether this object or event really is as it emotionally appears to be. A number of conclusions would seem to follow from this. First, in so far as the perceptual theorist insists that emotions in normal circumstances silence the justificatory question, or proposes that we usually take the content of our emotional experience at face value, then she can be accused of ignoring a central aspect or element of emotional experience, namely that emotions can motivate the search for reasons through the capture and consumption of attention. Second, emotional experience makes more of an epistemic contribution than the provision of an initial evaluative take on our situation. It can, in addition, play the important role of facilitating an improved or enhanced representation of the evaluative realm or our evaluative circumstances. In this way emotional experience can facilitate reappraisal of its own initial evaluation. Third, by raising rather than silencing justificatory questions, emotions demonstrate an element of *independence* from the particular circumstances in which they are elicited, and from the initial, reflexive, and automatic evaluative responses that partly constitute the emotions themselves. Emotions are, in other words, more flexible and more dynamic with regard to evaluation and assessment than the perceptual model has supposed. And finally, the idea that emotion facilitates its own reassessment or reappraisal goes beyond traditional, common-sense thinking about the epistemic yield and value of such experience, and indicates that emotions can do more than simply constitute the initial evaluative input to which evaluative judgement is the output. The way that emotional experience can elicit and justify evaluative judgement is considerably more complex than the traditional picture supposes.[22]

---

[22] Once again, I do not claim that emotions *guarantee* an enhanced representation or more accurate appraisal through the capture and consumption of attention. As I'll explain in Chapter 5, sometimes emotions won't involve the persistence of attention. And sometimes the maintenance of attention can have deleterious effects. What I do want to say is that without emotional persistence it is doubtful that reassessment or reappraisal of our initial emotional appraisal will happen, or at least will happen as efficiently. As I'll soon explain, reason alone is typically insufficient to provide the necessary check-and-balance on emotional appraisal. So even if emotional persistence does not guarantee accurate evaluations, it is unlikely that we will successfully achieve such accuracy, as a result of reassessment or reappraisal, in the absence of emotion.

The idea that emotions can have epistemic importance or value in these distinctive ways requires, of course, more in the way of support. So in the following sections I will argue that the consumption of attention and the motivation to search for reasons can be regarded as central features of emotional experience, and which serve important epistemic and practical needs.

3.3   An emotional solution to an emotional problem

We saw earlier that some emotions, in some circumstances, resemble what Ekman terms "affect program responses". Thus fear is often an automatic, reflexive, and very rapid response to potentially threatening objects and events. As we also saw, affect program responses function independently of higher-level conscious thought, since such thought tends to be relatively time-consuming; and there are obvious evolutionary advantages to a system that can facilitate a very fast and psychologically frugal response to potential threats, contamination, et al. In addition, although affect program responses do not themselves involve evaluative thought or judgement, they can nevertheless be understood as appraisals of objects and events in one's environment: affect program disgust can thus be understood as an appraisal of disgustingness or contamination, without necessarily involving thoughts about such things.

There is, however, a serious downside to a system that facilitates very fast responses to potentially important objects and events, which is that the responses are relatively *indiscriminate*. In other words, the appraisals involved in affect program responses are "quick and dirty": very rapid but relatively coarse responses to emotional objects and events. This is why people are reflexively, automatically, and indiscriminately afraid of things such as crawling insects, loud noises, looming objects, and the like, only some of which will actually be dangerous.[23] So discrimination is the cost that has to be paid for ensuring speed of response; it is, nevertheless, a price that is worth paying *in certain circumstances*, given that it is better to have an emotional system that responds very quickly to all such things than it is to

[23] See, for instance, Barrett, L., 'Adaptations to Predators and Prey', in Budd, D. (ed.), *The Handbook of Evolutionary Psychology*, New York: John Wiley & Sons (2005).

have a more discriminating evaluative system that responds more slowly.[24]

Given that affect program responses are relatively indiscriminate, how-ever, and given the importance of accurate evaluative information, then there seems a clear need for a more discriminating evaluative system. There is, in other words, a need for appraisals of emotional objects and events that are more discriminating than those generated by affect pro-grams, and which can thereby function to ensure that our emotional take matches up with evaluative reality. Without a secondary system for reappraisal, we would be stuck with our quick and dirty emotional responses, and this would clearly be problematic from both epistemic and practical standpoints. This is not just a point we can make about affect program responses. For there is also a need for reassessment and reappraisal of less "basic", more "cognitive" emotions such as resentment, guilt, and pride. As with affect program emotions, the higher cognitive emotions are also typically passive responses to things that are (potentially) relevant to our values, our cares and concerns. And as with affect program emotions, the higher cognitive emotions have a significant effect on our behaviour: think of how powerful resentment, guilt, pride, and shame can be when it comes to motivating action. It is therefore important that our emotional responses here track what is *genuinely* important or significant to us. But there is no guarantee that our initial emotional responses in such cases, which tend to reflect our social and cultural background, are any more discriminating than our affect program responses—indeed, given the wide variation in social and cultural environments, there's some reason to think that there will be *more* variety in the objects of guilt and pride than in the objects of the transcultural emotions of fear and disgust. There is thus a need for critical reflection on our higher cognitive emotions, and on the legitimacy of the inherited cultural norms that such emotions reflect, with a view to ensuring that here too emotional appearance matches evaluative

---

[24] As Phoebe Ellsworth writes, "one of the central functions of emotion is to motivate the organism to respond quickly and effectively to environmental threats as they arise. Generally the costs of failing to respond soon enough are far greater than the costs of responding when it is not really necessary . . . It is far safer for an organism to be calibrated to feel emotion when it is not warranted—to have a hypersensitive system—than it is to have a system that postpones the initiation of emotional processes until there is no question that they are justified." In Ellsworth, P., 'Levels of Thought and Levels of Emotion', in Ekman and Davidson (1994), p. 194.

reality. So speed of response speaks to the value of having a fast, reflexive, and frugal evaluative–motivational system that affect program emotions can fill. And accuracy of response speaks to the value of having a slow, reflective, conscious, and relatively costly evaluative–motivational system to assess our initial emotional responses and, where necessary, to counteract and countermand them.

At this point it is common for philosophers and psychologists to appeal to our capacity for *reason* as a solution to the problem of the lack of discrimination in our emotional responses. For there is a long-standing and venerable tradition according to which emotion needs to be monitored and controlled by reason: it is our capacity for rational reflection on our emotional situation that is essential as a check-and-balance on our emotional reactions.[25] A more contemporary expression of this idea is found in the literature on "dual-process" theories, a recent example of which is due to Keith Stanovich, and appeals to a distinction between "System 1" and "System 2" thinking. Dual-process theories of cognitive functioning "propose that within the brain there are two cognitive systems each with separable goal structures, and separate types of mechanisms for implementing the goal structures".[26] System 1 (or "intuitive" or "on-line") processing "is characterized as automatic, heuristic-based and relatively undemanding of computational capacity".[27] System 2 (or "analytic" or "off-line" or "rational") processes are "rule-based, often language-based, computationally expensive—and they are the focus of awareness".[28] For Stanovich, "[o]ne important function of the analytic system is to serve as a mechanism that can override inappropriately overgeneralized responses generated by the heuristic system—hence the tendency to link aspects of analytic processing with notions of inhibitory control."[29] In other words, System 2 (or rational) thinking can check and override System 1 (or intuitive) thinking, where the former is too crude, quick, overgeneralized, and indiscriminate.[30] To relate this to our discussion about emotional

---

[25] This point is familiar from Plato, Aristotle, and others in the 'intellectualist' tradition. Contemporary supporters include Dancy, Korsgaard, and Nagel. But the point also gains support from those more sympathetic to the role of the passions, such as Hume.

[26] Stanovich, K., *The Robot's Rebellion*, University of Chicago Press (2004), p. 34.

[27] Stanovich (2004), p. 34.

[28] Stanovich (2004), p. 36.   [29] Stanovich (2004), p. 36.

[30] See also Slovic, P., who claims that "one of the important functions of System 2 [processing] is to monitor the quality of the intuitive impressions produced by System 1", in '"If I Look at the Mass I Will Never Act". Psychic Numbing and Genocide', *Judgment and*

experience, affect program responses would seem to be System 1 responses, whilst the evaluative judgements we form as a result of reflection on considerations for and against the initial emotional appraisal are System 2 responses. The latter provide the necessary additional, overarching, and regulatory evaluative perspective on the former. So traditional thinking and contemporary cognitive science maintains that there is a need for reappraisal of our initial, intuitive, fast, and frugal emotional responses, and that it is reason which facilitates such reappraisal, in the form of evaluative judgements.

In light of this, why do I claim that it is *emotional* persistence that is central to such reappraisal, through motivating us to search for and discover reasons that bear on the accuracy of our initial, reflexive, and relatively indiscriminate emotional responses? Why think that the beneficial re-evaluation of our emotional construals is facilitated *via* the persistence of emotional experience? Although emotional persistence can have negative effects on accurate re-evaluation, as I'll discuss in the final chapter, I want to argue that emotion plays a central role in re-evaluation, and in the main because reason alone will generally be insufficient for the task of reappraisal. Without emotion, therefore, genuinely effective reappraisal will typically not occur.[31] At the very least, I want to argue that there are good reasons to think that reappraisal will be both more effective and less costly if reason is assisted by emotion, rather than if it operates alone. In order to make this argument, I'll garner phenomenological, psychological, philosophical, and neuroscientific support.

3.4 Why emotion is helpful for reappraisal

I maintain that emotion is central to reappraisal of emotional construals, both because of evidence that shows that emotion motivates reassessment,

Decision Making (2007), 2(2): p. 158. Peter Goldie comments: "The point is really a general one . . . If we assume that humans do have, broadly speaking, dual processes of thinking, intuitive and deliberative, then Slovic is surely right that at least one of the roles of deliberative thinking is a 'monitoring' one—to act as a kind of epistemic check and balance on fast and frugal intuitive thinking". In Goldie, P., 'Misleading Emotions', in Brun, G. Doğuoğlu, U. and Kuenzle D. (eds), *Epistemology and Emotions*, Farnham: Ashgate Publishing (2008), p. 208.

[31] I therefore support Michael Lacewing's scepticism about the extent to which "reason can and should autonomously and independently evaluate our emotional responses to situations". See his 'Emotional Self-Awareness and Ethical Deliberation', *Ratio* (2005), p. 81.

and because of evidence that reason alone is not up to the task of keeping our attention fixed on potentially important objects and events.

To see this, consider first some phenomenological evidence for the claim that it is emotion that typically motivates reappraisal of our initial emotional responses and thus helps to satisfy the need for reassessment of our evaluative situation. As we saw earlier, we often *feel the need* to discover reasons and evidence when emotional. Thus, recall the case where one is woken up by a noise downstairs, and think of the experience of one's senses being on "red alert" for other noises that could confirm (or hopefully, in this instance, disconfirm) the appraisal that one is in danger. Or think of the jealous person feeling the motivation to seek confirming (or disconfirming) evidence that her partner is unfaithful. Here the need for discovery is felt in so far as the emotional experience persists.[32]

But this is not simply the point that when emotional we feel the need to discover reasons or evidence; it also seems true that when we are no longer emotional we usually *lack* the motivation to check or assess the accuracy of our initial emotional appraisals. If, for instance, I no longer feel uneasy about the stranger, it is unlikely that I'll feel much motivation to seek evidence of his trustworthiness. Or if I no longer feel afraid, then it is unlikely that I'll bother myself much with seeking evidence as to whether or not I'm in danger. At least, it is unlikely that I'll be moved to seek confirming or disconfirming evidence with respect to what is now a non-emotional appearance of untrustworthiness or danger, which is I take it that which remains when we are no longer emotional. This is not surprising. A non-emotional appearance of danger is akin to Roberts's non-emotional evaluative construal, i.e. a construal that is not grounded in or based upon one of my cares or concerns—as when, for instance, I construe the shape of the cloud as an anvil. But in so far as the evaluative appearance

---

[32] This suggests that traditional versions of the feeling model don't get the phenomenology of emotion quite right. For if emotional experience involves feeling the need to search for and discover reasons that bear on the accuracy of our emotional responses, then the phenomenology of emotional experience will partly involve a feeling of changes in our attentional and cognitive resources. In other words, traditional and contemporary feeling theories have tended to ignore the fact that it *feels like something* to have one's attention fixed on some emotional object or event with a view to determining its accuracy, just as it feels like something to be fascinated by a puzzle or to be wrapped up in one's intellectual endeavours. The phenomenology of emotional experience is not simply therefore the feeling of bodily changes; it is also the feeling of cognitive changes that facilitate reappraisal of our emotional situation.

is not based upon my cares or concerns, then why would it matter to me whether the construal is accurate or not, and hence why should I check whether it is accurate? If this is the case, then there is a strong connection between the persistence of emotional experience and feeling the need to assess the accuracy of one's initial emotional appraisal.[33]

. Phenomenological support for the idea that emotions facilitate reappraisal, through effects on attention, fits in nicely with views in psychology which suggest that appraisal and reappraisal is an ongoing process in emotional experience. Thus, Klaus Scherer has argued that "emotion *decouples* stimulus and response", allowing a "latency period between stimulus evaluation and reaction".[34] On his view, "the first major function [of the latency period] is the ongoing analysis of the stimulus event, which allows the organism to arrive at a more detailed or more realistic conclusion and may lead to a re-evaluation and consequently a revision of the original appraisal".[35] On my account, the latency period coincides with the persistence of emotional experience, and hence with our attention being fixed and focused on the relevant object or event. In the same vein, Richard Lazarus writes:

For people to react with an emotion, the relevance of what is happening to their well-being must be sensed, as well as whether this has negative or positive implications. We do not stop with a hasty and incomplete cognitive evaluation—this constitutes an incompleted task, which the person or animal is compelled to pursue further—until what is happening can be understood in a way that is relevant to efforts at coping. Although the initial appraisal may be hasty and limited, if the opportunity for further investigation of what is happening presents itself, it would be a strange creature that let things drop before a full functional understanding has been achieved.[36]

On my account, it is the fact that attention is consumed in emotional experience that is a central element in presenting the opportunity for further investigation of what is happening, since it keeps what is happening, and its importance, at the forefront of our minds. And if

[33] As we'll see in the next chapter, another reason why it is important for us to discover reasons that bear on the accuracy of our emotional appraisals is that this is an effective way of controlling or moderating our emotional responses. If so, then this is another reason not to be surprised when the motivation to search for reasons dissipates when the emotional experience ends—for then the need to control one's emotion has also disappeared.

[34] Scherer, K., 'The Function of Emotions', in Ekman and Davidson (eds) (1994), p. 128.

[35] Scherer (1994), p. 129.

[36] Lazarus, R., 'Appraisal: The Long and the Short of It', in Ekman and Davidson (eds) (1994), p. 215.

Lazarus is right, the compulsion or motivation to investigate further and to attain a more accurate appraisal is the norm: it is not just that we sometimes feel the need to investigate when we have the opportunity, but rather that feeling the need to investigate when we have the chance is what normal humans do.

The idea that emotion plays the role of facilitating reflection and reappraisal through the capture of attention, and that reason alone is not up to this task, also finds support in the writings of Thomas Reid, who is one of the few philosophers to be concerned with the connection between emotion and attention. Reid claims that "[i]t requires a strong degree of curiosity, or some more important passion, to give us that interest in an object which is necessary to our giving attention to it. And, without attention, we can form no true and stable judgement of any object."[37] And

[a]ttention may be given to any object, either of sense or of intellect, in order to form a distinct notion of it, or to discover its nature, its attributes, or its relations and so great is the effect of attention, that, without it, it is impossible to acquire or retain a distinct notion of any object of thought.[38]

So for Reid, emotion (or "passion") is necessary for us to pay attention to some object or event, and paying attention is necessary for us to form an accurate ("a true and stable") judgement about that object or event. Reid would therefore be sympathetic to the idea that emotional control of attention facilitates a better grasp of our evaluative situation, by making us aware of the reasons that have a bearing in these circumstances.

Now although Reid's claims about necessity are too strong, since we can voluntarily fix our attention onto some object in the absence of emotion, he is nevertheless surely correct to stress the importance of emotion in the direction and control of attention, and the importance of attention to an accurate evaluation of our circumstances.[39] Although we *can* voluntarily fix and direct our attention onto some object or event, this is usually very costly in terms of mental resources, in which case there is a significant advantage in having a system which keeps our attention fixed

---

[37] Reid, T., *Essays on the Active Powers of the Human Mind*, Brody, B. (ed.), Cambridge, MA: MIT Press (1969), pp. 184–5.

[38] Reid (1969), pp. 76–7.

[39] See Faucher and Tappolet (2002) for the distinction between voluntary and involuntary maintenance of attention.

with little in the way of conscious effort on our part. If considerations of mental economy speak in favour of the automatic and reflexive direction and focus of attention in emotional experience, then similar considerations speak to the emotional consumption of attention. But it is not simply a matter of cost: an interest in some object that is motivated by emotion would seem to be more stable and persistent than a non-emotional interest maintained through sheer strength of will. In the absence of emotion, it is all too easy to lose interest in some object or event, partly because of the effort involved, but also partly because a lack of emotion usually means that some object or event doesn't *matter* to us (or doesn't matter to us *as much* any more), in which case there's little point in our continuing to take an interest in it. If an accurate appraisal of some object or event typically requires more than a fleeting interest in it, then attentional persistence will typically be needed to facilitate such an appraisal. Even if the emotional capture and consumption of attention is not strictly necessary for us to get an accurate picture of our evaluative situation, therefore, the emotional governance of attention for this end is extremely valuable. This is why it is plausible to think that it is emotion, rather than reason alone, which is best suited to facilitating reappraisal of our emotional situation.

There is, in addition, considerable neurophysiological evidence for the proposal that at least certain emotions involve attentional capture and consumption, and that this helps to facilitate an enhanced representation of the relevant emotional object and event. A central part of this evidence rests upon the idea that emotions involve increased *cortical arousal*, and that this is a central element in attentiveness.[40] Thus, Joseph LeDoux writes that

It has long been believed that the difference between being awake and alert, on the one hand, and drowsy or asleep on the other is related to the arousal level of the cortex. When you are alert and paying attention to something important, your cortex is aroused. When you are drowsy and not focusing on anything, the cortex is in the unaroused state.[41]

---

[40] The evidence concerns the emotion of fear; and similar things might be said for a small category of biologically basic emotions, perhaps including disgust, surprise, anger, and joy. It is not clear that there is similar neurophysiological evidence with respect to more "cognitive" emotions such as jealousy, resentment, and guilt. Nevertheless, it is not obviously implausible that similar stories could be told with regard to these, if we think of jealousy as involving fear of rejection, resentment as involving anger of a particular kind, and so on. So perhaps this kind of evidence could cover more of the things that philosophers identify as emotions.

[41] LeDoux (1996), p. 287.

For LeDoux, "[e]motional reactions are typically accompanied by intense cortical arousal . . . This high level of arousal is, in part, the explanation for why it is hard to concentrate on other things and work efficiently when you are in an emotional state."[42] Increased arousal is itself in part a matter of increased sensitivity of cells in the cortical and thalamic regions, and this results in increased processing of emotional stimuli. LeDoux continues:

While much of the cortex is potentially hypersensitive to inputs during arousal, the systems that are processing information are able to make the most use of this effect. For example, if arousal is triggered by the sight of a snake, the neurons that are actively involved in processing the snake, retrieving long-term memories about snakes, and creating working memory representations of the snake are going to be especially affected by arousal. Other neurons are inactive at this point and don't reap the benefits.[43]

Moreover, additional sensitivity of cells in the cortical and thalamic regions typically results in a "feedback loop" of arousal, since sensitivity of such cells triggers further arousal of the amygdala, which is the area of the brain which initially activates arousal systems in response to emotional stimuli. As a result, "arousal locks you into whatever emotional state you are in when arousal occurs".[44] Arousal of the amygdala is thus responsible for the persistence of attentional focus in emotional experience, which results in increased processing of emotional stimuli. Consequently, we can say that emotions often involve the mobilization and direction of attentional mechanisms, and that this can "provoke a more detailed stimulus analysis [and] enhance the representation of the relevant stimuli".[45]

If this is correct, then emotions involve cortical arousal, cortical arousal is needed for us to be alert and attentive, and attentiveness facilitates the processing of information that is involved in appraisal and reappraisal of emotional stimuli. So contemporary neurophysiology suggests that the persistence of attentional focus in emotional experience serves to facilitate a better evaluation of our emotional situation, through promoting awareness of, and reflection about, our emotional circumstances. This does not, by itself, show that reason alone does not do this. Nevertheless, given the

---

[42] LeDoux (1996), p. 289.   [43] LeDoux (1996), pp. 287–8.
[44] LeDoux (1996), p. 290.
[45] Vuilleumier, P., Armony, J., and Dolan, R.J., 'Reciprocal Links between Emotion and Attention', in Frackowiak, R. et al. (eds), *Human Brain Function*, 2nd edition, San Diego: Academic Press (2003), p. 432.

previous points about the difficulty of remaining focused and attentive when non-emotional, the conclusion that emotion facilitates enhanced or accurate representation more easily than reason alone is difficult to resist. Neurophysiology therefore suggests that emotions have value because they facilitate the reassessment of our initial emotional responses.

A final reason to think that the persistence of attention in emotional experience has a central or primary function of facilitating a reappraisal can be seen if we consider a rival proposal for the point of attentional persistence. For it might be argued that the most important function or role of the maintenance of attention in an emotion like fear is not to determine whether something that appears dangerous really is dangerous, but is rather to monitor something that is taken to be dangerous. In such a case, attention will remain on the object for the purpose of monitoring its behaviour—as when one's fear maintains one's sensory attention on the dog running wild in the park—without motivating one to reassess one's initial appraisal of the dog as dangerous. And it might be argued that the former is more plausibly identified as the function of attentional persistence, on the grounds that monitoring the dog in this instance is needed to figure out how to respond to the dog, and this goal has priority over re-evaluating one's initial emotional take. After all, monitoring serves our *overall* goal of responding appropriately to an object of importance or significance, and so this explanation of the point of attentional persistence fits nicely with our guiding platitude about what emotions in general enable us to do.

However, I want to argue that these are not rival explanations of the point of attentional persistence, but are in fact compatible. Indeed, the thought that emotions help us monitor something that is taken to have an evaluative property so that we can respond appropriately would seem to *require* that emotions help us to re-evaluate or reappraise the emotional object: recall Lazarus's claim that "we do not stop with a hasty and incomplete cognitive evaluation—this constitutes an incompleted task, which the person or animal of compelled to pursue further—until what is happening can be understood in a way that is relevant to efforts at *coping*".[46] In other words, my proposal that emotions have the function of reassessing or reappraising the emotional object would seem to *follow from*

---

[46] My italics. I take "coping" here to refer to a behavioural response.

the thought that the maintenance of attention facilitates monitoring the said object. For if emotional persistence enables us to monitor something with a view to determining the appropriate behavioural response, then emotional persistence *ought* to motivate reappraisal, on the assumption that the object in question might turn out to *lack* the evaluative property in question, in which case the appropriate behavioural response will be to *do nothing*. For instance, if the point of monitoring the dog in the park is to determine the appropriate behavioural response, then a search for reasons that bear on the accuracy of one's initial appraisal of the dog as dangerous would seem to be required for this determination, on the grounds that an appropriate response if the dog turns out to be harmless is neither fight nor flight but inaction. There might, after all, be significant costs to be borne if one chooses either of the two standard options when faced with dangerous animals—namely to run away or to attack   should the dog actually turn out to be harmless. (Think of how the dog owner might respond to your unprovoked assault on his prized corgi.) It is, therefore, implausible to think that the point of attentional persistence is the narrow one of monitoring some object in order to determine how one should respond to an object that *has* some property, rather than the broader one of monitoring some object in order to determine the appropriate behavioural response where this *includes* the possibility of doing nothing because the object lacks the property that it initially appeared to have. So if one has the time and the opportunity for further investigation with a view to determining whether emotional appearance matches evaluative reality—which is precisely the time and opportunity that the persistence of attention typically provides—then one should seek out reasons and evidence that have a bearing on this question. For, to repeat, what the appropriate behavioural response to some object will be clearly *depends upon* whether one's initial emotional take on this object is accurate. The claim that attentional persistence enables the subject to monitor some object with a view to determining the appropriate behavioural response, and the claim that attentional persistence enables the subject to reassess or re-evaluate her original emotional take, are not therefore rival views of the function of the maintenance of attention in emotional experience. Instead, monitoring some emotional object in order to determine the appropriate behavioural response requires the subject to reappraise or re-evaluate her initial emotional construal, since this is needed in order for a proper determination of what the appropriate response in these conditions will be. If so, then there is an epistemic need for reassessment of one's initial emotional response, given the chance that such a response is relatively indiscriminate; and there is a more directly practical need for reassessment of one's initial emotional response, given the chance that the object lacks the evaluative property that it seems to have in the first emotional blush. We have, therefore, a further reason to think that emotion has value in so far as it captures and consumes attention, and thereby facilitates a reappraisal and re-evaluation of emotion itself.

If these arguments are convincing, then we have phenomenological, psychological, philosophical, and neurophysiological support for the idea that emotions motivate the search for reasons and evidence, i.e. for considerations that are relevant to the accuracy of our initial emotional appraisals. Emotions help to motivate, in other words, their own re-appraisal. In so doing, emotions both serve a need that stems from the nature of affect program emotional responses and higher cognitive emotions, and facilitate appropriate behaviour. For affect program responses are often too indiscriminate to be relied upon, whilst higher cognitive emotions are often too dependent upon social and cultural background to be accepted without reassessment; and appropriate behaviour can often involve doing nothing when one realizes that the object lacks the property that it appeared to have in the first emotional blush. This suggests the following conclusion: emotions have developed to solve a problem that emotions themselves are responsible for setting up. Emotions are both the cause of and solution to an evaluative problem. The epistemological implications of this conclusion, and in particular the implications for the perceptual model of emotion, will now be considered.

3.5 Against the perceptual model

The previous sections strongly suggest that there is an epistemological difference between emotional and perceptual experience, and that this difference stems from the very nature of emotion. It seems plausible, as many philosophers suggest, that (absent defeating evidence) we automatically take the representational content of perceptual experiences at face value when forming the relevant empirical beliefs. And it seems plausible that, except in very unusual circumstances, we are entitled to do so. In this way perceptual experience does indeed silence the demand for justification. One reason for confidence here is that perceptual experiences are not fast and indiscriminate responses to external stimuli, and therefore there is no general need for us to keep attention focused on the relevant objects and events in order to reappraise our initial perceptual experience of them. Another reason is that perceptual experience is much less susceptible to cultural or social influences than emotional experience.[47] As a result, there is much less variation in perceptual experience, and thus much less of a need for reassessment in order to balance potentially misleading social and cultural influences. This might explain why perceptual experiences do not involve the persistence or consumption of attention: as LeDoux notes, even novel visual stimuli fail to capture the attention for more than a moment, at least in the absence of an emotional connection.

But if emotional responses are often indiscriminate, and if it is a common feature of our emotional lives that we search for reasons that bear on the accuracy of our initial emotional appraisals, then it is a mistake to suggest that in normal circumstances we take the representational content of emotional experiences at face value when forming evaluative beliefs. Rather, given that emotions capture and consume attention, and given that this facilitates the search for considerations that confirm or disconfirm our initial emotional appraisal of our circumstances, we might think instead that it is normal for us to endorse the content of our emotional experience only after we have discovered (or on some occasions invented or fabricated) reasons to think that our emotional appearance is veridical. It is usual, in other words, for emotional experience to *raise* rather than *silence* the justificatory demand with respect to our initial emotional appraisal; the persistence of emotional experience makes the demand for justification of this appraisal pressing. Moreover, absent the discovery (or invention) of such reasons, it is by no means obvious that we regard ourselves as entitled to take the content of our emotional experiences at face value. All of this strongly suggests, as noted earlier, that there is a difference in the strength of reasons or evidence provided by perceptual and emotional experiences. In normal circumstances our perceptual experiences constitute sufficient reasons for non-evaluative empirical judgements; but in normal circumstances our emotional experiences do not constitute sufficient reasons for evaluative judgements. If they did,

---

[47] Recall de Sousa's claim that emotions, unlike perceptions, are "typically susceptible" to "social and ideological factors" (1987), pp. 152–3.

then we would be at a loss to explain or accommodate a central feature of emotional experience, namely the fact that we are moved to seek reasons or evidence to confirm, or disconfirm, our initial emotional appraisals. The widespread tendency to engage in this form of epistemic activity would be inexplicable if the epistemic yield of emotional experiences matched that of perceptual experiences in normal circumstances. As a result, the claim that the epistemic role and value of emotional experience mirrors that of perceptual experience is mistaken, and the confidence that the perceptual theorist has in the similarity between emotional and perceptual experience at the epistemic level is misplaced.

At this point the defender of the perceptual model might respond as follows. We do indeed search for reasons in support of our emotional appraisals, and typically do not with respect to our perceptual experiences. But this merely reflects the fact that, as Elgin puts it, our emotional experiences are less reliable than perceptual experiences, and thus "need more collateral support in order to be [fully] tenable".[48] On this view, emotional experiences "start out with less initial tenability"[49] than perceptual experiences. Nevertheless, Elgin claims that "to have less initial tenability is not to have none. The very fact that [emotional experiences] present themselves as indicators of how things stand gives them some degree of initial tenability".[50] It is therefore compatible with the search for reasons that emotions provide *some*, albeit not sufficient, support for our evaluative beliefs.[51] Emotions can still constitute reasons or evidence for evaluative beliefs, in other words, despite the fact that we are often motivated to look for additional evidence when it comes to emotional experience. If so, then the perceptual theorist can maintain that a difference in how attention is governed in perceptual and emotional experience does little to undermine the claim that such experiences play a similar epistemic role, if we understand that epistemic role more broadly as being that of *reason- or evidence-providing*.

We might wonder whether this is a concession too far for the perceptual theorist to make. After all, the central unifying theme of perceptual theories would seem to be the distinctive epistemological claim that emotional experience is just like perceptual experience in its epistemic

---

[48] Elgin, C., 'Emotion and Understanding', in Brun, Doğuoğlu, and Kuenzle (eds) (2008), p. 40.

[49] Elgin (2008), p. 40.   [50] Elgin (2008), p. 40.

[51] On p. 34 of 'Emotion and Understanding', Elgin (2008) is explicit about the fact that emotions might not provide conclusive reasons.

role and value. This claim is supposed to mark some theory out as "perceptual", even if the theory claims that in all other respects emotions and perceptual experiences are merely analogous. Now we are being asked to accept that emotional experience is merely similar to perceptual experience in some respects at the epistemic level. The comparison with perceptual experience is becoming so attenuated that some might question the appropriateness of the analogy at all. Even if we ignore this, however, I think that Elgin's response is overly optimistic. For it can be argued that emotional experience doesn't, even in normal conditions, provide *any* kind of reason for evaluative judgement. If so, then emotional experience is not at all like perceptual experience at the epistemic level.

To see this, note first that there is another point of disanalogy between emotional and perceptual experiences: the former, but not the latter, can themselves be *responses to reasons*. It is because of this that many people think that at least some emotions can be assessed for rationality as well as for accuracy. For instance, it is common to think of "recalcitrant" emotions as in some sense irrational: it is irrational to be ashamed of things that one does not judge to be shameful, or to feel guilt when one believes that one has done nothing wrong. And it is irrational to be ashamed or guilty in these circumstance because nothing about the object or event constitutes a good enough reason for shame or guilt: recalcitrant shame of one's Glaswegian accent is irrational because there is nothing about a Glaswegian accent that is shameful; and recalcitrant guilt about hanging up one's washing on a Sunday is irrational because there is nothing about hanging up one's washing on a Sunday that constitutes a reason to feel guilty. Conversely, it seems perfectly rational for me to be afraid while driving in heavy traffic in fog, or to be angry when the University Principal awards himself a 20 per cent pay rise at the same time as I'm forced to take a 10 per cent cut, or to feel guilty when the homeless person is in need of my help and I walk past without offering any. This is because such considerations constitute good reasons for fear or anger or guilt. And this marks a contrast with perceptual experiences. Even though perceptual experience can diverge from belief, as in the case where the perceiver knows that they are subject to a visual illusion, it is not irrational to perceive the lines in the Hering illusion as being curved when one knows that they are straight. And it is not irrational to see the lines in this way because it makes little sense to talk of features of the depicted figure as reasons to see the lines as straight. It makes little sense, in other words, to talk about features of an object as reasons to see or hear it in some way.

This illustrates a general point: the considerations that constitute good reasons for an emotional response are *equally* good reasons for the relevant evaluative judgement; and, by the same token, considerations that constitute good reasons for some evaluative judgement are equally good reasons for the relevant emotional response.[52] So reasons to think that something is dangerous are equally reasons to fear that thing; reasons to think that one has just been insulted are equally reasons to be angry; reasons to think that one has done something wrong are equally reasons to feel guilt; and similarly for other central cases of emotions. To illustrate, the fact that the bull in the farmer's field has sharp horns and is advancing rapidly towards me is a good reason for me to be afraid *and* a good reason for me to judge that the bull is dangerous. Or the fact that Jones keeps changing his story under questioning, refuses to meet his interlocutor's eyes, and stands to gain financially from testifying against the defendant are all good reasons for us to feel mistrust towards Jones *and* judge that he is untrustworthy as a witness for the prosecution. In each case, the considerations in question are the non-evaluative features of the object or event which seem directly relevant to the rationality of the emotional response and, by the same token, to the correct ascription of the evaluative property. These considerations are, moreover, precisely the kinds of consideration that we seek out when assessing the accuracy of our initial emotional appraisals; they are the kinds of reason or evidence that we are moved to discover through the persistence of emotional experience.

Our question, then, is this: is the fact that we have some emotional experience a consideration of this kind? In other words: is it plausible to maintain that our emotional experience of the bull and of Jones are *additional* reasons to judge that the bull is dangerous and that Jones is untrustworthy, over and above the considerations already mentioned? The answer to such questions is clearly "no". The fact that a reason for an evaluative judgement is equally a reason for the relevant emotional response rules out the possibility that emotional experiences can themselves be reasons for evaluative judgements, for then such experience would appear to be capable of justifying itself. That is, my fear of the bull cannot

---

[52] See Goldie, P., 'Emotion, Reason, and Virtue', in Evans, P. and Cruse, P. (eds), *Emotion, Evolution, and Rationality*, Oxford: Oxford University Press (2004), p. 254.

be a reason to judge that the bull is dangerous, since then we would have to conclude, from the fact that I am afraid of the bull, that I have good reason to be afraid of the bull. And fear, we might think, cannot justify itself in this way.

We might make the same point in a different way, by focusing on the concepts that form the content of the relevant evaluative judgements. A plausible position in metaethics, and one that might appear conducive to the aims of the perceptual theorist, is that evaluative concepts like "dangerous", "insulting", "disgusting", "amusing", and so forth are best understood along *sentimentalist* lines. At least, many prominent philosophers have maintained that these kinds of evaluative concepts can only be understood in terms of particular human emotions or sentiments. Sentimentalist accounts propose that we are to understand what it is for something to be dangerous or shameful, let's say, in terms of its "eliciting or meriting" certain emotional responses, namely fear and shame. On such views, having emotional responses is required for a complete grasp of the concept—a point which, as we've seen, is stressed by Döring, Goldie, Johnston, and others. Now the most promising versions of sentimentalism about value are second-order accounts, according to which "to apply a response-dependent concept Φ to an object X (i.e. to think that X is Φ) is to think it *appropriate* (merited, rational, justified, warranted) to feel an associated sentiment F towards X".[53] These are the kinds of accounts favoured by 'sensibility theorists' such as Simon Blackburn, Allan Gibbard, John McDowell, and David Wiggins. It is important to note that all of these philosophers reject *dispositionalist* theories of evaluative concepts.[54] Sensibility theorists deny, that is, that an evaluative concept Φ is to be understood in terms of the sentiments that people are disposed to feel under normal conditions. Instead, they maintain that we must understand evaluative concepts in terms of appropriate or fitting or merited or rational emotional responses. On this account, to judge that X is Φ is to judge that it is rational or appropriate or fitting to feel F in response to X; to say that

---

[53] D'Arms, J., 'Two Arguments for Sentimentalism', *Philosophical Issues* (2005), 15: p. 3.

[54] See Blackburn, S., *Ruling Passions*, New York: Oxford University Press (1998); Gibbard, A., *Wise Choices, Apt Feelings*, Cambridge, MA: Harvard University Press (1990); McDowell, J., 'Values and Secondary Qualities' and 'Projection and Truth in Ethics', collected in his *Mind, Value, and Reality*, Cambridge, MA: Harvard University Press (1998); and Wiggins, D., 'A Sensible Subjectivism?' in his *Needs, Values, Truth*, Oxford: Blackwell Publishers (1987).

some object is dangerous is, therefore, to say that it merits fear, or that fear in this instance would be appropriate, or warranted, or rational, or fitting.

Now sensibility theorists face difficulties in spelling out just what it is for an emotional response to be appropriate, merited, or fitting. Despite this, the approach has a good deal of initial plausibility when it comes to evaluative concepts like "dangerous", "insulting", and "shameful".[55] At the very least, it is a good deal more plausible than standard dispositionalist accounts that appeal to emotional responses in normal conditions. If a rational version of sentimentalism is correct, however, then our emotional responses cannot be reasons or evidence for the associated evaluative judgements. My fear of the bull, for instance, cannot be a reason to judge that the bull is dangerous, for then my fear would be a reason to judge that fear in these circumstances is appropriate or merited or fitting; and we have good reason to doubt that fear can justify itself in this way. The very fact that I am afraid of the bull cannot, by itself, be evidence that it is fitting or appropriate for me to be afraid of the bull. On a sentimentalist account of evaluative concepts, therefore, emotional experience cannot provide reason or evidence for evaluative judgements.

It is important to note that this form of argument cannot be used to show that perceptions cannot be reasons for perceptual beliefs. If a response-invoking or response-dependent account is to be plausible with respect to sensory or perceptual properties like colours, then in all likelihood it *will* be a dispositionalist account. On this view, we are to understand colour concepts, let us say, in terms of the colours that people are disposed to see under normal conditions. We should not be tempted here to propose that we should understand the concept "red" in terms of the *rational* appropriateness of what people see, or in terms of responses to *reasons* to see, simply because we do not assess seeing red in terms of its rational appropriateness; to see something as red is not a response to reasons. As a result, seeing something as red can *be* a reason to believe that it is red; but since reasons for perceptual beliefs are not, in and of

[55] See, for instance, the following important papers co-authored by D'Arms, J. and Jacobson, D.: 'The Moralistic Fallacy', *Philosophy and Phenomenological Research* 61 (2000a); 'Sentiment and Value', *Ethics* 110 (2000b); 'The Significance of Recalcitrant Emotion' (2003); and 'Anthropocentric Constraints on Human Value', in Shafer-Landau, R. (ed.), *Oxford Studies in Metaethics Vol. 1*, Oxford: Oxford University Press (2006).

themselves, reasons to perceive things, then seeing something as red does not constitute a reason for itself.

3.6 Conclusions

In this chapter I have argued that emotional experiences are not sufficient reasons for evaluative judgements, and as a result are dissimilar to perceptual experiences at the epistemic level. The core of this argument appealed to a distinctive feature of emotion, which is that emotional experience captures and consumes our attention, motivating the search for reasons that bear on the accuracy of our initial emotional responses, and helping to satisfy an epistemic and a practical need for reappraisal. As a result of this, we do not normally treat our emotional experiences as sufficient reasons for evaluative judgement. Moreover, I argued that we are *right* not to take our emotional experiences at face value or to regard them as silencing the need for justification. One reason for this is that behaviour on the basis of emotion alone is often unjustified in normal conditions, which reflects the unjustified nature of the underlying evaluative belief or judgement. If emotional experiences were like perceptual experiences in providing sufficient reasons in normal circumstances, this central feature of emotional experience in motivating reappraisal would be inexplicable. And if emotional experience were like perceptual experience at the epistemic level, then behaviour on the basis of emotional experience *wouldn't* normally be unjustified—on the plausible assumption that behaviour on the basis of what we seem to see and hear is, except in abnormal circumstances, and all things considered, justified behaviour.

This left open the possibility that emotional experiences were, nevertheless, a weaker kind of reason and so retained some epistemological similarity with perceptual experiences. However, I then argued that emotional experiences are not reasons at all when it comes to our evaluative judgements. This argument depended upon the thought that reasons for evaluative judgements are equally reasons for emotional responses. If so, then emotional responses cannot themselves constitute reasons for evaluative judgements, on pain of being capable of justifying themselves. And this, we might plausibly think, they cannot do.

These arguments and conclusions generate a puzzle, however. For common-sense suggests that emotional experiences themselves can and do tell us about the evaluative world. And if such experiences themselves inform us about value, then it seems right to hold that they can and do constitute reasons or evidence for evaluative judgements. If so, then the plausibility of these arguments puts us under some pressure to jettison our common-sense take on emotion's epistemic role and value. But this would be premature. In the following chapter I'll argue that we can accommodate common-sense thinking about the epistemic value of emotional experience, but only if we relinquish the strict comparison to or analogy with sensory perceptual experience. As such, the perceptual model, far from being the most plausible explanation of our common-sense thinking about the epistemic value of emotional experience, is in fact a barrier to a proper explanation of how emotions inform us about value. Moreover, I'll argue that this indicates how emotional experience can have epistemic value beyond the ways envisaged by traditional or common-sense thinking about this issue. Criticism of the perceptual model thus illustrates how emotions can have epistemic value, and in new and hitherto unexplored ways.

4

Emotion and Understanding

In the previous chapter I argued that emotional experiences are not, in normal conditions, sufficient reasons for evaluative judgements. I then claimed that emotional experiences do not seem to constitute reasons of *any* kind for evaluative judgements. If they did, emotional experiences would seem to be capable of justifying themselves—which is something that we can doubt. This, however, leaves us with something of a puzzle, since common-sense tells us that emotional experience certainly seems to provide information about the evaluative world, at least under certain conditions. In the first half of this chapter I attempt to resolve this puzzle. My main argument here will rest upon the claim that emotional experiences can be *proxy* or *pro tempore* reasons—useful substitutes or stand-ins for considerations that constitute genuine reasons. This indicates how common-sense views about the epistemology of emotional experience can be preserved, but at the cost of rejecting the perceptual model. As such, the perceptual model is actually a *barrier* to capturing the idea that emotions can inform us about value.

In the second half of the chapter I continue the development of my positive account of the epistemic role and value of emotion. In order to do this, I propose and defend an idea that was implicit in the previous chapter, namely that emotions, through the capture and consumption of attention, facilitate or promote *evaluative understanding*. This illustrates, moreover, that the perceptual model is not only guilty of overstating the epistemic role and value of emotional experience, by claiming that such experience is just like perceptual experience at the epistemic level; it is also guilty of *understating* the epistemic value that emotional experience has, in so far as it ignores the role that emotional experience itself plays in promoting understanding of value. Furthermore, this general idea about emotion's epistemic role can be expanded to include understanding of one's own values, in addition to understanding of value "in the world". The fact that emotional experience constitutes a different kind of reason from that provided by perceptual experience does not therefore suggest that we discount the former's epistemic role and value. Instead, the difference between emotional and perceptual experience that I am proposing gives us reason to be *more* confident in the epistemic importance of emotion than the perceptual theory, and indeed traditional common-sense thinking, allows.

To begin, I want to consider a response that the perceptual theorist might make to the argument that emotional experiences are not sufficient reasons for evaluative beliefs.

4.1 In defence of the perceptual model

In the previous chapter I made a number of claims about emotional experience in normal conditions. For instance, I claimed that we do not usually take such experience for granted or think that it silences the demand for justification. I claimed that emotions motivate us to search for and discover reasons that bear on the accuracy of our initial emotional construals through the capture and consumption of attention. I also claimed, as a corollary, that we don't, in normal conditions, endorse or reject such construals until we discover (or in some cases invent or fabricate) reasons that speak for or against them. Finally, I claimed that although there were circumstances in which our emotional experience does indeed silence the need for justification, such as the feeling of disgust one experiences at the venison shank on one's plate, these are relatively rare. In normal circumstances we do not regard the need for justification as silenced; and we are, moreover, right to think that we need more in the way of evidence. So the jealous man searches for evidence of infidelity, the angry woman seeks out considerations that justify her rage, the guilty teenager tries to discover whether she really has done something wrong, and so forth. As a result, I argued that we do not usually regard emotional experiences as sufficient reasons for evaluative judgements, and to this extent at least the former differ in their epistemic role and value from perceptual experiences.

At this point the perceptual theorist might claim that these claims about emotional experience in normal conditions are not true—or at the very least, such claims are open to challenge. Although emotions *can* motivate the search for reasons, particularly when there is a lot at stake, it is a mistake to generalize on the basis of these examples and claim that we normally or typically seek reasons to confirm or disconfirm our emotional appraisals. For one thing, general claims about what emotions normally or typically do seem too imprecise to have truth values. That is, claims about normality and rarity need a clear and detailed specification of the *type* of emotion involved, and the *type* of circumstances in which the emotional response occurs, if they are to be themselves assessable for truth or falsity. In this they mirror claims about the reliability of some process or system. For another, the perceptual theorist can appeal to a whole range of cases in which a subject takes her emotional experiences for granted, or does not search for confirming or disconfirming evidence for her emotional construals. Once we see these cases in detail, we should accept that it is not rare for emotional experience to silence the justificatory demand; instead, this happens all the time. As a result, my claim that we do not, in normal circumstances, take our emotional experiences for granted, or regard our emotions as providing sufficient reasons for evaluative judgements, is undermined.[1]

A first case is provided by young children: we might doubt that children are often, if ever, motivated to seek out reasons that bear on the accuracy of their emotional appraisals. Instead, young children would seem to form evaluative beliefs—such as the belief that they are in peril—directly as a result of experiencing fear. Here it is the child's feeling of fear which is the reason why she believes that she is in danger; and since it is highly unlikely that the child formed this belief as a result of endorsing her emotional construal after reflection on other considerations that constitute reasons, it seems obvious that the child simply takes her fear at face value. For the child at least, her emotional experience is a sufficient reason to believe that she is in danger.[2]

A second case is where evaluative judgements are *habitually* and *immediately* formed as a result of emotional experience. Think, for instance, of someone prone to road rage, who habitually and automatically endorses

---

[1] A different way of making the same point is to argue that my account is guilty of over-intellectualizing the emotional–evaluative life of normal people in normal conditions. The objector therefore thinks that it is false that the search for and discovery of reasons to validate or disconfirm our initial emotional construals is a feature of our normal, everyday emotional experience.

[2] I owe this example, and objection, to Tim Bayne.

the representational content of his anger at other road users, or of the teenager who immediately and unthinkingly accepts the representational content of his feelings of shame. There's little in the way of distance between emotional experience and evaluative judgement in these cases; rather, the emotional experiences quickly and automatically cause the evaluative judgements. By the same token, there's not much in the way of evidence gathering and reappraisal of an initial emotional response for these subjects; rather, the content of their emotional experience is accepted as true as a matter of habit. Here too it seems as though the subjects take their emotional experiences at face value, or treat them as sufficient reasons to believe as they do.[3] In these cases, emotional experience leads to evaluative judgement without any mediating process, in the same way that perceptual experience leads quickly, automatically, and without mediation to non-evaluative judgement.

A third sort of case is provided by moral judgement.[4] Recent research by the psychologist Jonathan Haidt suggests that moral judgement often follows immediately from an initial emotional response, rather than being mediated by the search for reasons and subsequent endorsement or rejection of our emotional construal.[5] Instead, Haidt proposes that the search for reasons is a matter of *post hoc* rationalization. In this way the search for reasons resembles the way in which a lawyer makes his case for a pre-assigned position: the position is fixed, and the lawyer *then* searches for reasons to support it.[6] Haidt's experiments also indicate that subjects will hold on to their moral judgements even in the absence of such reasons, although they will profess to feeling "morally dumbfounded" in this case— "that is, they would stutter, laugh, and express surprise at their inability to find supporting reasons, yet they would not change their initial judgments of condemnation".[7] For instance, subjects were told a story about a

---

[3] I do not claim here that such treatment involves the subject explicitly thinking of such experiences as reasons, any more than other kinds of habitual activity—whether intellectual or practical—involves explicit thought.

[4] This case, and its relevance to the question of the epistemic role and value of emotional experience, were suggested to me by Robert Cowan. For Cowan's own view, see his *Ethical Intuitionism*, University of Glasgow PhD dissertation (2011).

[5] See Haidt, J., Bjorklund, F., and Murphy, S., 'Moral Dumbfounding: When Intuition Finds No Reason' (2000), unpublished manuscript; and Haidt, J. 'The Emotional Dog and Its Rational Tail: A Social Intuitionist Approach to Moral Judgment', *Psychological Review* (2001), 108(4): 814–34.

[6] Haidt (2001), p. 814.   [7] Haidt (2001), p. 817.

brother and sister having sex. The subjects judged this to be morally wrong, but the story is such that all of the usual reasons for thinking so—the dangers of inbreeding, the possibility of psychological harm—were not applicable. In such instances, the subjects maintained that they knew on the basis of their emotional experience that some action was wrong, even though they could not explain why it was wrong. This seems, therefore, like another case where subjects take their emotional experiences at face value: it is the emotional experience alone that grounds their claims to evaluative knowledge, even when they lack supporting evidence.

A fourth kind of case is where we do not search for reasons because we *trust* in the reliability of our emotional responses. After all, if emotions can play the role of alerting us to objects and events of potential significance, then emotions can do this more or less reliably. It hardly needs pointing out that our emotions can be trained or calibrated so that they function more efficiently in bringing to our attention important aspects of our environment. Moreover, it seems true that we can learn to associate emotional responses with the relevant values. As a result, perceptual theorists like Elgin claim that we commonly "take ourselves to be able to reliably correlate emotions with circumstances", at least given "a sophisticated understanding of when and to what extent they are trustworthy".[8] That is, "we can often tell which emotional reactions reflect the presence of emotional [evaluative] properties. So under certain recognizable circumstances, an emotional reaction affords epistemic access to such properties."[9] Here there is no re-evaluation or reappraisal, no search for and discovery of reasons, because we recognize that in these circumstances our emotional experience gets it right. Emotional experiences, in these circumstances, are ones that we trust in the absence of additional reasons.

A fifth possibility is where some emotional object or event is not re-evaluated or reappraised since the relevant reasons are in principle unavailable. This might be the situation if there are *ineffable* values. If there are, then clearly there is little point in searching for reasons, and as such we will take our emotional responses at face value. The clearest examples of ineffable values seem to be those that are closely related to feelings of

---

[8] Elgin, C., 'Emotion and Understanding', in Brun, G., Doğuoğlu, U., and Kuenzle, D. (eds), *Epistemology and Emotions*, Farnham: Ashgate Publishing (2008), p. 37.
[9] Elgin (2008), pp. 40–1.

pleasure. Consider, for instance, the wonder one feels when viewing a glorious sunset, or the satisfaction one experiences when drinking a cold glass of beer on a hot day, or the delight one feels when experiencing a first tender kiss. I imagine that the case in favour of trusting our emotional responses to disclose value in these instances has to do with the fact that there seems something seriously amiss in reflecting critically upon what it is that makes the sunset so wonderful, the beer so satisfying, the kiss so delightful, at least when one is experiencing such emotions. (Think of how the person you're kissing would regard such reflection, for instance.) If so, then it seems as if we will treat our emotional experiences in these cases as sufficient reasons for the relevant judgements.

A final set of cases concern situations where we are not motivated to search for reasons because the features to which our emotions are responses are unlikely to be available to us as the result of some other factor. As such, there is no *point* to our seeking to discover such reasons. One such case is where I lack a certain sensibility or education, which precludes me from identifying reasons. I might judge, for instance, that the piece of music is beautiful on the basis of aesthetic feelings, even though I am unable to tell—because I lack the right kind of musical education—precisely what it is about the music that generates my emotional response or justifies my judgement. Another sort of case is where there are pragmatic consider-ations that tell against a search, such as time-constraints. I might judge, for example, that a certain answer is the right response to an interviewer's question on the basis of feeling confident in the answer, in a situation where reflection on why the answer is right would have negative conse-quences. Reflection and hesitation might, after all, give the impression that I am not suitably decisive, and the capacity to make quick decisions is a desideratum for the job in question. There can be other practical con-straints that argue against searching for reasons: consider a situation where I walk into a pub, immediately feel fear, and as a result turn on my heels and make a quick exit. Here too I might rely upon my fear as evidence for my judgement that the pub was dangerous and neglect to search for reasons, since staying put, staring intently at the denizens, and trying to identify the reasons that ground my fear would raise the threat-level considerably. So there is a range of cases where a subject will put her trust in her emotional responses to provide her with evaluative infor-mation, because there are reasons against searching for reasons that have a bearing on the adequacy of these responses. In these situations, the relevant considerations are (for a variety of reasons) beyond our ken.[10]

To summarize, we have a number of cases where subjects take their emotional experiences at face value. These are cases where: (i) the subject is incapable of seeking out and reflecting upon reasons and evidence that have a bearing on the accuracy of their own emotional experiences; this is, I take it, the situation with young children when they form evaluative beliefs on the basis of emotional experience. (ii) The subject forms evaluative beliefs automatically and habitually on the basis of emotional experience. Here questions of justification don't seem to arise for the subject, and certainly don't interpose themselves between his emotional experience and the formation of the subsequent evaluative judgement. (iii) The subject's search for reasons will be unsuccessful, but she will, nevertheless, continue to regard her emotional experience as a sufficient reason to hold her evaluative judgement. (iv) The subject takes her emotional experience at face value because she has learnt to associate emotional experience in these circumstances with the relevant value. (v) The subject takes her emotional experience at face value because the relevant object or event is ineffable or inexplicable in terms of reasons. And (vi) the subject takes her emotional experience at face value and does not search for reasons, because she realizes that the search would be fruitless or problematic: either she lacks the sensibility to discover them, or the search will be too time-consuming, or too costly in some other way.

There are, therefore, a number of recognizable cases where a subject regards her emotions as providing sufficient reason for her evaluative judgements, and refrains from searching for reasons that have a bearing on her emotional–evaluative situation. Indeed, it looks as though taking one's emotional experience at face value, far from being rare, might in fact

---

[10] The argument here mirrors that made by Rob Hopkins, on conditions in which it is legitimate to trust the testimony of others on aesthetic matters. Hopkins argues that trusting the testimony of others is sometimes appropriate, in circumstances where one cannot remain agnostic on some issue—e.g. when one has to decide which film to see—but where one cannot investigate the matter of which film is most worth watching for oneself, since this would take too long and cost too much money. See Hopkins, R., 'How to be a Pessimist about Aesthetic Testimony', *Journal of Philosophy* (2011) 108(3): 138–57. By the same token, there seem to be conditions in which one cannot remain agnostic on some evaluative issue—e.g. whether to give a particular answer in a job interview—but where one cannot investigate whether this is the right answer, at the time, without incurring significant practical costs. The question of whether it is equally legitimate to trust one's emotions in these kinds of cases will be discussed shortly.

be the norm. If so, perhaps emotional experience is closer to perceptual experience, at the epistemic level, than the previous chapter suggests.

4.2 A further argument against the perceptual model

The perceptual theory will only be vindicated, however, if there is a wide range of cases in which we are *right* or *entitled* to take our emotional experiences at face value. And it is not clear that all of the cases cited here are instances where the subject is so entitled. If so, the range of cases in which emotional experiences can constitute sufficient reasons, because it is right to take those experiences at face value in the relevant circumstances, might be narrower than the above suggests. This is not all. For I will argue that even if we consider only the best cases from the standpoint of the perceptual theory, emotional experiences are still a lesser kind of reason than those features and properties that emotional experience motivates us to seek and discover. As such, emotional experiences still differ from perceptual experiences in their epistemic role and value. But as I'll also point out, this is a good thing; for it allows us to keep hold of the common-sense idea that emotions can, in certain circumstances, constitute reason and evidence for evaluative judgements. In so far as the perceptual theory maintains that emotions are reasons *of the same kind* as those supplied by perceptual experiences, it cannot capture our common-sense intuition.

It seems clear that in the first two types of case considered, the emotional responses in question, although causes of the relevant evaluative judgements, are not good reasons or evidence for those judgements. In both cases, the subjects take their emotional experiences for granted, and are not motivated to search for reasons bearing on the accuracy of these responses. But we can doubt that they are *right* to do so, since we can doubt that the emotional reactions of young children, and of those who habitually and unthinkingly form judgements on the basis of their reactions, are suitably reliable 'trackers' of reasons. In other words, such subjects have emotional experiences that are not reliably correlated with danger, insult, and shamefulness. At best, such experiences are causes of, or *motivating* reasons for, evaluative judgements.

A more tentative conclusion is warranted with respect to the moral judgements made by the subjects in Haidt's experiments. On the one hand, we might deny that such subjects were justified in believing as they did, either because the actions in question are not wrong, or because, even though the actions are wrong, the subjects could not explain why they were wrong; we might then claim that the capacity to cite one's evidence is a necessary condition to be justified. On the other hand, even if the emotional responses of the subjects were reliably correlated with wrongness such that they could be justified on reliabilist lines despite being unable to cite supporting reasons, the fact that the subjects were disturbed or left dumbfounded by the experiment suggests that they did not regard the justificatory demand to be silenced *even by their own lights*. There would be no ground for disturbance, after all, if emotional experience in this instance could be taken for granted in much the same way that perceptual experience is taken for granted in normal circumstances. As such, this kind of case isn't a good illustration of a circumstance in which the subject both regards, and is right to regard, her emotional response as a sufficient reason. Moreover, I think that any support for the perceptual theory that is generated by this kind of example simply reflects the plausibility of our final three cases, where the subject trusts her emotional responses but does *not* search for reasons or evidence. The perceptual theorist's claim that we are often right to take our emotional experiences at face value seems most plausible in these latter cases after all; so it is to these I'll now turn.

In our fourth case, our subject trusts that her emotional experience is reliably correlated with value, but this time does not search for reasons because she recognizes that her emotional reactions in these circumstances "reflect the presence of emotional [evaluative] properties".[11] Here the subject refrains from searching, because she sees no need for confirmation, given her "sophisticated understanding" that her emotional responses in these circumstances are to be trusted. Given the *de facto* reliable connection between emotion and value, we might think that the subject in this instance *is* entitled to take her emotional response at face value. But this is by no means obvious either. One explanation, after all, for why the subject is not motivated to discover additional reasons or evidence is that she is already aware of such reasons or evidence, in virtue of her "sophisticated understanding" of when and to what extent her emotional responses are reliable. For we might think that a sophisticated capacity to recognize

---

[11] Elgin (2008), pp. 40–1.

conditions in which emotional responses can be trusted *just is* the capacity to recognize certain features of those conditions as reasons or evidence for the relevant evaluative judgement, and certain other features as irrelevant to the correct ascription of the evaluative property. What else, after all, could our sophisticated understanding of the conditions in which our emotions are reliable be picking up on? But if the trust that we have in our emotional experiences is grounded in a recognition of reasons that make it the case that some value is present, then it looks as if it is the recognition of the reasons that is doing the justificatory work, rather than the emotional experience. In other words: we do not, in these circumstances, take our emotional experience at face value. Instead, the emotional experience is backed up by our awareness of reasons for the relevant evaluative judgement.[12]

A similar conclusion is warranted when we consider the so-called ineffable values. The fact that there is something amiss in reflecting upon these values, at least when experiencing them, does not show that such values are ineffable, or that there are no reasons that reflective scrutiny would uncover. On the contrary, these values seem clearly understandable, and indeed expressible in words: cold beer on a hot day is valuable because it quenches thirst, cools one down, makes one more relaxed and sociable, expresses one's endorsement of a splendid summer tradition of idly sitting around in a beer garden instead of working, and so on. And these are features of which we are, of course, usually aware when drinking cold beer on a hot summer's day, since they typically constitute our reasons *to* drink beer on days like this. By the same token, a first tender kiss is valuable because it is the initial physical expression of mutual attraction, or the first step of a meaningful relationship, or a moment of shared intimacy, and so on—again, features we are usually aware of when sharing a first kiss. (Think of how the person you're kissing would regard your *failure* to understand or grasp that these features are in play in the circumstances. Try simply citing the pleasure that *you* felt when the person you were kissing asks what the kiss meant to you.) Similarly, the sunset is wonderful because it illustrates the vastness of the solar system, the small and fragile place we occupy in it, the community we share with other humans experiencing

---

[12] Even if we deny that the relevant capacity is the capacity to recognize reasons, we might still think that there is something wrong with the subject's resting content with her emotional responses in these circumstances. I'll explain why shortly.

the same thing as the world turns, and so on. Given this, then, the strangeness of consciously reflecting on all of these things isn't grounded in the fact that they are not themselves responses to reasons. Rather, the strangeness is grounded in the fact that human beings normally *possess* the relevant evaluative knowledge, such that (further) reflection on them is pointless. Indeed, reflection about such values seems amiss, as it would expresses a child-like ignorance of the relevant values. Children might genuinely wonder about the value of cold beer or a wonderful sunset or a first kiss; the anomaly of an adult wondering about these things presupposes, rather than rules out, the fact that the values are capable of being grasped. Since I suspect that something similar can be said about all so-called ineffable values, then these cases do not provide an illustration of circumstances in which we both take our emotional experiences at face value, and are right to do so. Instead, the emotional experience is backed up by our awareness of reasons for the relevant evaluative judgement.

However, the idea that it is sometimes legitimate to put one's trust in one's emotional responses and take these at face value is rather more plausible when it comes to the range of examples in our last kind of case. Here, if we recall, the subject takes her emotional experience at face value and does not search for confirming or disconfirming evidence, because (i) she trusts that her emotional experience is reliably correlated with value, and (ii) she realizes that there is little or no point in her searching for reasons, given practical constraints on her searching. Suppose that our subject is right on both of these counts. If so, then, other things being equal, it seems as though she is right to trust in the deliverances of her emotional experiences. What else, after all, can our subject go on in an attempt to determine her evaluative situation? And if her emotional responses are reliably correlated with value, then what could be wrong in our subject's putting her trust in the only reliable indicator of value available to her? So in this final case, it seems that our subject is right to trust in her emotions to give her evaluative information, and that such experiences therefore constitute sufficient reasons for the relevant evaluative judgement.

This conclusion ultimately does little to rescue the epistemic analogy between emotional and perceptual experience. For I now want to argue that even in this final case, emotional experiences lack the epistemic role and value possessed by perceptual experiences. Emotional experiences in these conditions, I maintain, are not *genuine* reasons for evaluative judgements, but are merely proxy or *pro tempore* reasons: they are, in other words, useful stand-ins or surrogates for genuine reasons for evaluative beliefs, but lack that status themselves. If so, then although we might take such experiences at face value in certain circumstances, such experiences are nevertheless inferior, from the epistemic standpoint, to the reasons they are surrogates for. Moreover, even when we trust our emotional responses, and are right to do so, our emotional experiences still fail to have the epistemic status or value possessed by perceptual experiences, since perceptual experiences are clearly not substitutes or stand-ins for genuine reasons in the non-evaluative realm. We can therefore maintain that there is an important epistemic difference between emotional and perceptual experiences even in those instances which constitute the strongest case for the perceptual model.

There is another motivation for the claim that emotional experiences are mere proxy or *pro tem* reasons for evaluative judgements, and one which is directly relevant to the puzzle highlighted at the beginning of this chapter. Viewing emotional experiences in this way will allow us to capture the common-sense idea that emotions *can*, in certain circumstances, provide us with information about the evaluative world, whilst avoiding the criticism that emotions must thereby be capable of justifying themselves. If so, however, the interesting conclusion is that the supporter of common-sense thinking about emotion can resolve the relevant puzzle only if they accept that emotional experiences are proxy or *pro tem* reasons, and hence different, in epistemic role and value, from perceptual experiences. Common-sense thinking about emotion can thus be captured, but only at the cost of the central claim of the perceptual model. Or so, at least, I'll argue in the following section.

4.3 Emotional experiences as proxy reasons

I have been proposing that emotions can motivate us to search for reasons or evidence that bear on the accuracy of our initial emotional responses. Such reasons are considerations that speak to the question of whether some object or event really is dangerous, contaminated, lovable, an achievement, shameful, morally wrong, and so forth. So the fact that some piece of legislation treats citizens differently on the basis of arbitrary factors is a good reason to think that it is wrong or unjust; the fact that the road is icy and the fog is descending is a good reason to judge that driving is dangerous; the fact that it is the highest mark an undergraduate has achieved in ten years is a good reason to think it is an achievement; the fact that a funeral is a solemn occasion is a good reason to think that my telling jokes was shameful. I'll term such reasons—perhaps tendentiously, but to help clarify my argument—"genuine reasons" for evaluative judgments. But the important thing to note is that these are the kinds of considerations that our emotional responses are *supposed to* be responsive or sensitive to. In other words, the emotional responses in question, namely resentment, fear, pride, and shame, *ought* to be responsive to such things, rather than to features of objects and events that do not ground reasons to think the object or event morally wrong, dangerous, an achievement, or shameful. Moreover, the supporter of the perceptual theory must maintain that it is only in so far as our emotional experiences are reliably caused by genuine reasons that we are entitled to trust them and therefore entitled to take them at face value. After all, it is only on the assumption that our emotional experiences are reliably correlated with features that ground genuine reasons that such experiences stand a chance of being reasons or evidence themselves. A key assumption, therefore, in the account of epistemic justification proposed by the perceptual theorist must be that emotional experiences are indicators of value, or are reasons for evaluative judgements, only when they are reliably correlated with features of objects and events which ground genuine reasons for such judgements.

This suggests, however, that when we form evaluative beliefs on the basis of emotional experience, trusting that our emotions are reliably correlated with the relevant values, or taking those experiences at face value, we are treating our emotions as *proxies* for genuine reasons, as experiences which *stand in for* experiences of features that we assume reliably cause and justify this form of emotional response. To put things slightly differently: when we believe on the basis of emotional experience, we are believing on the basis of *pro tempore* reasons, reasons "for the time being", which we rely upon precisely because we presently lack awareness of features that constitute genuine reasons for our judgements. For note that if we *did* become aware of such features, then the justificatory force of our emotional experience would seem to disappear. This is because the justificatory force of our emotional experience would seem to be exhausted by the justificatory force of the features that we take our emotional experience to reliably track—it is, to repeat, only *because* our emotions reliably track such features that they can function as signs or indicators of value. Awareness of such features, and of the relation between such features and value, would thus seem to render the emotional experience otiose from the justificatory perspective. To think of our emotional experience in these circumstances as an *additional* reason for the evaluative judgement would seem to be to engage in an illicit form of double-counting: the features to which our emotion is a response would be counted once in their own right, when we become aware of them and form the evaluative judgement on this basis, and once again *via* our taking the emotional response to such features as a further reason for the evaluative judgement.[13]

In order to illustrate how the justificatory force of emotional experience can disappear or be rendered otiose in this way, consider an analogy: let us assume that the consequentialist is right to think that the rules of common-sense morality are mere rules of thumb, i.e. useful devices for when we have to figure out how we should act, but not in themselves part of any "standard of rightness". Here we might claim that the fact that some act would be an act of promise-breaking, let's say, is a reason for me to believe that the act is wrong, given the reliable connection between promise-breaking and bad consequences. But it is clear that this fact is only a proxy or *pro tem* reason. For suppose that I now become aware of the fact that the act in question resulted in bad consequences, and believe that it is wrong for this reason. It would be a mistake to think that the fact that the act is a case of promise-breaking is or continues to be an *additional* reason to believe it wrong. For the justificatory force of this fact dissipates once

---

[13] To see another instance of double-counting, consider the following: if you believe that p on the basis of evidence, it would be a mistake to take your believing as you do to be an *additional* piece of evidence in favour of p. As Thomas Kelly writes, "The fact that you believe as you do is the *result* of your assessment of the probative force of the first-order evidence: it is not one more piece of evidence to be placed alongside the rest. That is, you do not treat the fact that you believe [p] as a further reason to believe that [p], above and beyond the first-order considerations that you take to rationalize your belief". In Kelly, T., 'The Epistemic Significance of Disagreement', in Hawthorne, J. and Gendler Szabo, T. (eds), *Oxford Studies in Epistemology, Vol. 1*, Oxford: Oxford University Press (2005), pp. 167–96. So Kelly thinks that treating the fact that one believes that p as a further reason is to engage in illicit double-counting. I think something similar can be said in a case where one is aware of the reasons that one's emotional response tracks. Such reasons play the role of "first-order evidence" on my account. Given this, it would be a mistake to take one's emotional response to this first-order evidence as an additional first-order reason for one's evaluative judgement.

I become aware of the wrong-making feature, and hence the genuine reason for moral judgements, that the rule about promise-breaking is meant to reliably track.[14]

It seems to me that this undermines the perceptual theorist's claim that emotional experiences *can* have a justificatory role and value that mirrors the justificatory role and value of perceptual experiences, and hence undermines the response on the basis of the 'best case' considered in the previous section. For we can now see that the epistemic analogy will not hold. The epistemic role and value of emotional experience is significantly different from the epistemic role and value of perceptual experience, for clearly *perceptual* experiences are not proxy or *pro tem* reasons for non-evaluative judgements. It is hardly plausible to think that our perceptual experiences are merely helpful stand-ins or surrogates for our real reasons to judge that external reality is thus-and-so, for the simple reason that it is difficult to think of a better way in which we could access the external world than *via* the senses. As a result, we can maintain that there is a significant difference when it comes to the epistemic role and value of perceptual and emotional experiences: whilst the former are rightly regarded as genuine reasons for non-evaluative judgements, emotional experiences are merely proxy or *pro tem* reasons for evaluative judgements. The perceptual model is thus overly optimistic in its assessment of the epistemic credentials of emotional experience.

However, far from this being damaging to the idea that emotional experiences have epistemic value, this conclusion actually allows us to accept our pre-theoretical, common-sense claim that emotional experiences can inform us about value, or can be reasons or evidence for evaluative beliefs. The problem with regarding emotions as reasons, if

---

[14] Might there not be some emotional experiences whose epistemic force does not dissipate? Think of love. Suppose I claim that my feeling of passion for someone is a pro tem reason to think her adorable. Suppose now I seek out the reasons why she is adorable, and form an evaluative judgement on the basis of such reasons. Still, my feelings might be doing epistemic work. For I might realize that another person has similar features to my beloved, and hence that there are similar reasons to think her adorable, and yet *not* find her adorable, precisely because I lack the relevant feelings. I'm not convinced by such examples, however. If I realize that these are reasons to think the second person adorable, then presumably I will judge that she is. What won't happen is that I have *feelings* of love towards her. What we need is a case where I do recognize that someone has the features that make my beloved adorable and yet I *don't* think that she is adorable for these reasons. But it is difficult to understand how this could happen.

we recall, is that reasons for evaluative judgements seem to be equally reasons for emotional responses—in which case emotions would seem to be capable of justifying themselves, which is something that we can doubt they can do. However, the circumstances in which emotions are proxy reasons for evaluative judgements are precisely circumstances in which what is doing the justifying are the reasons for which the emotions are proxies. That is, emotions can play a positive justificatory role only in virtue of the fact that they are proxies for genuine reasons, in which case it is the reasons to which the emotions are a response, and for which the emotions are a surrogate or substitute, that provide the ultimate justification for the evaluative judgement. So emotions can inform us about value, or can constitute reasons or evidence of a particular type, without this entailing that the fact that I am afraid gives me good reason to be afraid. What gives me good reason to be afraid are the considerations to which my fear, and hence my judgement that I am in danger, is a response.

If this is the case, then the idea that emotions are proxy or *pro tem* reasons plays a central role in enabling us to capture the common-sense view about the epistemic value of emotion, whilst allowing us to avoid the charge that if emotions are reasons, then they must be capable of justifying themselves. But a consequence of this is that we must give up the idea that emotional experience is akin to perceptual experience at the epistemic level. For perceptual experience, to repeat, is not plausibly viewed as a proxy or *pro tem* reason for empirical belief. So it is the *difference* between emotion and perception at the epistemic level that allows us to capture the idea that emotions can inform us about value.

4.4 Emotion and understanding

The supporter of the perceptual model might nevertheless still maintain that emotional experiences—as proxies—have a similar kind of value to genuine reasons for evaluative beliefs, and are analogous to this extent to perceptual experiences. In other words, the perceptual theorist might try to accommodate the previous arguments by accepting that emotional experiences are proxies, but by then claiming that emotional proxies can have a similar epistemic value, and can play a similar epistemic role, to sensory perceptual experiences. After all, if our feelings are indeed reliable indicators of value in certain circumstances, and if it is legitimate for us to trust that our feelings provide us with information about value in those circumstances, then why think that emotional experiences are *epistemically* less valuable than genuine reasons, even if they are proxies for such reasons? In what sense are we epistemically worse off by using reliable proxies rather than genuine reasons in forming our evaluative beliefs? Might it not be *equally* appropriate to form evaluative beliefs on the basis of different methods—on the one hand, by taking our (reliable) emotional experiences at face value; on the other, by an awareness of the features to which our emotions reliably respond? And if so, why deny that emotional experiences are as valuable as genuine reasons? It might be true that, were we to be aware of the latter and of their relation to value, the justificatory force of the emotion-as-proxy would disappear. But it doesn't follow from this that it is somehow illicit to rely on our reliable emotional experiences if we are not aware of such features. Nor, importantly, does it follow that it is somehow illicit to rely on our emotions in a situation where we could become aware of such features but do not: if there is no epistemic pressure for us to become aware of the features which constitute genuine reasons and believe on this basis, then there seems no epistemic loss when we don't. The idea that reliable emotional proxies are epistemically inferior to genuine reasons (and hence, by analogy, epistemically inferior to perceptual experiences) therefore requires more support. In particular, it requires an argument that we ought to believe on the basis of genuine reasons where these are available, rather than resting content with our reliable emotional responses.[15] In the absence of such an argument, a version of the perceptual model, which maintains that there is an analogy between emotional and perceptual experiences at the level of epistemic value, remains intact.

In support of this response on behalf of the perceptual model, consider another analogy. Suppose I believe that England's cricketers won the test

---

[15] The qualification "reliable" is important here. For in the previous chapter we saw the argument that there are good reasons for us to seek out considerations that bear on the accuracy of our initial emotional construals, given the nature of affect program responses as quick and dirty, and the nature of more highly cognitive emotion as influenced by social and environmental factors. These are considerations that bear on the question of whether our emotional response is, in the circumstances, a reliable indicator of value. What I am now concerned with is whether there is an argument that we should search for and believe on the basis of genuine reasons even when we are sure that our emotional responses *are* reliable or accurate. This is why we can't just appeal to the considerations adduced in the previous chapter in order to make the relevant argument here.

match against Australia on the basis of your testimony. Suppose too that your testimony is based upon watching the highlights of the final day that are being shown on the sports news channel. If I now watch the same highlights on the same channel later in the evening, it seems that the justificatory force of your testimony dissipates. For if I become aware of the very same source that grounded your testimony, then it is difficult to see how your testimony constitutes an *additional* reason for me to believe that England beat Australia. But it does not follow from this that I would be doing anything wrong, from the epistemic standpoint, were I to rely solely on your testimony in a situation where your grounds for believing that England won are readily available to me—because I have easy access to the highlights on the rolling sports channel, say. It is doubtful, that is, that I am doing anything illicit in relying solely on your testimony in this instance, even though I *could* easily become aware of your reasons for thinking that England's cricketers won. So if the evidence provided by emotional experience is akin to that provided by testimony, then it is not obvious why emotional proxies are epistemically inferior to genuine reasons, and hence not obvious that emotional and perceptual experiences differ in terms of their value in contributing to the justification of the relevant judgements.

Can we therefore provide an argument that we ought to form our evaluative judgements on the basis of genuine reasons where these are available, rather than resting content with our (reliable) emotional responses? Can we, in other words, supply a reason to think that there is something dubious about forming evaluative judgements on the basis of our (reliable) emotional responses alone, in those situations where we could become aware of the reasons that our emotions reliably track? I think that we can. In the remainder of this section, I'll provide a brief outline of one such argument, and in the sections to follow I'll show how this outline can be filled in. To begin, let us look again at the features I have termed "genuine reasons" for evaluative judgements.

Suppose that I'm crossing a farmer's field on a pleasant Sunday stroll, when I suddenly spot a bull turning towards me. The bull is very large, sports sharp horns, and starts to run at speed in my direction. I take it that these are all features of the bull that constitute genuine reasons for me to believe that he is dangerous. But unlike other reasons for the same belief—such as the farmer's sign that there is a dangerous bull in the field, or a fellow rambler's testimony—these features are also reasons *why* the bull is dangerous. They are, in short, among the collection of things in virtue of which the bull has the property "dangerous"; they are the "danger-making" features of the animal.[16] Now note that if we are aware of these features, and of the fact that the bull counts as dangerous in virtue of these features, then we are not simply possessed of the knowledge *that* the bull is dangerous. We also know *why* the bull is dangerous. Awareness of these reasons, as opposed to the other sorts of reasons, like the farmer's sign or the rambler's testimony, therefore facilitates *understanding of* or *insight into* our evaluative situation.[17]

This provides the framework for the argument that we need.[18] For if the goal of thinking about emotional objects and events is understanding rather than evaluative belief or evaluative knowledge, then there is a clear reason why we ought to make ourselves aware of such reasons, rather than resting content with the information provided by our emotional experiences alone. This is because the fact that we are afraid of something, let's say, is clearly not sufficient for an understanding of the dangerousness of our situation. If, then, the goal of thinking of emotional objects and events is understanding rather than belief or knowledge, we have an explanation for why it is illicit to rely upon our emotional experiences in forming evaluative judgements, in those circumstances where we could be aware of the features that such experiences reliably track. In resting content with our emotional experiences, we would be failing to pursue our primary epistemic goal of gaining evaluative understanding.[19] Ultimately the perceptual model fails, I want to argue, because it misidentifies

---

[16] In different terminology, they are the "determinables" of the "determinate" *dangerous*.

[17] From hereon I'll confine myself to talking about "understanding" rather than "insight", given the prominence of the former term in the literature. But I take the terms to refer to the same kind of positive epistemic standing with respect to value.

[18] The general structure of this argument borrows from work in aesthetics by Rob Hopkins, and work in moral epistemology by Alison Hills. Hopkins and Hills suggest that there is something illicit in forming aesthetic or moral judgements purely on the basis of testimony, when we could form such beliefs on the basis of experience or reflection. Hills thinks that this is because the goal of moral thinking is understanding, rather than mere knowledge. I wish to make similar points but with respect to emotions and evaluative judgements. See Hopkins (2011) and Hills, A. 'Moral Epistemology', in Brady, M. (ed.), *New Waves in Metaethics*, London: Palgrave Macmillan (2010).

[19] This does not mean, when the goal of understanding is unavailable, we shouldn't settle for a lesser epistemic goal of justified belief or knowledge with respect to such objects. So relying upon emotional proxies is perfectly legitimate when understanding is out of reach. What is not appropriate, I want to say, is resting content with these secondary goals when our primary goal is attainable.

our epistemic goal with respect to emotional objects and events. The reason why we are not satisfied with taking our emotional experiences at face value, or why we do not think that emotional experience silences the demand for justification, is that our epistemic goal is to understand our emotional–evaluative situation, rather than merely attain justified evaluative belief or evaluative knowledge.[20]

4.5 Understanding as our ultimate epistemic goal

How might we show that our epistemic goal with respect to the dangerous, the shameful, the insulting, and other emotional objects is understanding rather than justified belief or knowledge? One possibility is to argue that understanding is, in general, more valuable than justified belief or knowledge; the idea that understanding, rather than mere justified belief, is our primary goal in the evaluative realm then follows from this. In support of the general claim, we might then argue that understanding is more valuable than knowledge on the grounds that the former satisfies our natural curiosity. When we are curious about a certain topic or subject, we do not simply want to amass a range of facts about that subject; instead, we want to see how these facts fit together, in a systematic, coherent, and unified way. Stephen Grimm puts it as follows: "as Aristotle noted long ago, there is something inherently satisfying about being able to gratify our deep wonder and curiosity about the world—a curiosity which goes farther than piecing together the facts of the world in the fashion of a reliable computer."[21] In a similar vein, Jonathan Kvanvig writes that "organized elements of thought [that result when we understand something] provide intrinsically satisfying closure to the process of inquiry, yielding a sense or feeling of completeness to our grasp of a particular subject matter".[22] Understanding therefore has greater value

---

[20] As such, the point of making ourselves aware of the reasons that our emotional experiences track isn't *simply* to secure accurate evaluative judgements. The need for us to understand our evaluative situation thus constitutes an *additional* reason to search for and discover reasons to those we discussed in the previous chapter.

[21] Grimm, S., 'Ernest Sosa, Knowledge, and Understanding', *Philosophical Studies* (2001), 106(3): p. 186.

[22] Kvanvig, J., *The Value of Knowledge and the Pursuit of Understanding*, Cambridge: Cambridge University Press (2003), p. 202.

than knowledge in so far as it addresses our curiosity and completes our inquiries. We might therefore think that the greater value of evaluative understanding, and its status as our primary epistemic goal in evaluative thinking, is just a particular example of this general point.

Despite the *prima facie* plausibility of this line of thought, I want to construct a different set of arguments for the conclusion that our ultimate aim, in thinking of emotional objects and events, is understanding rather than justified belief or knowledge. This is because I think that understanding emotional objects and events has some special value, over and above any it gains by satisfying our natural curiosity, and so generates a distinctive argument as to why it is understanding that we ought to pursue, at least when it is available to us. I'll begin by providing a brief explanation of what understanding is, and then proceed to argue that understanding emotional objects and events serves a number of needs, and as such has greater value than mere justified belief or mere evaluative knowledge—at least if such epistemic states are themselves understood, as perceptual theorists propose and as we saw in Chapter 2, as involving internalist and externalist elements.[23]

A full and detailed account of understanding is beyond the scope of this chapter. But what I can do is highlight certain features that seem essential to understanding, and see how these have a bearing on our understanding of emotional objects and events.[24] First, as Jonathan Kvanvig notes, attributions of understanding have various logical forms: there are noun forms, as when we say that someone has an understanding of first aid; adjectival forms, as when we say that he is an understanding sort of boss; and verb forms, as when say that he understands German, or understands that he was driving too fast, or understands why the budget cuts are necessary, or understands how to ride a unicycle, or understands the flimsiness of his argument.[25] This illustrates the fact that understanding can have different kinds of *object*: we can understand people; we can understand

---

[23] Recall that supporters of the perceptual model favour a mixed internalist/externalist perspective on evaluative knowledge in so far as they push a general reliabilist line. Recall, for instance, the perceptual theorist's talk of "default entitlements" to form evaluative beliefs on the basis of emotional experiences, without anything in the way of inference from our experiences, which suggests an externalist element to the justificatory picture.

[24] For an excellent overview of certain aspects of understanding, see Grimm, S. 'Understanding', *Routledge Companion to Epistemology*, Bernecker, S. and Pritchard, D. (eds), London: Routledge (forthcoming).

[25] Kvanvig (2003), pp. 188–9.

languages; we can understand subjects or disciplines; we can understand facts; we can understand concepts; we can understand works of art. It also highlights that there are different *kinds* of understanding: we can understand *that* things are the case; understand *how* things work or how to do things; understand *why* things happened or why things are the way they are.²⁶ Now for our purposes the relevant objects will be emotional objects and events. In particular, the relevant objects are the *values* of emotional objects and events: the dangerousness of the neighbourhood, the shamefulness of the drunken behaviour, the adorableness of the beloved. Given this, the relevant kind of understanding would seem to be understanding *why*: in particular, understanding why the object or event has the value it has. This is because the other kinds of understanding seem inappropriate with respect to emotional objects and events. For instance, understanding *that* something is shameful or beautiful seems equivalent to *knowing that* something is shameful or beautiful; as Grimm writes, "ascriptions of understanding [along these lines] seem to be more or less synonymous with corresponding ascriptions of knowledge".²⁷ But it seems plausible to hold that achieving an understanding of emotional objects and events involves more than knowing that the objects and events have the evaluative properties that they do. Similarly, to say that I understand the shamefulness of my behaviour isn't best regarded as a case of my understanding *how* to do anything, although if I achieve the former then typically I will understand how to respond appropriately, e.g. with apologies and reparations.²⁸

What, then, is involved in understanding why some emotional object or event is the way that it is from an evaluative standpoint? Here we arrive at a second important feature of understanding, which is that it seems to involve a grasp or awareness of connections or links between various items; it involves seeing how things fit together, how features are related,

---

²⁶ See Elgin, C., *Considered Judgement*, Princeton: Princeton University Press (1996), p. 123.
²⁷ Grimm (forthcoming), p. 3 in MS.
²⁸ The idea that understanding emotional objects and events is a matter of understanding why something has the value it has ties in with a general view that certain forms of understanding have priority over others. Thus, Duncan Pritchard thinks that understanding *why* something is the case, rather than *that* it is the case, is central. He writes: "One problem that afflicts any direct comparison between knowledge and understanding is that knowledge . . . is concerned with *propositions*, whereas understanding usually isn't, at least not directly . . . I want to take the paradigm usage of 'understands' to be statement like 'I understand why such-and-such is the case'", 'Knowledge, Understanding and Epistemic Value', in *Epistemology*, O'Hear, A. (ed.), Cambridge: Cambridge University Press (forthcoming), p. 11 in MS.

how facts support and explain other facts, and so on. Indeed, the notion of explanation would seem to be central: for instance, many people think that *scientific* understanding simply is a matter of grasping a correct explanation of that thing. As Strevens writes, "[s]cientific understanding is that state produced, and only produced, by grasping a correct explanation."[29] Similarly, Grimm writes that "understanding involves some degree of explanatory coherence, where being able to explain a given fact typically means seeing its interconnectedness with other facts".[30] And: "it seems to be a hallmark of having understanding that we can typically articulate (or explain) what it is in virtue of which we take ourselves to understand."[31] Kvanvig too holds that

[t]he central feature of understanding . . . is in the neighborhood of what internalist coherence theories say about justification. Understanding requires the grasping of explanatory and other coherence-making relationships in a large and comprehensive body of information. One can know many unrelated pieces of information, but understanding is achieved only when informational items are pieced together by the subject in question.[32]

Suppose, to illustrate, that I have done something shameful. In order for me to understand my evaluative situation, I need to grasp why my behaviour was shameful. And this involves grasping the connections between pieces of information—that it was important to maintain a polite and formal atmosphere for the honoured guests, that my crude stories were embarrassing for my hosts and the visitors, that my colleagues now regard me as rude and inept in social situations—and the shamefulness of my behaviour. Understanding therefore seems to be, as Pritchard puts it, "an essentially internalist notion"[33] involving access to reasons, whereas the kind of justified evaluative belief or knowledge that results from emotional experience on the perceptual model might leave our reasons opaque.[34] As Grimm writes: "understanding . . . differs from knowledge

---

[29] Strevens, M., (2008), *Depth: An Account of Scientific Explanation*, Cambridge, MA: Harvard University Press (2008), p. 3.

[30] Grimm (2001), p. 173

[31] Grimm, S., 'Is Understanding a Species of Knowledge?', *British Journal for the Philosophy of Science* (2006), 57: 517.

[32] Kvanvig (2003), p. 192.   [33] Pritchard (forthcoming), p. 18.

[34] Pritchard (forthcoming), pp. 13–14. Later, at p. 18, Pritchard writes: "Understanding clearly is amenable to an account along internalist lines, in the sense that it is hard to make sense of how an agent could possess understanding and yet lack good reflectively accessible grounds in support of that understanding. Understanding thus cannot be 'opaque' to the subject in the way that knowledge, by externalist lights at least, can sometime be."

in that it involves the ability to give reasons, or grasp causes, or make connections—whereas genuine, reliable knowledge need involve none of these things."[35]

However, we might question whether this kind of ability to give reasons or grasp causes or make connections is sufficient for understanding. This is because one can connect large numbers of facts and in a way that gives (apparent) answers to many questions and still lack understanding of some phenomenon. To illustrate, suppose that Roy Race, the player–manager of Melchester Rovers, thinks that there is a conspiracy against his team by the Football Referees' Association, and that this explains the large number of decisions going against the Rovers. And suppose that Roy has good but misleading evidence for the conspiracy: he overhears two referees talking about a conspiracy against his team, but fails to realize that the conversation he is hearing is intended as a malicious prank against him, in return for his habit of eavesdropping outside the referees' office. Here Roy is in a position to "grasp" the connection between the relevant pieces of information, and can give "reasons" for the numbers of decisions going against his team in terms of the conspiracy. The relevant internal conditions for understanding therefore are in place, we might think; but we are not inclined to say that Roy understands the unjustness of what is happening to his team.

If so, then understanding requires more than seeing rational connections or grasping coherence-making relations between facts or pieces of information. In addition, we can say that the connections that we grasp have to reflect (causal and/or explanatory) relations that genuinely hold. Since there isn't, in fact, a conspiracy against Melchester Rovers, then Roy Race's explaining the number of decisions going against his team by appeal to such a conspiracy results in a mistaken explanation and a lack of understanding: the interconnectedness that we grasp when we achieve understanding must, therefore, be genuine interconnectedness. Grimm puts the point as follows:

> Let us think of *subjective understanding* as the kind of understanding one achieves by grasping a representation of the world (a model, perhaps, or an explanatory story of some kind) that fits or coheres with one's "world picture". On the other hand, let us think of *objective understanding* as the kind of understanding that comes not just from grasping a representation of the world that fits with one's world picture, but

---

[35] Grimm (2001), p. 185.

also from grasping a (more or less) *correct* representation of the world. Objective understanding therefore entails subjective understanding but goes beyond it, requiring that the grasped representation in fact obtains.[36]

So understanding emotional objects and events is a matter of understanding why the objects and events have the evaluative properties that they do. And understanding why requires a correct representation of the evaluative world, and of the rational and explanatory relations within that world. In particular, this kind of objective understanding is a matter of correctly grasping why something is shameful, dangerous, lovable, disappointing.

Given this account of understanding, can we explain why it is understanding, rather than knowledge, which should be our goal when it comes to the objects and events in our emotional lives? Can we, in other words, provide a further explanation for why we ought to pursue and make ourselves aware of the reasons that our emotional experiences track, and to form or modify our evaluative beliefs on the basis of such reasons, even in situations where we trust that our emotional responses are reliable? I think that we can, and I want to present two reasons in support. The first concerns morality and virtue. It is uncontroversial to hold that moral development requires that subjects gain an understanding of why certain actions are right and wrong, in addition to knowing that such actions are right and wrong. This doesn't require that subjects engage in extensive high-level moral theorizing; all that is claimed is that people grasp that certain actions are wrong because of certain features of the actions—for instance, that they cause unnecessary pain, or violate trust, or involve treating people differently on the basis of arbitrary factors, and so forth.[37] Moreover, it is uncontroversial to suppose that understanding is necessary for moral virtue; it is hardly plausible to suppose that the benevolent person has a reliable grasp of which actions are benevolent but no awareness of why such actions are required, for instance. So moral development and moral virtue would seem to require moral understanding.[38] But understanding is not only necessary for having a certain character; we

---

[36] Grimm (forthcoming), p. 15 in MS.

[37] See Hills (2010), and the lack of a requirement that reasons "go all of the way down".

[38] A quicker route to this conclusion might be to recall that the virtuous person is the person of theoretical and practical wisdom, and then note that understanding would seem an essential element of wisdom.

might think that awareness of the reasons why something is right or wrong is a necessary condition for one's *actions* to have a certain kind of moral value. As Alison Hills writes:

> moral understanding plays an important role in certain kinds of moral action. If you know what to do, you can do the right action. But what will be your reason for action? That you are doing what you are told? You might do the right action, but you will not be acting for the right reasons. Your action will not be *morally worthy*. Morally worthy action is right action for the right reasons, that is, for the reasons that make the action right. If you have moral understanding, if you grasp why your action is right, and you act on that basis, you will act for the right reasons.[39]

We need not be Kantians to accept this sort of argument, since there should be widespread agreement among moral theorists of all stripes that the good person is someone who does the right thing for the right reason; the difference is that non-Kantians will think that "right reason" can include considerations that are unrelated to duty. If so, then understanding is essential to morally valuable behaviour as well, since the good person will need to be aware of which considerations constitute right reasons in order to do the right thing for those reasons.

How does this show that understanding *emotional* objects and events is our epistemic goal, however? The simple answer is that a certain category of emotions is intimately linked with morality, and so gaining an understanding of the features which constitute reasons for these emotions would seem to be essential to moral development, moral virtue, and morally valuable action. These "moral emotions" include shame, guilt, remorse, empathy, gratitude, indignation, contempt, regret, and the sense of justice. There are, in addition, "moralized" versions of non-moral emotions such as disgust, as when we're disgusted by the candidate's views on immigration, as well as other non-moral emotions (such as fear) that are necessarily linked with virtues (such as courage). Given this, moral development and moral virtue would seem to require more than mere knowledge that certain things are wrong or unjust or shameful or contemptible or regrettable. By the same token, morally worthy or valuable behaviour would seem to require an understanding of why something is unjust, or a proper object of indignation, or a legitimate target of contempt, or an appropriate

---

[39] Hills (2010), p. 258. Again, we need not think that acting from such understanding requires conscious reflection or deliberation on the subject's part, any more than acting on reasons in general requires conscious reflection or deliberation.

source of shame. For instance, apologies or reparations for shameful or contemptible behaviour require that one understand what one did and *why* it was shameful or contemptible: apologizing because you know that you have done something wrong, without knowing why it was wrong, seems lacking in moral worth or value. This is an instance of the more general point that understanding has value because it is often necessary to facilitate the right behavioural response. One reason it is good to be aware of the features in virtue of which an object is dangerous is that such awareness allows one to take appropriate action to avoid the particular sort of danger involved. Merely knowing that something is dangerous is less practically useful than knowing that it is dangerous because it will bite or sting or con me.[40] Given the goals of moral development, moral virtue, and morally valuable behaviour, we ought not to rest content with mere evaluative knowledge or evaluative belief, if understanding is within our reach.

This gives us reason to achieve understanding with respect to a large class of emotions, both moral and non-moral. Moreover, since we cannot tell when understanding of non-moral emotions outwith this class might be required for moral development and virtuous behaviour, we might think that there is a standing reason to gain such understanding whenever we can. But even if we ignore this, there is another reason for us to pursue understanding rather than mere knowledge of emotional objects and events. This is because we have a general need to *control* and *regulate* our emotional responses, and one of the most effective ways of doing so is to gain an understanding of our evaluative situation.

As D'Arms and Jacobson have pointed out, there are a number of reasons why it is important for us to control our emotional responses. I'll focus on two. First, "emotions involve powerful motivational tendencies, so regulating them is an indirect way of regulating behaviour".[41] As D'Arms puts things elsewhere,

states such as anger, envy, and shame, for instance, involve motivational tendencies: toward retaliation, competition, or concealment, respectively. Because it matters very much to each of us how we act, there's reason to think about what to be angry, envious or ashamed of. These facts generate an important role for

---

[40] Thanks to Fiona Macpherson for this point and this example.

[41] In D'Arms, J. and Jacobson, D., 'Anthropocentric Constraints on Human Value', in Shafer-Landau, R. (ed.), *Oxford Studies in Metaethics, Vol. 1*, Oxford: Oxford University Press (2006), pp. 99–126.

intrapersonal criticism and reflection that an agent can undertake concerning the appropriateness of these irruptive, motivating emotions.[42]

Second,

there are especially powerful reasons to seek coordination of social emotions (such as anger, shame, and contempt), stemming from the need to avoid and resolve conflict. Indeed, the desire to coordinate with others, even over feelings that have no direct connection to action, runs deep. People seek shared standards for feelings such as amusement, disgust, and sorrow, and find it unsettling to discover that they have idiosyncratic sensibilities.[43]

There are various methods we might employ in order to control and regulate our emotions. But one of the most effective ways is to come to an understanding of our emotional situation, since emotions are typically responsive to understanding.[44] Thus, my fear tends to dissipate when I come to understand why I am not in danger—since the noise I thought was a burglar at the front door is only my neighbour fumbling with his keys; my guilt usually recedes when I grasp why I didn't do anything wrong—since the accident was his fault, not mine; my anger tends to peter out when I come to understand why he didn't insult me— for the remark was made in jest, rather than out of spite; and so on. Although such control and regulation is not guaranteed—emotions such as guilt can persist, even when one understands why one did nothing wrong—nevertheless it seems plausible to suppose that understanding is generally more effective than other methods, and in particular more effective than belief or knowledge that is *not* grounded in awareness of reasons. My guilt might recede if I merely judge that I did not do anything wrong; but unless I'm aware of the reasons why I did nothing wrong, there is a significant chance that it is my judgement that will change in the face of my guilt, rather than vice versa. If we are unaware of any genuine reasons that support our evaluative judgement, it is likely that our judgement will lack normative authority in the face of conflicting emotion. Understanding therefore promises to be

---

[42] D'Arms, J., 'Two Arguments for Sentimentalism', *Philosophical Issues* (2005), 15: p. 8.

[43] D'Arms and Jacobson (2006), p. 111.

[44] D'Arms and Jacobson make this point in terms of the regulatory efficacy of evaluative judgements; D'Arms and Jacobson (2006) p. 112. But I think that a stronger case can be made for the efficacy of evaluative understanding, for the reasons cited.

more *stable* than evaluative judgement or knowledge, and thus significantly more effective in controlling and regulating our emotional responses.[45]

To summarize: we have seen that understanding emotional objects and events—especially those connected with the moral emotions—is essential for moral development and moral virtue. We have also seen the importance of such understanding to the control and regulation of emotion, at least when understanding is contrasted with justified evaluative belief or evaluative knowledge understood on externalist lines. All of this strongly suggests that we have good reason to understand our emotional situation when possible, rather than relying solely on our emotional responses—however reliable these might be as trackers of value. If so, then the argument that emotional experiences are unlike perceptual experiences at the epistemic level is secured: there is indeed something epistemically dubious about relying upon our emotions when we have access to the reasons that emotions reliably track, such that we should believe on the basis of the latter in so far as we are able. However, there is nothing epistemically dubious about relying upon our perceptual experiences when *these* are reliably correlated with external reality. It is not the case that we need to grasp the reasons for such experiences (should there be such reasons, which we can doubt) in order to control our perceptual responses or promote perceptual development. And it is not the case that understanding why things are as they are is our epistemic goal when we undergo perceptual experiences in normal circumstances.[46] This is why it is no epistemic failing when we take our perceptual experiences at face value in normal conditions and lack the motivation for further inquiry. And this is ultimately why emotional experiences differ in epistemic role and value from perceptual experiences.

---

[45] A second way in which understanding can help control and regulate emotion is when we understand *why* we have some emotion, in the sense of grasping the causal history of it. Thus, I might be able to better control and regulate my feelings of anger to my boss when I realize that he looks just like the kid who tormented me at school, and that that's the origin of my feelings.

[46] This is not to deny that sometimes understanding why we see how we do can improve our perceptual capacities—for instance, when we understand why colour vision is unreliable in dim light, or why straight objects appear bent in water.

4.6 How emotions facilitate understanding

In this section I want to argue that the perceptual model, in so far as it maintains that emotional and perceptual experiences play a similar epistemic role and have a similar epistemic value, is in fact guilty of *underestimating* the epistemic value of emotions. For by insisting that emotional experiences are akin to perceptual experiences, the perceptual model ignores the contribution that emotions themselves make to our understanding of our evaluative situation—and, as I'll argue in the next section, to self-understanding. Recall that on my account, emotion can promote the search for and discovery of reasons that bear on the accuracy of our emotional responses: the features, that is, that constitute genuine reasons why some object or event has some evaluative property like "dangerous" or "shameful". Emotions do this by keeping our attention fixed on the emotional object or event, thereby enabling us to better assess whether it really is as our emotional construal initially presents it as being. And as we saw in the previous chapter, emotion facilitates this reassessment or reappraisal of our emotional–evaluative situation more effectively than reason alone. If emotion fades prior to the search for and discovery of reasons, then there is a tendency for such inquiry to halt. Part of the reason for this is that it is difficult and costly to keep one's attention fixed on some object when emotion is no longer involved. But another part of the reason is that the object or event will typically no longer strike one as important or significant in the absence of emotion, in which case it doesn't matter whether one's construal is accurate or not. As a result, emotions help to facilitate reassessment through the capture and consumption of attention; emotions enable us to gain a "true and stable" evaluative judgement, in Reid's terminology.

But in so doing, emotions promote our understanding of our evaluative situation, since to discover the reasons why some object or event has some evaluative property *just is* to come to understand one's evaluative situation with respect to that object or event: to discover the reasons that make it the case that the pub is dangerous just is to understand the dangerousness of the pub, and hence to understand one's evaluative situation. So we can see that the reappraisal or reassessment of emotional objects and events discussed in this chapter and the previous one is a process whereby we come to understand our emotional–evaluative situation. Moreover, as we also saw in the previous chapter, the epistemological story we tell about how we discover such reasons and how we thereby gain evaluative understanding is one that *involves* emotion, in so far as emotion directs attention to and keeps attention on potentially important objects and events, and one that involves a measure of *independence* from emotion, in so far as the reasons that have a bearing on the accuracy of our emotional responses do not include the emotional responses themselves.

As I also suggested in the previous chapter, this latter kind of independence from emotion does not mean that my account of how we gain evaluative understanding raises any particular epistemological problems. As we saw then, experience and reflection can ground beliefs in the relevance of some natural property to the presence of some evaluative property. This is because reflection and experience can help us to identify the natural property or properties that our emotional experience is responsive to, and then help us to assess whether this property is one that our emotional experience ought to be tracking. Indeed, in the absence of beliefs that are grounded in this way it is difficult to see how we could ever come to characterize our initial System 1 emotional responses as crude, quick, overgeneralized, and relatively indiscriminate in the first place, or ever come to acknowledge that in certain circumstances our emotional experiences fail to be reliably correlated with value. The fact that we are able to see a mismatch between emotional appearance and evaluative reality speaks to our capacity to recognize and identify the kinds of features or considerations that make (and do not make) things wrong, wonderful, or dangerous, and hence the kinds of features that we think our emotions ought (and ought not) to reliably track. The epistemological story to be told here about our access to and awareness of reasons for emotions is no more mysterious than the epistemological story we standardly tell about our access to and awareness of reasons for *action*, in which reflection and experience inform us of the kinds of things that we can do to make it more likely that our goals are satisfied. Practical reasons are, after all, and other things being equal, considerations that raise the likelihood of goal-satisfaction. By the same token, reasons that bear positively on the accuracy of emotional experience are, other things being equal, considerations that raise the likelihood of the evaluative property presented in emotional experience being instantiated. Similarly, reasons that bear negatively on the accuracy of emotional experience are, other things being equal, considerations that lower the likelihood of the evaluative property being instantiated. To acquire this information we need decent teaching, suitable reflection, and sufficient experience; and to access this information we need a decent memory. The epistemological story we tell about how emotion promotes understanding is, therefore, relatively straightforward.[47]

Again, we can illustrate this commonplace and everyday capacity with examples: the fact that the large, aggressive gentleman in the pub is approaching me with a pool cue is a good reason to believe that I am in danger; I can endorse my fear in this case because I have good reason to think that my fear is responsive to the danger-making features of the gentleman in question. Or the fact that the witness stands to gain materially from testifying against the defendant is a good reason to believe that he is untrustworthy; I can endorse my feelings of mistrust in this case because I have good reason to think that my feelings are responsive to this untrustworthy-making feature of the witness. Or the fact that my son scores a hat-trick in the final of the schools' cup competition is a good reason to believe that someone close to me has achieved something valuable; I can endorse my pride in this case because I have good reason to think that my pride is responsive to something that constitutes a genuine achievement that is suitably related to me. As such, there is no great epistemological mystery as to how emotions promote evaluative understanding through the capture and consumption of attention; all that this requires is belief in the normal capacity that human beings have to discover and recognize the sorts of things that do, and that do not, make a difference to our evaluative situation.

To relate all this to our guiding question of the epistemic value of emotional experience: the case made in the last chapter that there is an epistemic need for a reassessment or reappraisal of our initial emotional responses—because affect program responses are relatively indiscriminate, and higher cognitive emotions grounded in specific social and cultural norms—can now be supplemented by the arguments in this chapter that there is a need for us to gain an understanding of our emotional–evaluative situation—because such understanding is essential for moral development

---

[47] This does not commit me to the view that identifying such features is always easy, or that there are no legitimate disputes about whether or not some feature is a reason for shame or envy. It is obviously true that many such disputes are legitimate and difficult to settle. But this doesn't count against my claim that we can often discover reasons that have a bearing on emotional accuracy, any more than the fact that there are sometimes legitimate and difficult disputes about what we have reason to do counts against the claim that we can often discover our practical reasons.

and virtue, and for controlling and regulating our emotional behaviour. Taken together, these constitute a very strong case for the conclusion that there is significant value in the search for and discovery of reasons that bear on emotional accuracy across a whole range of situations. But in so far as emotions facilitate this search and discovery through the capture and consumption of attention, the arguments in these two chapters also constitute a very strong case for the conclusion that emotional experience has significant, and seldom recognized, epistemic value. As such, the perceptual model, which stresses the epistemic similarities between emotional and perceptual experience, actually *understates* the epistemic value of emotion. For ordinary perceptual experiences do not move us to seek out better reasons for our judgements about the non-evaluative, empirical world, and so do not facilitate our understanding of that world in a similar way. The claim that emotions are just like perceptions on the epistemic level therefore does emotions a disservice. Emotions are more important to our epistemic goals and our epistemic needs than the perceptual model suggests.

4.7 Emotion and self-understanding

In the penultimate section of this chapter I'll discuss another way in which emotional experience facilitates understanding of one's evaluative situation through the capture and consumption of attention, and as such another way in which emotions can play an epistemic role that is not played by sensory perceptual experiences. For emotions can motivate us to reflect upon and appraise the cares and concerns that underlie our emotional response. Now on the one hand, this is another way in which emotions move us to re-evaluate our emotional situation, since such reflection might lead us to reject the concern that grounds such things as pride or shame. Emotions can therefore move us to seek and discover reasons that bear on whether or not we ought to care for certain things in the way that we do. On the other hand, this is a way in which emotions can facilitate *self*-understanding, by bringing to light the fact that we have certain concerns, and thus by making us aware of the kind of person that we are. Emotions can therefore promote understanding of our evaluative landscape *and* of the values that we ourselves hold.

We saw in the first chapter one important link between emotions and desires, where I am construing 'desire' broadly so as to encompass cares, concerns, preferences, likes, dislikes, and needs. The link is that emotions are based upon or grounded in desire. So, as Nico Frijda puts things,

the "ends" are what give the emotional event its emotional valence. Personal loss produces sadness because it conflicts with one's attachment to the lost person, frustrations madden because we desire to complete progress toward our goals, and so on . . . Emotions signal the relevance of events to concerns.[48]

Or as Gerald Clore claims, "[t]he idea is that one has a variety of general goals, standards, and attitudes. These are cognitive prerequisites for emotion because without these structures nothing matters to the person."[49] Such thoughts are clearly supported by common-sense. It is because I care for bodily integrity that I'm afraid when I see the storm front approaching as I reach the mountaintop; and it is because I'm concerned with what others think of me that I'm embarrassed by my being scruffily dressed at the formal party.

We have also seen that emotions can bring to our attention *the fact that* we have the concerns and desires that underlie our emotional experiences. Emotions can make salient the fact that certain things matter to us. Michael Stocker writes: "emotions provide evidence for what one values: for example, your guilt at not paying your taxes shows that you think you should pay them."[50] And:

Emotions can . . . *reveal* values: the values they contain and that help make them up . . . I found out that I was still a fan of a team, and not just interested in watching a football game, by finding myself annoyed at that team's failures and pleased by its successes. Turning to a serious matter, I found out part of how very bad I thought the start of a recent war was by finding myself very upset and saddened almost to distraction upon hearing that it had begun.[51]

So emotions can be epistemically valuable in promoting self-awareness and self-knowledge.

But this is not the only valuable epistemic contribution that emotion can make in this area. For emotions can not only alert us to our underlying concerns and desires, but can, through the capture and consumption of attention, promote and facilitate reflection upon and reappraisal of those

[48] Frijda, N., 'Why Emotions are Functional, Most of the Time', in Ekman and Davidson (eds) (1994), p. 113.

[49] Clore, 'Why Emotions Require Cognition' (1994b), p. 188.

[50] Stocker, M. and Hegeman, E., *Valuing Emotions*, Cambridge: Cambridge University Press (1996), p. 3.

[51] Stocker and Hegeman (1996) pp. 56–7.

very concerns and desires. Moreover, just as there is a need for critical reflection on the accuracy of our initial emotional appraisals, and for (as we have seen) a variety of reasons, there is also a need for critical reflection on the adequacy of our underlying concerns and desires, given that such desires might be ones that we ought to reject. As such, emotions can help to serve another epistemic (and practical) need, this time with respect to the cares and concerns that underlie the emotional experiences themselves.

In order to support this proposal, note that emotionally motivated self-awareness of one's underlying concerns can, as a matter of fact, lead to reflection on and reassessment of one's *other* evaluative attitudes. To take one instance, self-awareness of underlying concerns can motivate reassessment of our consciously held evaluative judgements. Consider, to illustrate, Nomy Arpaly's example of Emily, whose

best judgement has always told her that she should pursue a Ph.D. in chemistry. But as she proceeds through a graduate program, she starts feeling restless, sad, and ill-motivated to stick to her studies. These feelings are triggered by a variety of factors which, let us suppose, are good reasons for her, given her beliefs and desires, not to be in the program.[52]

Suppose that Emily takes her persistent emotional responses, as well she might, to reveal that she has no deep concern or desire that is satisfied by studying chemistry. In light of this self-knowledge, Emily could surely reassess her initial evaluative judgement, and now come to judge that continuing a PhD in chemistry is a very bad idea. In this way, Emily's emotional responses reveal to her something about her concerns, and the persistence of her emotion facilitates reflection on and reappraisal of her other evaluative attitudes.

Emotional revelation can do more than cause reassessment of our other values, however. For what is revealed in emotional experience might lead us to reflect upon, and deliberate about, the concerns and values that underlie this very experience. This is because, as we saw in the first chapter, our emotions sometimes tell us things about ourselves that we do not like—for instance, suppose that I feel disappointed when my son tells me that he is gay. This emotional response reveals to me an aspect of my character, and an underlying concern, that I do not want myself to

⁵² Arpaly, N., *Unprincipled Virtue*, Oxford: Oxford University Press (2003), p. 49.

have, that I reflectively *reject*. In so far as emotional experience can both focus and keep attention fixed on such things, it can facilitate reflection on and deliberation about them; and it can, in doing so, be an important part of a process of self-improvement.

In order to support the idea that there is a *need* for such critical reflection, recall the argument that one of the ways in which emotions are epistemically important is that they alert us, quickly and at little mental cost, to objects and events of importance or significance. Now I have glossed what is important or significant in terms of things that are relevant to our current cares and concerns. But this doesn't seem quite right, in light of the fact that emotions can be grounded in concerns that we would reflectively reject. Suppose, to illustrate, that I become anxious, walking through the city at night, when I encounter groups of Asian men but not groups of European men. This counts as an *emotional* failing, and by my own lights, since I regard ethnicity as irrelevant with respect to the question of whether or not I should be fearful. Here what is emotionally salient for me is not something that I ought to pay attention to; it is not something that I regard as significant. So what is important or significant for me, or what *merits* my attention, isn't simply a matter of what I in fact care about or am concerned with. Instead, we might think that it is a matter, in part, of the cares and concerns that I would reflectively endorse. If so, then there are two ways in which emotions might be unreliable indicators of value. The first way is when emotions are unreliable in alerting us to the presence of objects and events that are relevant to our current concerns and desires: so my fear might be unreliable in alerting me to objects that are relevant to my concern for safety, either because it draws my attention to things that are perfectly harmless, or because it fails to draw my attention to things that are authentically dangerous. But the second way in which emotions can be unreliable is when they alert us to things that are relevant to concerns that we ought not to have: so my anxiety is unreliable when it draws my attention to groups of Asian men but not groups of European men, since ethnicity is not important in my circumstances and as such should not be salient for me. In this latter kind of case, emotions can be unreliable with respect to alerting us to things that *merit* our attention, even if they reliably alert us to things that are relevant to what we *in fact* care about.

This suggests that there is a need for critical reflection to check and regulate emotions along two dimensions: first, there is a need to check on the accuracy of our initial emotional construals; second, there is a need to check on the adequacy of our underlying concerns. Given that emotions, through the capture and consumption of attention, can promote the first kind of reappraisal and regulation, and given that emotions often draw our attention to the fact that we have some desire or concern, it is not implausible to suppose that emotions themselves can help to serve this second need. On this view, then, emotions can motivate the search for information relevant to whether some emotional object or event really is as it initially appears, *and* for information relevant to whether the concern underlying our emotion is one that we ought to have. The capture and consumption of attention can serve our epistemic needs by enabling *two* critical searches rather than just one.

We might make this argument in a different way. Examples clearly show that what we notice and care about can diverge from what we ought to notice and care about. One way in which this can happen is when cares and concerns are no longer relevant in our current circumstances. These are cases of what Peter Goldie terms *environmental mismatch*, where something that used to be advantageous is no longer so, because our environment has changed. Goldie provides a nice example of such mismatch—of something that was "once adaptive" and is "now dysfunctional"—when he asks us to consider "fear and mistrust of strangers—xenophobia. The xenophobe tends immediately and unreflectively to react adversely to those who are 'not like us', and to treat them with suspicion or ever worse".[53] Whilst such mistrust and behaviour might once have had a point or value, in ensuring group cohesion and survival where resources are scarce, for instance, circumstances now are sufficiently different, which casts doubt upon the need for us to retain xenophobic attitudes and reactions. This is especially true, given the harm that such attitudes can do to both others and the xenophobe herself. Or consider a concern for sexual purity, which plausibly grounds emotions relating to chastity and celibacy. In certain circumstances a strong emotional commitment to sexual abstinence (at least, outside of marriage) will be advantageous. In a society where sex before marriage is severely punished by the authorities, or where sexual activity promises significant risks to health because there is little access to safe contraception, let's say, then it will be in the subject's

---

[53] Goldie, P., 'Misleading Emotions', in Brun, Doğuoğlu, and Kuenzle (eds) (2008), p. 156.

best interests to have a strong concern to remain pure, and to therefore develop a pattern of emotional responses that is centred on this concern. But if circumstances change—if, for instance, sex before marriage becomes widely accepted as a norm, and if there is little danger to health by engaging in sex with numerous partners—then we might doubt the need to continue to care for one's sexual purity and to respond with the pattern of emotions connected to this concern. This suggests that there is significant practical value in having concerns that are suitably flexible and responsive to changes in our environment and circumstances: there is, in other words, a significant practical advantage in avoiding mismatches between our concerns (and overlying emotions) and our environment. Emotions can themselves help to ensure this flexibility and matching, by fixing our attention and by facilitating reflection on what we care about. As such, emotions, through the promotion of self-understanding and the motivation to reflect on our cares and concerns, serve another important epistemic need.

4.8 Conclusions

This chapter began with a puzzle: to accommodate the common-sense idea that emotions can be sources of information about the evaluative world, in a way that allows us to avoid the objection at the end of the previous chapter. In order to solve this puzzle I proposed that emotions are proxies or surrogates for genuine reasons. This enables emotions to play a role in the justification of evaluative judgement, in so far as the emotion is reliably correlated with the relevant value. At the same time this indicates why emotional experience does not, in this instance, justify itself. For the relevant justificatory work is being done by the considerations to which our emotional experience is a response, and for which the experience is a proxy. An interesting consequence of this is that we can save our common-sense intuition only if we *reject* the perceptual model's claim that emotional experience constitutes reason or evidence in the same way that perceptual experience constitutes reason or evidence. For perceptual experience is not a proxy or a surrogate reason for non-evaluative belief.

I then turned to a possible response that the perceptual theorist might make, which is to accept that emotional experiences are proxy or *pro tem* reasons, but argue that forming evaluative judgements on the basis of such reasons is equally respectable, from the epistemic standpoint, to forming such judgements on the basis of genuine reasons. As such, there is not a difference in the role or value of emotional and perceptual experiences, when it comes to the justification of their relevant beliefs. Emotional and perceptual experiences are, according to this response, *equally good ways* of forming the relevant judgements. However, I proceeded to argue that this wasn't correct: there is something illicit about forming evaluative judgements on the basis of emotional responses, and hence with taking one's emotional responses at face value, when one could make oneself aware of, and form beliefs on the basis of, genuine reasons. This is because our epistemic goal, when it comes to thinking about emotional objects and events, isn't justified belief or even knowledge, but evaluative *understanding*. The epistemic difference between emotional and perceptual experience remains, therefore, given that there is nothing illicit about forming non-evaluative judgements on the basis of perceptual experience in normal conditions; for understanding of our non-evaluative world is not necessarily our epistemic goal with respect to very many of our perceptual interactions with that world in ordinary circumstances.

I then claimed that the perceptual model is in fact guilty of underestimating the epistemic importance of emotion, in so far as it neglects the extent to which emotion itself promotes evaluative understanding, both of our environment and of ourselves. In this way our emotions can be seen to have a measure of independence from both reason and desire. In motivating us to search for and discover reasons, emotions assist reason in the promotion of understanding; but emotions do so in a way that is initially independent from conscious reflection or reasoning. As we've seen, in many cases attention is automatically directed and fixed upon some emotional object and event, independently of any conscious awareness of a need for attention and reappraisal. In motivating us to reflect upon the adequacy of the cares and concerns that underlie our emotional responses, emotions, although triggered by objects and events that are relevant to our concerns, facilitate the reassessment of those very concerns. In this way emotions have a measure of independence from the desires that partly constitute them. As a result, emotions facilitate their own reassessment along a couple of dimensions; in so doing, they promote, in a relatively autonomous way, understanding of value. I propose that this is the most important contribution that emotions make to our epistemic lives; and the fact that emotions can help us to attain these epistemic goods is the main reason why we ought not to rest content with our emotional responses in normal conditions—at least, if this implies taking such responses at face value and thinking of the need for justification as silenced.

In the final chapter, I'll turn my attention to an issue that has been in the background to the discussion thus far, and which threatens to undermine the positive case I've been making for the epistemic value of emotion. For clearly, emotional effects on attention can have a negative impact on the accuracy of our evaluative judgements and on the acquisition of understanding. I need to say something more, then, about the conditions in which emotional experience can promote evaluative understanding. This requires a detailed investigation of the links between emotion, attention, and virtue.

5

Emotion, Attention, and Virtue

In previous chapters I have presented the view that emotions can play a number of important epistemic roles. In particular, I have argued that emotions can promote our understanding of the evaluative world, by motivating us to search for reasons that have a bearing on the accuracy of our emotional responses and upon the adequacy of our underlying concerns. Emotions perform this role by capturing and consuming our attention. On this picture, an emotion such as fear involves an initial appraisal of some threat, and a search for reasons that are relevant to whether or not something that we care for is thereby threatened. In so far as these are reasons *why* some object or event is or is not dangerous, they are considerations which enable us to understand the dangerousness (or otherwise) of our environment. The fact that emotions can promote understanding, by motivating us to search for reasons, suggests that their epistemic role and value is different from that of perceptual experience. As we put things in the last chapter, emotional experiences are at best *proxies* for the reasons that they reliably track, whereas perceptual experiences are not proxies for reasons for empirical beliefs. Perceptual experiences enjoy, instead, a privileged position when it comes to perceptual justification. There is thus no need for us to search for additional reasons when it comes to perceptual experience—for there are, typically, no better reasons—and this might explain why our perceptual experiences do not motivate us to search for reasons. We saw, further, that a view of emotional experiences as proxies for genuine reasons has additional merit, as it enables us to capture the common-sense idea that emotions can inform us about value, without thereby being capable of justifying themselves.

This general picture of the relation between emotion, attention, and reflection on the accuracy of our emotional responses needs further development and defence, however. For the account has, up to this point, been silent about a rather obvious fact, namely that sometimes emotional governance of attention (or lack thereof) can have a deleterious effect on our epistemic standing; such (lack of) governance can, that is, generate epistemological problems as well as epistemological benefits. There are, for instance, times when the emotional capture of attention promotes too much reflection, or fails to promote reflection to a suitable extent, or is otherwise problematic from the epistemological standpoint.

We therefore need an account of how attention is governed or regulated in emotional experience so as to promote, rather than hinder, our epistemic goals, and so as to further explicate the common-sense idea that has been at the heart of this book, namely that emotions can, in the right circumstances, tell us about value. Given problems associated with attention, such an account will need to specify the conditions in which we are *right* to reflect on our emotional responses in the pursuit of evaluative understanding, and, by the same token, the conditions in which we are right to refrain from reflection and put our trust in our emotional proxies. My aim in this chapter is to provide such an account, and thereby complete the story about how emotions have a positive epistemic role and value.

The structure of the chapter is as follows. In the first section I'll describe some of the ways in which emotion can lead us astray through its effects on attention, which shows the need for us to say something about how attention is governed so that emotional experiences have a positive epistemic yield. I then develop my positive proposal, which rests upon the suggestion from Peter Goldie that emotions play a positive epistemic role to the extent that they are governed by *virtuous habits of attention and reflection*.[1] I argue, however, that we should reject Goldie's particular account of such habits, for reasons that will be familiar from the last two chapters, and maintain instead that the virtuous regulation and moderation of attention itself depends, in various ways, upon *evaluative understanding*. Finally, I show how this account of virtuous habits of attention is compatible with the idea

---

[1] The idea that virtue requires correct control of attention can also be found in Thomas Reid, who writes that "A great part of wisdom and virtue consists in giving a proper direction to our attention", in *Essays on the Active Powers of the Human Mind*, Brody, B. (ed.), Cambridge, MA: MIT Press (1969), p. 80. For discussion of this aspect of Reid's philosophy with respect to emotion, see Cuneo, T., 'Signs of Value: Reid on the Evidential Role of Feelings in Moral Judgement', *British Journal for the History of Philosophy* (2006), 41(1): p. 81.

that there are conditions in which the virtuous person will *not* pursue evaluative understanding, but will instead trust in her emotional proxies to themselves provide her with evaluative information. The overall account is therefore compatible with, and explanatory of, our common-sense views on the epistemic value of emotional experience.

5.1 Emotion, attention, and reflection

I have argued that the capture and consumption of attention in emotional experience can promote reflection upon the emotion itself, along two dimensions: first, upon the accuracy of our initial emotional construal; second, upon the adequacy of the concerns that ground the emotion. In this way emotions can facilitate their own reassessment or reappraisal: emotions therefore enjoy a measure of independence from the circumstances that trigger them, and from the desires, cares, and concerns that underlie such responses. But if this sounds plausible, we should also be open to accepting a broader picture where emotions promote reflection on and the gathering of information about their objects more generally. As de Sousa notes, emotions can make salient strategies for coping with some object or event; and emotions can also bring to mind memories of similar objects or events, our responses to these, other things of the same evaluative kind, and so forth. If so, then emotions would seem to promote thinking about and exploration of emotional themes in general.[2]

There are, nevertheless, a number of problems associated with emotional control over attention.[3] Some of these will be cases where emotion consumes attention too much. Some will be cases where emotion fails to capture and consume attention enough.[4] In other instances emotion

---

[2] Think, in support, of how love can move one to discover very many trivial things about one's beloved, as well as promote reflection on the characteristics that make her so lovable. I'd like to thank Adam Morton for pushing me to say a little more about a bigger picture here.

[3] For an interesting discussion of related problems, see Kent Bach's 'Emotional Disorder and Attention', in Graham, G. and Stephens, L. (eds), *Philosophical Psychopathology*, Cambridge, MA: MIT Press (1994). In what follows, I'll focus on problems that are more straightforwardly related to the epistemic effects of emotional control of attention.

[4] Peter Goldie stressed to me the extent to which emotional capture and consumption can lead us astray.

focuses attention too narrowly on an emotional target, leading to neglect of other things; in yet other instances emotion focuses attention too broadly, leading to neglect of the emotional target. These latter instances suggest, moreover, that there is a problem when it comes to generalizing my claim that emotions focus attention so as to motivate reflection on some emotional object and event. If so, then attentional difficulties pose an additional challenge to my thesis. Given all of this, there is reason to consider just what is required in order to ensure that emotions control attention in the right kind of way, and to consider how this might be achieved. Let us turn, then, to the problems.

5.1.1 Problems with emotional persistence

One notable instance in which emotional persistence appears problematic, and in the main because such persistence keeps attention fixed upon and motivates reflection about certain objects and events, occurs when emotions are *recalcitrant*. A recalcitrant emotion, as we saw in previous chapters, is one that appears to conflict with evaluative judgement. Thus, a subject's guilt at going to the theatre is recalcitrant when it persists in the face of the subject judging that they have done nothing morally wrong.[5]

Part of the problem with recalcitrant emotions, and part of the reason why they might seem to involve some form of *rational* conflict, is down to the feature of emotions that I have been proposing has an epistemic benefit, namely that emotions consume attention for the purpose of searching for reasons that bear on the emotion's accuracy. For such a search might seem irrational in at least some cases of emotional recalcitrance, where the subject seeks out reasons that confirm her emotional construal in the face of an evaluative judgement that counts as a disconfirmation of the construal. If, that is, the subject has already judged, after reflecting on her evaluative situation, that some emotional object or event is *not* thus-and-so, she has (by her own lights) no need to seek reasons that support her emotional appraisal of object or event as thus-and-so. In so far as persistence of attention facilitates this search, it represents, from the subject's perspective, a waste of cognitive and attentional resources. For example, when our subject experiences a recalcitrant episode of fear, she might expend cognitive and attentional effort seeking signs and evidence

---

[5] This example is due to John Rawls, in *A Theory of Justice*, Cambridge, MA: Harvard University Press (1971), p. 422.

that the object is dangerous, whilst judging that it is *not* dangerous. Recalcitrant emotions thus appear irrational in so far as they involve the capture and consumption of attentional resources in the service of a question that has, by the subject's own lights, already been answered.[6]

Recalcitrant emotions are a particular example of a more general emotional failing related to attentional persistence. For it is widely thought that attention to and reflection on one's reasons can, in certain circumstances, constitute an overly cautious or an unduly suspicious attitude on the subject's part. In so far as such reflection is motivated by the capture and consumption of attention in emotional experience, emotion can lead to what might be regarded as excessive checking and reflection on emotion itself. For surely (the objection goes) it is not necessary for us to check on the accuracy of our emotional responses *whenever* emotion persists. This not only wastes cognitive and attentional resources; it can also constitute a form of epistemological and practical paralysis, where the subject fails to arrive at a judgement or decision as a result of excessive checking and reflection. Persistence of emotion can therefore *prevent*, rather than facilitate, the formation of evaluative judgements and the achievement of evaluative understanding.[7]

There is a third problem generated by attentional persistence in emotional experience. As we saw in our discussion of recalcitrant emotion, subjects often search for reasons that confirm, rather than disconfirm, their initial emotional construals. In this way we are often susceptible to a 'confirmatory bias'.[8] Emotional persistence can therefore support a tendency that leads us to endorse, rather than critically assess, our initial and often relatively indiscriminate emotional appraisals, and can thereby lead us astray epistemically.[9] Goldie puts the point nicely:

---

[6] For more on this argument, see Brady, M., 'The irrationality of recalcitrant emotions', *Philosophical Studies* (2009), 145(3): 413–30.

[7] I owe this objection to Heather Battaly.

[8] In general, confirmatory bias is a psychological tendency to search for and accept evidence that confirms, rather than disconfirms, some idea or hypothesis. In some instances this can lead to the confabulation or invention of "reasons" or "evidence", as when a jealous partner interprets innocent behaviour as supporting the charge of infidelity. See, for instance, Evans, J., *Bias in Human Reasoning: Causes and Consequences*, London: Psychology Press (1990), ch. 3.

[9] Quite why we feel the pressure or need to confirm, rather than disconfirm, our initial emotional appraisals is an interesting question. Part of the reason, I assume, is simply that we don't like the prospect of getting things wrong, where this includes our initial emotional

one's emotions can distort perception and reason by *skewing the epistemic landscape* to make it cohere with the emotional experience . . . we seek out and 'find' reasons—reasons which are . . . supposed to justify the emotion. The emotion, and the related perception of the object as having the emotion-proper property, tend to be *idées fixes* to which reason has to cohere. The phenomenon is a familiar one: when we are afraid, we tend unknowingly to seek out features of the object of our fear that will justify the fear—features that would otherwise (that is, if we were not already afraid) seem relatively harmless.[10]

Our susceptibility to an emotional confirmatory bias can also be apparent with another sort of reflection that is motivated by emotional persistence, namely reflection upon the adequacy of our underlying concerns. For here too there is no guarantee that we will, when emotion persists, seek out in a fair and judicious manner information or evidence as to whether we should endorse or reject such concerns. We might, instead, seek out or adopt only information that supports the desires that ground our emotions. In this way we might "rationalize" concerns that we ought not to endorse, as when someone seeks out reasons that support the concern that grounds a feeling of disappointment upon learning that her son is gay, namely a latent dislike of homosexuals. This constitutes another instance where reflection motivated by the persistence of emotion can lead to epistemic—and not to mention moral, practical, and social—difficulties.

5.1.2 Problems of dissociation between emotion and reflection

I have been stressing the idea that the persistence of attention in emotional experience can motivate the search for reasons and evidence. But clearly emotional experience and the persistence of attention need not perform this role. For often emotion *doesn't* promote reflection. Even if emotion makes some aspect of our environment salient for us, it might not be the case that we are thereby motivated, as emotion persists, to reflect about the accuracy of our emotional construal. Perhaps we're just not reflective about such things most of the time. Or if we are reflective when

---

responses. Since we don't like to accept that we do get things wrong, there is a temptation to interpret evidence in a way that we don't have to accept this.

[10] Goldie, P., 'Emotion, Reason and Virtue', in Evans, D. and Cruse, P. (eds), *Emotion, Evolution, and Rationality*, Oxford: Oxford University Press (2004), p. 259. As we saw in the last chapter, Jonathan Haidt's view, on which emotion generates evaluative judgement and reason plays the role of lawyer or advocate in *post hoc* rationalization of such judgement, pushes a similar line.

experiencing an emotion, perhaps we focus or reflect, not on the accuracy of our initial emotional construal, but on other things: what to say in response to the construed insult, or how very pleasant it is to feel *schaden-freude*, or how my anxiety during the interview could affect my job prospects, and so on.[11]

Similar things can be said about emotional persistence and reflection upon our underlying cares and concerns. Even if emotion has epistemic value in making us aware of some grounding concern, it is not obvious that we will be motivated to reflect upon its adequacy. Again, perhaps we're just not a reflective kind of person. Or perhaps what emotion reveals about our character is so unwelcome as to prevent further reflection or even denial: someone might react to the emotional suggestion that she harbours homophobic attitudes by ignoring the suggestion, and by continuing to believe that she doesn't.

As such, it is often the case that the attentional persistence characteristic of emotional experience fails to promote effective reflection about the accuracy of our emotional construals and about the adequacy of our underlying concerns. As such, we face an explanatory burden, namely of specifying the conditions in which emotions succeed in promoting reflection, and promoting it to the right degree.

5.1.3 Problems with emotional focus

The thought that emotions capture and consume attention, and motivate a search for reasons or evidence, implies that different emotions have the same or at least similar effects on attention. But this is something that we can doubt. For empirical evidence suggests that the links between emotion and attention are more complicated than it at first appears. In particular, there is a lot of evidence to indicate that whereas "negative" emotion focuses attention narrowly, "positive" emotion broadens attentional focus.[12] If this is true, then we can identify two further epistemological

---

[11] As we saw in Chapter 3, reflection on the accuracy of one's initial emotional appraisals is but one of the things that attentional capture and consumption can lead to. Another obvious effect of the capture and consumption of attention is focus on and reflection about strategies for coping with one's evaluative situation.

[12] The many studies that support this line include Wells, A. and Matthews, G., *Attention and Emotion: A Clinical Perspective*, Hillsdale, NJ: Erlbaum (1994); Fredrickson, B. L. and Branigan, C., 'Positive emotions broaden the scope of attention and thought-action repertoires', *Cognition & Emotion* (2005), 19(3): pp. 313–32; Kimchi, R. and Palmer, S. E., 'Form and texture in hierarchically constructed patterns', *Journal of Experimental Psychology: Human*

problems that individuals might face due to the persistence of attention, and in addition one significant problem for my thesis. The two epistemological problems are as follows. First, if negative emotion narrows attention such that we are emotionally focused on certain objects or events, this might mean that we fail to concentrate on or pay attention to more important things; as a result, emotional capture of attention can hinder, rather than promote, reflection on what is all-things-considered important or significant for us.[13] Second, if positive emotion broadens attention, it would seem to facilitate a "global" rather than a "local" assessment of our evaluative situation or environment; and this might mean that we neglect or fail to concentrate enough on the relevant object or event. As a result, emotional capture of attention in positive emotion can hinder, rather than promote, reflection on whether some object or event is as it emotionally appears. Both of these problems suggest a third problem, namely that my thesis doesn't *generalize*. For my claim that emotional experience captures attention and thereby motivates reflection upon the accuracy of our initial appraisal of some emotional object or event will be plausible, if at all, only with respect to negative emotions, as negative emotions narrow attentional focus on to the relevant object and event. Since positive emotions broaden attentional focus, this seems to tell against the idea that such emotions facilitate an enhanced representation *of the object or event in question*. So the idea that positive emotions involve a broader attentional focus and promote more "global" ways of seeing and thinking would seem to be incompatible with the idea that emotions have

Perception and Performance (1982), 8: 521–35; Basso, M. R. et al., 'Mood and global-local visual processing', *Journal of the International Neuropsychological Society* (1996), 2: 249–55; Gaspar, K. and Clore, C. L., 'Attending to the big picture: Mood and global versus local processing of visual information', *Psychological Science* (2002), 13: 34–40; Frederickson, B. L., 'What good are positive emotions?', *Review of General Psychology* (1998), 2: 300–19; and Frederickson, B. L., 'The role of positive emotions in positive psychology: The broaden-and-build theory of positive emotions', *American Psychologist* (2001), 56: 218–26; Derryberry, D. and Tucker, D., 'Motivating the Focus of Attention' (1994); Isen, A. M., 'Positive affect and decision making', in Lewis, M. and Haviland-Jones, J., *Handbook of Emotions* (2000).

[13] Recall LeDoux's claim that "[e]motional reactions are typically accompanied by intense cortical arousal . . . This high level of arousal is, in part, the explanation for why it is hard to concentrate on other things and work efficiently when you are in an emotional state." In LeDoux, J., *The Emotional Brain*, New York: Simon & Schuster (1996), p. 289. As a result of our attention being consumed by an emotional object or event, we might not give enough thought to more significant tasks that we face.

epistemic value in so far as they facilitate our understanding of emotional objects and events.[14]

To illustrate these problems and the empirical backing for them, consider first the host of studies indicating that differently valenced emotions give rise to different biases on global–local visual processing tests. Such studies show that negative emotions involve a bias for local processing (or evaluation), whilst positive emotions involve a bias for global processing (or evaluation). This suggests that differently valenced emotions have different effects on the breadth of attention. The paradigm for this kind of experiment was a global-local visual processing task in Kimchi and Palmer.[15] Basso, Gaspar, and Clore, and Frederickson have all conducted versions of this experiment.[16] In what follows I'll describe the experiment as conducted by Frederickson and Branigan.[17]

Frederickson and Branigan's primary hypothesis was that positive emotions such as amusement and contentment would "produce a global bias on a global–local visual processing task, consistent with a broadened scope of attention"; they also wished to "test the corollary hypothesis that, relative to a neutral state, two distinct negative emotions (anger and anxiety) [would] . . . produce a local bias on a global–local visual processing task".[18] In order to test this, the researchers divided subjects into three groups, and showed each group a film clip intended to elicit a positive, negative, or neutral emotional response. The former were clips about

---

[14] There is some empirical work that suggests that attentional focus varies with *intensity* rather than valence, so that high-intensity positive *and* negative emotions narrow attentional focus whereas low-intensity positive *and* negative emotions broaden focus. See Gable, P. and Harmon-Jones, E., 'The Blues Broaden, but the Nasty Narrows: Attentional Consequences of Negative Affects Low and High in Motivational Intensity', *Psychological Science* (2010), 21(2): pp. 211–15. However, the preponderance of empirical work suggests that valence does affect attention in the ways suggested, so I will work on the assumption that it is valence, rather than intensity, which is the important factor here.

[15] Kimchi, R. and Palmer, S. E. (1982), 'Form and texture in hierarchically constructed patterns', *Journal of Experimental Psychology: Human Perception and Performance* 8(4): 521–35.

[16] Basso et al. (1996); Gaspar and Clore (2002); Frederickson (1998; 2001).

[17] Fredrickson and Branigan (2005).

[18] Fredrickson and Branigan (2005), p. 318.

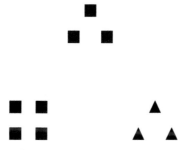

Figure 1 Originally appeared in Kimchi and Palmer (1982), p. 526.

"penguins waddling, swimming, and jumping" which primarily elicited enjoyment, and a film about nature showing "fields, streams, and mountains in warm, sunny weather" which primarily elicited contentment. The middle category involved a film featuring "a group of young men taunting and insulting a group of Amish passers-by in the street" which primarily elicited anger and disgust, and a film of "a prolonged mountain climbing accident" which primarily elicited anxiety and fear. A final clip—of "an abstract display of coloured sticks piling up"—served as a neutral control condition, and elicited "virtually no emotion".[19]

Participants were then assessed using a global–local visual processing task involving the following kind of display [Figure 1], where a triad of figures was presented that contained a "standard" figure on top, and two "comparison" figures underneath. Subjects were asked

to indicate which of the two comparison figures was more similar to the standard figure. Judgements could be based either on the global–configural aspects of the standard figure, or the local elements comprising it. In [Figure 1], for example, the standard figure's configuration is of a triangle made up of square elements. If participants choose the comparison figure that is a triangle made up of triangular elements . . . their choice is based on the global configuration of the standard figure. By contrast, if they choose the comparison figure that is a square made up of square elements . . . that choice is based on the local detail elements of the standard figure. Participants were instructed to give their first, most immediate impression of which comparison figure looks more like the standard figure.[20]

---

[19] Fredrickson and Branigan (2005), p. 319.
[20] Fredrickson and Branigan (2005), pp. 319–20.

The results were that "the two positive emotion film clips—*Penguins* and *Nature*—produced the largest global biases" when compared with the neutral film and negative emotion films. As a result, this suggests that "people experiencing positive emotions exhibit broader scopes of attention than do people experiencing no particular emotion or people experiencing negative emotion". In other words, it was found that "personality traits associated with negative emotions (anxiety and depression) correlate with a local bias consistent with a narrowed attentional focus. By contrast, traits associated with positive emotions (subjective well-being and optimism) correlate with a global bias consistent with a broadened attentional focus."[21] Similar results were seen in global–local visual focus tests conducted by Basso et al. and Gaspar and Clore, although in these cases the findings indicated that positive and negative *moods* promote attention to global and local information, respectively.

A different kind of study indicates that negative emotion during a search test leads to an impairment in the subject's ability to detect peripheral targets—in particular, empirical evidence indicates that negative feedback (or "failure") causes an increase in response times for targets far from the central feedback signal, when compared to response times for subjects in neutral or positive affective states.[22] In addition, there is considerable empirical work showing that valence has effects on attention more generally, i.e. not just visual attention. Derryberry and Tucker note that

although anxiety effects have...been examined most often in studies of visual attention, there is also evidence that anxiety constricts attention within the verbal cognitive domain as well...Mikulincer, Kedem, and Paz [found that] anxious subjects tended to reject non-prototypical exemplars of categories, the breadth of their categories was reduced, and they perceived less relatedness between different categories.[23] In subsequent research,[24] Mikulincer, Paz and Kedem found that anxious subjects categorized objects with less inclusive and more discrete categories, suggesting to these authors that anxiety may lead to conceptual fragmentation.[25]

---

[21] Fredrickson and Branigan (2005), p. 316.

[22] See Derryberry and Tucker (1994).

[23] Mikulincer, M., Kedem, P., and Paz, D., 'The impact of trait anxiety and situational stress on the categorization of natural objects', *Anxiety Research* (1990a) 2: 85–101.

[24] Mikulincer, M., Kedem, P., and Paz, D., 'Anxiety and categorization. Part 1: The structure and boundaries of mental categories; Part 2: Hierarchical levels of mental categories', *Personality and Individual Differences* (1990b) 8: 805–21.

[25] Derryberry and Tucker (1994), p. 182.

By the same token, there is evidence that positive emotion and positive mood influences attention in the opposite direction. Isen has, in a number of studies over the last two decades,[26] found that subjects

> in whom positive affect has been induced, in any of a variety of simple ways (e.g., watching five minutes of a comedy film, receiving a small bag of candy...) have a broader range of associates, and more diverse associates, to neutral material... Similarly, people in such conditions are able to categorize material more flexibly, seeing ways in which nontypical members of categories can fit or be viewed as members of the category.[27]

As a result, subjects who are experiencing positive emotion or affect tend to "create and use categories more inclusively, to group more stimuli together, and to rate more low-prototypic exemplars as category members than did control subjects".[28] In one such experiment to show the latter, subjects who have been induced to experience positive affect were more likely to judge 'fringe examplars' of a category such as *vehicle*—for instance, *elevator* and *camel*—as included within that category (Isen and Daubman, 1984).[29] So Isen's work suggests that positive emotion or affect produces a flexibility in organization and a capacity to integrate diverse material.[30]

If we take these results seriously, we can see how the effects of valence on attention might lead to epistemological problems—of neglecting the emotional object in the cases of positive emotions, and of failing to see the "big picture" in the case of negative. We can also see how such empirical evidence poses a generalization problem to my thesis that emotions can have epistemic value in so far as they promote the understanding of some emotional object or event.

In light of all of these epistemological problems, I need to provide an account of how attention is regulated so that emotional governance of attention promotes, rather than hinders, our epistemic goals. Part of this will be a specification of the conditions in which we are *right* to reflect on our emotional responses in the pursuit of evaluative understanding, and, by the same token, the conditions in which we are right to refrain from reflection and put our trust in our emotional proxies. But another part of

---

[26] See Isen, A. M., 'Positive affect and decision making', in Lewis and Haviland-Jones (eds) (2000), for a summary and details.

[27] Isen (2000), p. 418.   [28] Derryberry and Tucker (1994), p. 184.

[29] Isen, A. M. and Daubman, K. A., 'The influence of affect on categorization', *Journal of Personality and Social Psychology* (1984), 47: 1206–17.

[30] See also Frederickson and Branigan (2005), p. 316.

this will be an explanation of how the different effects that valence has on attention is compatible with my general thesis about the epistemic role and value of emotion. So where should we turn in search of such an account? The obvious answer is: to the virtues.

5.2 Virtuous habits of attention

In the previous section we saw a number of problems relating to emotion and attention. In the rest of this chapter I will discuss a solution to these problems, which is to maintain that emotions can play a positive epistemic role to the extent that they are governed and regulated by *virtuous habits of thought and attention*. In this section I consider one development of this idea, due to Peter Goldie,[31] As we'll see, Goldie's proposal draws an analogy between the virtuous governance of attention in emotional and perceptual experience; to this extent, it would seem to represent a virtue-epistemological variant of the mixed internalist–externalist justificatory story that the perceptual theorist wishes to tell, and which we considered in detail in Chapter 2. It should come as no surprise, therefore, that I think that this picture of virtuous habits of attention ought to be rejected. In the following section I suggest that we should regard the virtuous governance of attention in emotion along different lines, which will illustrate why such governance of emotional experience is rather different from the virtuous governance of perceptual experience. I propose, in particular, that virtuous habits of attention in emotional experience depend, in various ways, upon evaluative understanding.[32] If true, this proposal provides further support for the central claim of the last chapter, namely that evaluative understanding is our epistemic goal. If such understanding is required for control and regulation of attention, in other words, then this is an additional reason for us to pursue understanding rather than resting content with some lesser epistemic state such as belief or knowledge. The proposal therefore puts further pressure on the epistemic analogy between emotional and

---

[31] In Goldie (2004).

[32] The idea that the positive epistemic yield of emotion depends upon evaluative understanding is a central part of Elgin's perceptual account. See Elgin, C., *Considered Judgement*, Princeton: Princeton University Press (1996) and Elgin, C., 'Emotion and Understanding', in Brun, Doğuoğlu, and Kuenzle (eds) (2008). However, my account differs from Elgin's in important ways. In particular, I claim that the presence of the sort of 'sophisticated understanding' that Elgin appeals to actually *undermines* the idea that emotions themselves have epistemic value in the relevant circumstances.

perceptual experiences. Before looking at this implication in more detail, however, let us consider how Peter Goldie addresses the relation between emotion, virtue, and attention.[33]

Goldie wishes to appeal to the virtues in order to explain how evaluative knowledge can be gained on the basis of emotional experience—a question he regards as pressing, given the possibility of divergence between emotional experience and evaluative reality. His solution is to appeal to virtuous habits of attention. According to Goldie, the virtuous person has a disposition to pay attention to, consciously reflect upon, and (if necessary) regulate the operation of his belief-forming mechanisms when, and only when, there is good reason to check up on their operation. In this he follows Christopher Hookway, who stresses that effective deliberation in general requires that "issues enter into our conscious deliberations if and only if their doing so is important for the success of [the] activities".[34] An important corollary of this idea is that in the absence of such attentional focus, the virtuous subject can *trust* that his belief-forming mechanisms provide him with accurate information about himself and his environment, and so can rely on such mechanisms as sources of knowledge. When attention is not drawn to the operation of these mechanisms, the virtuous subject is right to trust that appearance matches reality, and can come to acquire justified belief or knowledge as a result.

To see this picture in more detail, and to focus once again on the analogy that has been the unifying theme throughout this book, consider the story we are inclined to tell regarding the role that virtuous control of attention plays in the justification of perceptual beliefs or in the attaining of perceptual knowledge. It does not follow, from the fact that perceptual

---

[33] Philosophers have long been concerned about the relation between virtue and emotion, and some of the ancient and mediaeval writers were concerned with the (virtuous) control of emotion. For discussion, see for instance Sorabji, R., *Emotion and Peace of Mind: From Stoic Agitation to Christian Temptation*, Oxford: Oxford University Press (2002); Nussbaum, M., *The Therapy of Desire: Theory and Practice in Hellenistic Ethics*, Princeton, NJ: Princeton University Press (1994); Annas, J., *The Morality of Happiness*, New York: Oxford University Press (1993); Knuuttila, S., *Emotions in Ancient and Medieval Philosophy*, Oxford: Clarendon Press (2004). The more particular issue of the virtuous control of *attention* has received rather less coverage, however, and so here I focus on Goldie and Hookway as two people who have discussed this explicitly.

[34] Hookway, C., 'Epistemic Norms and Theoretical Deliberation', in Dancy, J. (ed.), *Normativity*, Oxford: Blackwell (2000), p. 64; see also Hookway, C., 'Affective States and Epistemic Immediacy', *Metaphilosophy* (2003), 34: 78–96, and Hookway, C., 'Reasons for Belief, Reasoning, Virtues', *Philosophical Studies* (2006), 130(1): 47–70.

experiences can diverge from reality, that the virtuous person is under an obligation to or is motivated to pay attention to all of her perceptual experiences and constantly check to see whether such experiences result from the proper functioning of her perceptual systems. Virtue does not require, as Goldie puts it, that "the content of each particular perceptual experience should be held in suspense pending a check on one's perceptual mechanisms or any other sort of second-order reflective endorsement".[35] One obvious reason why virtue does not require that we constantly check our perceptual mechanisms is that such attentional focus would be impossible, given the sheer number of our perceptual experiences. Goldie continues: "The epistemic requirement, rather, is the commonsense one that we need only consciously seek to satisfy ourselves that the deliverances of a particular perceptual experience are as they should be if there is good reason to do so on that occasion."[36] On this picture, virtue therefore involves habits of attention which enable us to exert what Karen Jones calls "regulative guidance" over our perceptual mechanisms, facilitating conscious reflection about their operation when this is required, and leading us to discount their deliverances or decide that the appearances are indeed veridical.[37] In the absence of attention being drawn to the operation of her perceptual mechanisms, the virtuous person is right to trust her perceptual experiences, and to regard them as providing her with information about how things really are. Virtuous habits of attention are therefore essential in the story of how our perceptual experiences provide us with information and knowledge about the sensory world, since virtuous habits of attention are required for the proper functioning and regulation of our perceptual systems.

Goldie wishes to say something similar about virtuous attention to our emotional systems, and so proposes an analogous account of how emotional experience can provide the virtuous person with justified evaluative belief or evaluative knowledge. Although what is emotionally salient might on occasion diverge from evaluative reality, here too it is not necessary for the virtuous person to pay attention to each and every emotional occurrence in order to check on the operation of her emotional

---

[35] Goldie (2004), p. 251.   [36] Goldie (2004), p. 251.
[37] Jones, K., 'Emotion, Weakness of Will, and the Normative Conception of Agency', in Hatzimoysis (ed.), *Philosophy and the Emotions*, Cambridge: Cambridge University Press (2003), p. 196.

systems, and in order to reflectively endorse or reject how things emotionally appear to her. Indeed, as we have seen, there are significant problems associated with such checking, in so far as it expresses an excessively cautious or overly suspicious attitude, and can prevent, rather than facilitate, the formation of evaluative belief or judgement. Rather, "it is part of being intellectually virtuous to check, when (and only when) the occasion requires, whether our emotions are distorting perception and reason".[38] In the absence of attentional focus on the operation of our emotional mechanisms, Goldie thinks that the virtuous person is right to trust the deliverances of such mechanisms, and to regard her emotions as providing her with genuine information about how things are in the evaluative world.[39] As a result, our emotions "can help us to find our way around the world, without our constantly having to consciously reflect on our reasons for our responses on each and every occasion".[40] Virtuous habits of attention are therefore equally essential in the story of how our emotional experiences provide us with information and knowledge about the evaluative world, since virtuous habits of attention are required for the proper functioning and regulation of our emotional systems.

It should come as no surprise that I want to reject this picture of how the virtuous governance of attention enables our emotions to provide evaluative information and facilitate evaluative knowledge. The fact that emotions capture and consume attention, whereas perceptual experiences do not, should indicate that the stories we tell with regard to the virtuous habits of attention governing each will be rather different. In particular, the story of virtuous governance of emotional experience will need to address attentional problems caused by attentional capture and consumption—such as emotional recalcitrance, confirmatory bias, and overly narrow or overly broad attentional focus—that are not problems with respect to perceptual experience. But I want to reject the picture above for an additional reason, which is that it fails to do what it advertises, namely to provide an explanation of how emotional experience can play a positive epistemic role. This is because Goldie fails to adequately explain

---

[38] Goldie (2004), p. 250.

[39] He writes that if one is virtuous, "and if there are no other undue influences on one's thinking, then one will see things as they really are", Goldie (2004), p. 258.

[40] Goldie (2004), p. 258.

the conditions in which the virtuous person will put her trust in her emotional experiences, and as such does not provide us with an account of how emotions inform us about value.

In order to see this, recall Goldie's claim that the virtuous person is right to trust the deliverances of her emotions, except when she is moved to check or reflect upon their operation. As such, Goldie seems to think that the virtuous person has what Döring describes as a "default entitlement" to believe on the basis of her emotional experiences. However, in so far as emotional experience captures and consumes attention, thereby motivating conscious reflection aimed at discovering reasons which bear on the accuracy of the emotional construal, we need a further story as to how emotional experience can be compatible with trusting that *this very experience* gives one good evidence about how things stand in the evaluative world. That is, if it is in the nature of emotional experience to promote reflection on emotional accuracy, then this would seem, on the face of it, to *preclude* one from taking the deliverances of one's emotions at face value. The by-now familiar thought that emotion captures and consumes attention, and in doing so motivates reflection on emotion itself, therefore undermines the thought that the virtuous person takes her emotional responses for granted *unless* her attention is drawn to their operation. If emotional experience raises questions about its own representational adequacy, we need a further story as to the conditions—if any—in which the virtuous person is *right* to trust her emotional responses.[41] In the absence of this, Goldie seems unable to capture the common-sense idea that we can sometimes trust our emotional experiences to provide us with information about value.

We might put this argument in a slightly different way. We saw in the previous chapter that the goal of evaluative thinking is understanding, rather than justified belief or knowledge. However, the picture of virtuous governance of attention presented by Goldie seems incompatible with this, and as a result he seems to be unable to explain the conditions in which the virtuous person takes her emotional experience at face value. For the virtuous person will be someone who is motivated to achieve her epistemic goal (if anyone is), and hence who will not rest content with merely reliably formed true beliefs about value. Goldie's picture of a

---

[41] I present an earlier version of this argument against Goldie in Brady, M., 'Virtue, Emotion and Attention', *Metaphilosophy* (2010), 41(1–2): 115–31.

subject who unreflectively trusts her emotional responses, because her attention is not explicitly drawn to their operation in the relevant circumstances, is in fact a picture of someone who *fails* to be virtuous. Resting content with one's reliable emotional responses is incompatible with genuine virtue, at least if we think that the virtuous person pursues wisdom and understanding rather than mere knowledge.

We have, therefore, good reason to reject Goldie's attempt to model the virtuous governance of attention in emotional experience on the virtuous governance of attention in perceptual experience. This should give us further pause about accepting any close analogy between emotional and perceptual experiences at the epistemological level. In the following section I'll present a different account of the relation between virtue, emotion, and attention, aimed at showing how the virtuous person will not be subject to the attentional difficulties described, and hence aimed at explaining the conditions in which our emotional experiences play a positive epistemic role.

5.3 Virtue and understanding

In §1 we saw that there are certain epistemological problems stemming from (faulty) relations between emotion and attention. But what is involved in the virtuous control and regulation of attention in emotional experiences, so that such problems are avoided or resolved? In this section I want to propose that the virtuous governance of attention itself depends upon, in a number of different ways, evaluative understanding. As a result, I want to claim that understanding facilitates virtuous control of attention in emotional experience, and that the virtuous control of attention in emotional experience facilitates evaluative understanding and other epistemic goods. In order to make this case, let us consider the specific attention-emotional problems in order, and see the role that evaluative understanding will play in their solution.

5.3.1 Problems with emotional persistence

The first set of epistemological problems stems from the persistence of attention and reflection in circumstances where such reflection is not needed. An instance of this is where a subject constantly checks the accuracy or reliability of her emotional responses, and as such betrays an overly cautious or unduly suspicious character. As a result, the subject suffers from a form of epistemological and practical paralysis, since she fails to arrive at a judgement or decision as a result of excessive checking and reflection. However, although it seems clear that constantly checking the accuracy or reliability of one's *perceptual* experiences would be an intellectual vice, given our default entitlement to take these at face value in normal conditions, it does not seem that the same can be said about checking and reflection on our *emotional* experiences, given that we have the epistemic goal of attaining an understanding of, rather than a merely reliable belief about, our emotional–evaluative situation. Indeed, if someone lacks evaluative understanding of her situation and is in a position to attain her epistemic goal, then (as we saw in the last chapter) this is something that she *ought* to do by subjecting her emotional responses to critical scrutiny. It is not obvious that the virtuous person will, therefore, refrain from checking the accuracy of her emotional responses in a situation where she lacks evaluative understanding. It follows from this that the virtuous person *will* refrain from such checking and reflection, in those situations (and only in those situations) where she *already* understands her evaluative situation. In these instances, there is no epistemic need for the virtuous person to check on the accuracy of her emotional responses, or attempt to discover reasons why things are evaluatively thus-and-so in these circumstances, since the point of checking and discovery has already been achieved. It is therefore understanding that is central to the virtuous control of attention in such circumstances, rather than any trust that the virtuous person has in the reliability of her emotional proxies.[42] Moreover, it is this kind of evaluative understanding that is plausibly at the heart of the *non-emotional* capacity to recognize value that we discussed in Chapter 1. After all, the virtuous person who possesses evaluative understanding is a person who both grasps the evaluative structure of her situation and *discounts* the deliverances of her emotional responses, since to take such deliverances into account would be to engage in an illicit form of double-counting. As such, invoking the idea of evaluative understanding makes it

---

[42] There is a *related* problem of caution and excessive checking, but this is more of a practical rather than an epistemological problem: it is the problem of checking the accuracy of one's emotional responses in a situation where one lacks the time or capacity to gain evaluative understanding, because (perhaps) an immediate *practical* response is demanded. I'll return to consider this kind of practical problem, and show how a virtuous solution to this is also grounded in a form of understanding, towards the end of the chapter.

intelligible as to how one could come to non-emotionally recognize value. Nevertheless, since emotion plays a vital or essential role in the development of evaluative understanding, our non-emotional capacity to recognize value will depend, to a great extent, upon our capacities for emotional appraisal and reappraisal. As a result, and to complete the argument in Chapter 1, this is why we would be worse off, from the standpoint of detecting important objects and events, in the absence of emotion and emotional experience.

The idea that our epistemic goal when thinking about emotional objects and events is understanding, and that the virtuous person is some-one who has (when possible) an understanding of her evaluative situation, also helps to explain why the virtuous person will be less susceptible (if susceptible at all) to a second form of excessive checking and reflection, namely that which occurs with recalcitrant emotions. Recall that when our emotions are recalcitrant, we continue to search for reasons that bear on the accuracy of our emotional construals, despite the fact that we have endorsed the opposing evaluative view in judging as we do. However, cases of recalcitrant emotion are considerably *less* likely if one has an understanding of one's evaluative situation, given that (again, as we saw in the last chapter) understanding puts one in a stronger epistemic position than justified evaluative belief or even knowledge. For it is plausible to assume that the weaker the epistemic credentials one has for a judgement, the higher the odds of a clash between one's judgement and one's emotional response. When one's evaluative judgement is epistemically insecure, in other words, it is less likely that one's contrary emotional response will change so as to align itself to the judgement. Now recalci-trant emotions seem closer to cases in which one is genuinely undecided or in two minds about some evaluative situation, than to cases in which one's evaluative judgement is securely held and strongly supported. There's a temptation, that is, to think that the subject of recalcitrant emotions remains, in a sense, *unconvinced* that flying is safe or that spiders are harmless or that the theatre isn't shameful, or doesn't *fully* grasp these things. In so far as evaluative understanding represents the strongest epistemic position one can be in with respect to some emotional object or event, however, it is plausible to think that someone with such understanding is far less prone, if prone at all, to further reflection on whether or not something really is dangerous or shameful. The possibility of emotional recalcitrance seems to recede, therefore, the closer we move to evaluative understanding. If so, then we have an explanation of why virtuous governance of attention in this direction will also be grounded in or dependent upon the understanding of value that the virtuous person has.[43]

A further problem generated by attentional persistence is the susceptibility of those undergoing emotional experiences to confirmatory bias. This occurs when attentional persistence generates or supports a tendency to discover or invent reasons that confirm, rather than disconfirm, one's initial emotional construals, or which support, rather than undermine, one's underlying cares or concerns. As such the subject of such bias is inclined to endorse, rather than critically assess, her emotional appraisals and/or concerns. Here too the thought that virtuous habits of attention and reflection are ultimately based in evaluative understanding can help to explain why the virtuous person will not be subject to such forms of bias. This is because the temptation to invent "reasons" or to rationalize emotional responses arises when attention persists and one *isn't* aware of features that constitute genuine reasons that bear on the accuracy of one's emotional construals or the adequacy of one's underlying concerns. But such awareness is precisely what someone who understands why an object or event is evaluatively thus-and-so possesses. As such, there is no psychological pressure or need for a virtuous subject, possessed of evaluative understanding, to fabricate reasons.

The thought that the virtuous person understands her evaluative situation can therefore provide a plausible explanation of why she is not subject to problems of attentional persistence in her emotional life. The virtuous person will not check on the accuracy of her emotional responses in those situations where she understands her evaluative situation, since there is no point to checking in these circumstances. Moreover, the virtuous person, possessing evaluative understanding, will not be subject to recalcitrant emotion or confirmatory bias.

---

[43] Of course, what the *search* for reasons and evidence that is motivated by emotional persistence might uncover is that it was the emotion that was getting things right all along. Cases of recalcitrant emotion are not necessarily cases where the failing or fault attaches to the emotion rather than to the belief or judgement. So emotional persistence and the search for understanding can prevent emotional recalcitrance from another direction, when one comes to understand one's evaluative situation, endorse how things emotionally appear, and reject one's initial judgement of the situation.

5.3.2 Problems of dissociation between emotion and reflection

A second set of epistemological problems occurs in situations where attention persists but the subject *doesn't* reflect on the accuracy of her emotional construals or the adequacy of her underlying concerns. Here too evaluative understanding is central to an explanation of why the *virtuous* person reflects on accuracy and adequacy when such reflection is needed. In this instance, we need to appeal not to the subject's understanding of the value of some object or event—for if the subject had such understanding, then she would hardly need to reflect upon the accuracy of her emotional construals. We need, instead, to make the plausible assumption that the virtuous person (i) grasps that her epistemic goal is evaluative understanding rather than reliably formed evaluative belief, and (ii) is motivated to achieve her epistemic goal.[44] The virtuous person, in other words, grasps the need for reflection on the accuracy of her emotional appraisals in circumstances where she doesn't possess an understanding of why things are thus-and-so.[45] As such, the virtuous person will feel the need to reflect on the accuracy of her responses and on the adequacy of her underlying concerns, as a result of her awareness that she presently lacks access to the reasons why the relevant object or event has (or does not have) the relevant evaluative feature, and hence lacks understanding on this matter.[46] This is why the virtuous person will not rest content with her initial emotional appraisals in circumstances where she lacks understanding, but will instead subject them to critical scrutiny.

---

[44] This assumption is plausible if we think we can at least partly define the virtuous person in terms of a motivation to pursue the goal or good that is appropriate to that virtue. Thus, the benevolent person can be partly defined in terms of her motivation to promote the welfare of others. Similarly, the intellectually virtuous person will be motivated to pursue various epistemic goods: truth, knowledge, and—the most valuable of all—understanding. For this line on virtue, see Linda Zagzebski's *Virtues of the Mind*, Cambridge: Cambridge University Press (1996).

[45] The thought that the virtuous person can suffer from an epistemic lack or limitation is surely plausible, if we think that the virtuous person need not be omniscient. I assume, therefore, that someone can be fully virtuous and yet be unaware of some evaluative information—for instance, in a situation where the virtuous person encounters some novel value, or some familiar value in a novel situation.

[46] If what I said in the last chapter was correct, such understanding will involve the recognition that understanding is expected of her as a moral agent, and hence recognition of the value of understanding as opposed to mere justified belief or knowledge understood on reliabilist lines.

One particular kind of understanding that motivates critical reflection is displayed by the virtuous person when she grasps that the conditions are such that her emotions might be leading her astray. For instance, the (otherwise) virtuous person who is in the throes of nicotine withdrawal will be aware that the anger he feels towards an apparently rude and inconsiderate colleague might not be entirely down to the latter's behaviour. Instead of simply accepting or endorsing his emotional–evaluative construal and reacting with angry behaviour, the virtuous subject who understands the effects of addiction to nicotine on mood will be inclined to reflect again on whether such behaviour really was inconsiderate or rude, and hence whether angry behaviour really is warranted. The virtuous regulation of attention in this direction is grounded in the sort of 'sophisticated understanding' of when our emotional responses might be unreliable that Elgin appeals to, and which Goldie identifies as a condition in which attention is rightly drawn to the operation of our belief-forming mechanisms. So to this extent I agree with Elgin and Goldie about the virtuous regulation of attention. But what I want to stress is that this sort of case is but an instance of a more general motivation to critically reflect upon our emotional responses, generated not out of concern for reliability of belief-forming mechanisms, but from a desire for evaluative understanding.

If so, then understanding features centrally in an explanation of the virtuous regulation of attention along this dimension: the virtuous person is one who grasps that her epistemic goal is evaluative understanding, and is suitably reflective about emotional objects and events as a result.

5.3.3 Problems with emotional focus and distraction

A third set of epistemological problems generated by attentional capture and consumption concerns emotional focus and scope. In particular, we saw that the different effects that valence can have on attentional focus can lead to particular epistemological problems. For if negative emotion narrows attention, this can lead us to focus too narrowly on some emotional object and event at the expense of seeing the "big picture": in so far as our attention is focused narrowly, we might fail to pay attention to what is all-things-considered important or significant for us. And if positive emotion broadens attention, this can lead us to neglect the emotional object or event, and can thus hinder, rather than promote, evaluative understanding of that object or event. Moreover, as we have seen, this suggests that my thesis might not generalize: the claim that emotional experience captures attention and thereby motivates reflection upon the accuracy of our initial appraisal of some emotional object or event will be plausible, if at all, only with respect to negative emotions. Given this, how might evaluative understanding play a role in the virtuous regulation of attention so as to avoid these two epistemological difficulties? And how might I show that my general thesis is compatible with the empirical evidence which indicates the different effects that valence can have on attention?

To take the latter question first, it strikes me that none of the evidence for valence having an effect on breadth of attention is telling against my account of the epistemic importance of emotion in facilitating understanding of emotional objects and events. Recall, to begin, Derryberry and Tucker's studies, which indicate that negative emotion during a search test leads to an impairment in the subject's ability to detect peripheral targets, whereas subjects experiencing neutral or positive affect do not suffer from this impairment. However, this evidence is not fatal to my account. The criticism of my account suggests that the broadening of attention in positive emotion would *not* facilitate an enhanced representation of the emotional object or event, but would have the opposite effect: namely positive emotion, by broadening attentional focus, would lead the subject to *neglect* the object or event that is the centre of attentional focus in negative emotional experience. But even if the evidence in question shows that negative emotion narrows attentional focus, it does nothing to show that positive emotion causes *neglect* at the local level, given that response times for targets closer to the central feedback signal were the *same* for negative and positive emotions.[47] If so, there is no evidence for positive emotion decreasing attention when it comes to the emotional object, assuming that the emotional object is that which plays the role of the central feedback signal in the empirical studies.

Indeed, it seems to me that we can doubt whether *any* of the three different types of empirical study cited causes a problem for my thesis. This is because all of the experimental work done to test the effect of valence on attention fixes on what I will call *consequential* attentional focus, rather than *constitutive* attentional focus. To explain, note that the focusing of attention onto some object or event is, plausibly, constitutive of emotional

---

[47] Derryberry and Tucker (1994), p. 180.

experience. For it seems impossible to think of someone as being afraid of the upcoming exam without the upcoming exam being the target of her attention. Similarly, it seems impossible to think of someone as being angry about the Principal's pay rise without the Principal's pay rise being the object or event that he attends to when angry. Let us therefore call the intentional target of emotion—that which the emotion is about—the object of constitutive attentional focus.

To say that some emotion involves, as a constituent, attention to some object or event does not entail, of course, that the subject's attention is *solely* focused on that object. My guilt at my bad behaviour might make me attend not only to what I did, but to ways in which I can make reparations; my disappointment at the team's defeat might lead me to pay attention not only to the loss, but to the possibility of alleviating my feelings with a trip to the pub. So emotion can also make us pay attention to strategies for coping with some emotional object or event. In addition, emotion can draw our attention to memories of similar events, as when my sorrow at my grandmother's death leads me to think about my grandfather's death. Emotion can motivate attention to imaginative possibilities, as when my happiness when she accepts my invitation to go on a date leads me to imagine where we might go for dinner, or our first kiss.

It is not obvious whether attention to strategies for coping are constitutive of emotional experience. The case might be made that fear necessarily involves thinking of attack or escape; but other emotional experiences don't seem to involve action tendencies or thoughts of coping. Consider, for instance, aesthetic contemplation, which certainly involves paying attention to an art object, but does not seem to involve much if anything in the way of action in response to, or in order to cope with, our emotional–evaluative situation. And it certainly seems true that memories and imaginings generated by emotion are not themselves constitutive of emotion, but are what we might call the objects of *consequential* emotional attention. In other words, emotional experience can generate attentional focus on things *other than* the object or event that elicited the emotion (my grandfather's death, her saying "yes" to my asking for a date), and which are consequential to the attentional focus on the emotional object or event itself, a focus that, as we've seen, is partly constitutive of the emotion in question.

Now my proposal about the epistemic value of emotion is a proposal about the epistemic value generated by attentional focus which is constitutive of emotion. This is because I argue that emotion can keep attention fixed on the object or event that elicited it, and in so doing can motivate the search for and discovery of reasons that bear on the accuracy of our initial evaluation of that event. So my proposal is a proposal about (the value of) constitutive attention. But it seems to me that all of the evidence cited about the effects of valence on attentional focus is evidence that fixes on consequential attention—that is, on attention paid to objects and events that are *other than* those objects and events that elicit, and are the focal target of, the emotional experience.

Consider, in this light, the experiments that purport to show that positive emotions lead to a global bias, and negative emotions to a local bias, in visual-processing tasks. In Frederickson's version of this experiment, which is pretty standard, emotion is first elicited by getting subjects to watch a film, and then they are asked which of the comparison figures most closely resembles the standard figure. But clearly the attentional focus in the latter cases is consequential attentional focus, since the object of attention in the experiment is *not* the object that generated, and was the intentional target of, the emotional itself. That is, when a subject gains enjoyment from watching *Penguins*, his constitutive attentional focus is on the film (or the behaviour of the penguins in the film); when he is asked to judge which of the comparison figures looks most like the standard figure, his consequential attention focus is on the figure. If so, then evidence from such experiments showing that enjoyment broadens attentional focus says nothing about whether positive emotion broadens *constitutive* attentional focus, and thus distracts the subject from attending to, and reassessing or re-evaluating, the object that elicits that emotion. For all that the evidence indicates, and as the 'target-detection' evidence cited suggests, positive and negative emotions do not differ in the extent to which they motivate focus on and reflection about the emotional object or event itself. The fact, therefore, that positive emotions lead to a broadening of consequential attentional focus is, from the standpoint of my thesis, simply beside the point.

A similar conclusion is warranted when we turn to the third body of evidence, generated by the research of Isen and her colleagues. Here too experimental evidence shows the influence of positive affect on categorization of objects that are not those that elicited the emotion, and hence that are the objects of consequential attentional focus. To quote Frederickson, "individuals induced to feel positive affect more often saw fringe exemplars of a given category as included within the category . . . report increased preference for variety and accept a broader array of behavioural options . . . [and display an] ability to integrate diverse material". But it is not the exemplars or behavioural options which were the objects of constitutive attention during the emotional experience, and so the fact that positive affect broadens attention so that fringe exemplars are more often included in a category says nothing about the effects of positive emotion or mood on attention to the intentional object of the emotion.

By the same token, and as Derryberry and Tucker write,

anxious subjects tended to reject non-prototypical exemplars of categories, the breadth of their categories was reduced, and they perceived less relatedness between different categories . . . subsequent research . . . found that anxious subjects categorized objects with less inclusive and more discrete categories, suggesting to these authors that anxiety may lead to conceptual fragmentation.

But again, exemplars and categories are the objects of consequential attentional focus, rather than constitutive, and so the fact that negative affect causes conceptual fragmentation says nothing about the effects of negative emotion or mood on attention to the intentional object of the emotion.

The empirical evidence of differing effects of valence on breadth of attention is, therefore, clearly fixated on consequential attentional spread or narrowing, rather than constitutive attentional focus. Such experimental evidence therefore fails to tell against my proposal, which concerned the epistemic importance of constitutive attention to objects and events. If so, then the charge that my account of the epistemic value of emotion suffers from a generalization problem, since it applies only to negative and not to positive emotions, is unwarranted.

The fact that my proposal is compatible with the empirical evidence is important when we turn to the two epistemological problems that the different effects of valence on attention are supposed to generate. One apparent problem was that if positive emotion broadens attention, this can lead us to neglect the emotional object or event, thus hindering evaluative understanding of that event. As we have seen, however, none of the empirical evidence shows that positive emotion does (usually, typically) lead to neglect of the emotional object or event. And whilst it is of course true that someone experiencing positive emotion or mood *could* thereby come to neglect the object or event that is the target of the emotion, it is equally true that the virtuous person would not behave in this way. For (as we saw in the previous section) the virtuous person will be someone who is motivated to understand her evaluative situation, and thus motivated to reflect upon and reassess her initial emotional response to the said object or event. As a result, it is evaluative understanding (as a goal) that plays a role in the virtuous regulation of attention, and thus evaluative understanding (as a goal) that provides the condition for emotion to have a positive epistemic yield.

What of the charge that if negative emotion narrows attention, this can lead us to focus too narrowly on some emotional object or event, and thus fail to pay sufficient attention to what is all-things-considered important or significant to us? Consider, for instance, the person consumed by jealousy and motivated to understand whether or not her new boyfriend is being unfaithful, and who thereby fails to see such attentional focus is damaging her health, her relationships with friends and family, etc. This worry is not addressed by pointing out that the virtuous person will be motivated to understand whether or not her new boyfriend is being unfaithful, since it is precisely this motivation and narrow focus that can cause someone to fail to attend to what are possibly more important matters. But the worry can be addressed if we make the plausible assumption that the virtuous person, while focused on the object in question, remains emotionally responsive to *other* important objects and events in her environment, such that she will be alert to the danger that a narrow pattern of attention might have on her health, friendships, and the like. It is, after all, no part of my picture that emotional capture and consumption of attention with respect to some particular object or event—the possibility of infidelity, one's shameful attire, how beautiful she is—rules out or blocks off other emotional responses, so that the subject is locked into, and only capable of, one emotional response. It seems clear that even someone who is consumed with jealousy (or shame or love) would still respond under normal conditions with anger when insulted in the street, or fear when accosted by the ne'er-do-well in the pub, or surprise when the phone rings late at night. As such, a narrow focus does not preclude paying attention to other important or significant things. In so far as we can characterize the virtuous person as someone who pays attention to *all* of the things that she ought to pay attention to, and in so far as the virtuous person is motivated to understand the values that emotional experience presents to her, then she will be someone who is motivated to understand what is all-things-considered important or significant in her environment. We can once again hold that it is evaluative understanding (as a goal) that plays a role in the virtuous regulation of attention, and evaluative understanding (as a goal) that provides the conditions for emotions to have a positive epistemic yield.

Taken together, these arguments present a strong case for the conclusion that the virtuous control and regulation of attention in emotional experience is related in various ways to evaluative understanding. For this account can explain why the virtuous person is not overly reflective or intellectually cautious, as I argued in the first subsection; it can explain why the virtuous person is nevertheless reflective enough, as I argued in the second; and it can explain why the virtuous person's reflections will be narrow enough to promote understanding of some emotional object and event, and also broad enough to promote understanding of the big evaluative picture. Central to these explanations is the conclusion from the last chapter, namely that understanding of emotional objects and events is the goal of evaluative thinking. For in so far as the virtuous person achieves this goal, she will not be overly reflective or cautious; and in so far as she hasn't yet achieved this goal, she will be suitably reflective in order to gain a broad understanding of her evaluative situation. The idea that virtuous governance of attention involves evaluative understanding thus seems to provide further support for that conclusion, and hence for the overall epistemological story about the epistemic role and value of emotion that I have presented in this book.

This epistemological story is not complete, however. For I still have to address the question of the conditions in which the virtuous person puts her trust in her emotional responses, or takes her emotional experience at face value. This will be the task of the penultimate section.

5.4 Does the virtuous person trust her emotional responses?

I have argued that we should reject Goldie's suggestion that the virtuous person is someone who puts her trust in her emotional responses in much the same way that she puts her trust in her perceptual experiences, and whose reflection on the operation of both belief-forming systems is governed by the same habits of attention. One implication of these arguments is that we have yet to see circumstances in which the virtuous subject trusts her emotional responses to give her information about the evaluative world and does *not* reflect further upon her evaluative situation. For to this point we have seen that the virtuous person will either understand her evaluative situation, in which case there is no need for her to rely upon her emotional responses to provide her with evaluative information—indeed, in so far as the subject has evaluative understanding, and thus is aware of the reasons that her emotions reliably track, she will regard the epistemic yield of her emotional proxies as nil. Or the virtuous person lacks understanding of her situation (and knows that she lacks it), in which case she will be motivated to achieve this by subjecting her emotional responses to critical scrutiny. In neither case will the virtuous person rest content with her emotional responses, in the way in which she typically rests content with her sensory perceptual experiences.

This raises the following question: under what conditions will the virtuous person rely upon her emotional experiences to provide her with evaluative information? In other words, what are the conditions in which the virtuous person puts her trust in her emotional experiences to inform her about value, and without further reflecting upon her evaluative situation? I think that we can answer these questions by turning to *pragmatic* or *practical* matters. For if we assume that the virtuous person is neither omnipotent nor omniscient, then it is plausible to hold that she is subject to practical constraints on her epistemic activities. As a result, there will be cases in which the virtuous person lacks the time for the pursuit of understanding, and other cases where the search for and discovery of reasons would conflict with the pursuit of her non-epistemic goals. Thus, even the virtuous person will on occasion have to make quick decisions on the basis of her emotional responses, where she lacks ready access to further evaluative information. For example, on the first night in a new city the virtuous person might trust in his anxiety and avoid walking home through a particular neighbourhood; and clearly this is not a situation in which the virtuous person should seek further information about whether the neighbourhood is actually dangerous, at least not then and there. Or the virtuous person might trust his positive feelings about this restaurant instead of that one, given that he wishes to eat, and yet lacks the time and money and indeed the motivation to investigate the reasons as to why this restaurant is better than that one—again, at least in circumstances where all that he wants is to find a nice restaurant for dinner on this occasion. So the virtuous person will be inclined to trust his emotional experiences in situations that are novel or unfamiliar—where he cannot remain agnostic as to his evaluative situation, as Rob Hopkins puts in—and where there are time- and other constraints on the pursuit of understanding.

In so far as the virtuous person puts his trust in his emotional experiences, he is like the rest of us: there are conditions in which the pursuit of our epistemic goal of understanding will be constrained, and in which we must rely upon our emotional responses for evaluative information. But an important implication of the picture developed in the past two chapters is that the occasions in which the virtuous person puts his trust in his emotional experiences will be significantly fewer than those in which the non-virtuous person does. As we saw in Chapter 4, one of the reasons for our failure to pursue understanding is a lack of the relevant sensibility: there's no point in my searching for reasons as to why this symphony is beautiful, given my lack of musical education. But this reason, we might think, doesn't apply to the virtuous person. If anyone has the right kind of sensibility and the right kind of education, it will be him. Moreover, as we have seen, the virtuous person is someone who achieves his epistemic goal of understanding if anyone does, and so we can assume that the virtuous person will have far more in the way of evaluative understanding than the non-virtuous person will. Given this, there will be fewer situations that strike the virtuous person as novel and unfamiliar from the evaluative perspective, and hence fewer situations in which he will have to trust his emotional responses *alone* to provide him with evaluative knowledge. If so, then the more virtuous someone is, the less reliant he will be on his emotional responses to themselves disclose evaluative information. As a result, emotional experiences will play a greater role in the formation of *our* evaluative beliefs than in the formation of the beliefs of the fully virtuous person. Moreover, since some of our emotional experiences will be reliably correlated with the relevant values, then there will be occasions when it is right for the virtuous person, and for us, to rely upon emotional responses alone to provide evaluative information. Emotional experiences can by themselves play a role in the justification of evaluative beliefs; but they will play a greater role in the justification of *our* evaluative beliefs than in the justification of the beliefs of the fully virtuous person. Emotional experiences therefore have epistemic value for us—as proxies or substitutes for reasons—in so far as we fall short of full virtue.

The resulting picture of the virtuous person's motivations is, then, as follows. If we assume that understanding is our epistemic goal, then in normal circumstances the virtuous person will either possess understanding of his evaluative situation, in which case he has no need to rely upon his emotional responses, or he will be motivated to achieve such understanding, in which case he will subject his emotional responses to critical scrutiny. In neither situation will the virtuous person rest content with, or rely solely upon, his emotional experiences in forming evaluative judgements. However, there are cases where the virtuous person lacks understanding but where the attempt to attain that understanding would have significant practical costs. In these circumstances, the requirement to pursue evaluative understanding lapses, and it is legitimate for the virtuous person to rely upon his best indication of value in his present circumstances, namely his emotional construal of the situation as thus-and-so. As such, this general account of the virtuous control and regulation of attention in emotional experience remains compatible with the commonsense view on the epistemic role and value of such experience. It is sometimes right for the virtuous person to put his trust in his emotions. Nevertheless, the occasions in which the virtuous person puts his trust in his emotions will be fewer than the occasions in which the non-virtuous person does. The more virtuous we become, therefore, the less reliant we are on emotions alone for evaluative information.

5.5 Conclusions

My initial goal in this chapter was to show how my account of emotion— as something which captures and consumes attention, and in so doing facilitates evaluative understanding—could accommodate the obvious fact that emotional effects on attention are sometimes epistemically deleterious. After illustrating a number of ways in which emotion and attention can lead us astray from an epistemic standpoint, I proceeded to examine the idea that the positive epistemic yield of emotional experience will depend upon virtuous habits of attention. I considered one such account, due to Goldie, that appeared to represent a virtue-epistemological extension of the justificatory story that the perceptual theorist wishes to tell. On this account, virtuous regulation of attention with respect to emotional experience mirrors virtuous governance of sensory perceptual experience:

in each case, the attention of the virtuous person is only drawn to such experiences when there is good reason to attend to the operation of the relevant belief-forming mechanism. Absent such attention, Goldie thinks that we are right to put our trust in our emotional and perceptual experiences, to take them at face value, and regard them as providing us with information about the evaluative and the non-evaluative world, respectively.

I then argued that we should reject Goldie's account, and with it this further analogy between emotional and perceptual experience, since it did not address the kinds of attentional failings previously detailed, and moreover failed to explain what needed explaining, namely the conditions in which the emotions can have a positive epistemic yield. For unless these attentional failings are discussed, the conditions in which the virtuous person puts her trust in her emotional responses will be unclear. I proposed that a more plausible account of the virtuous governance and regulation of attention in emotional experience will be grounded in the very thing I have argued is the goal of emotional–evaluative thinking, namely evaluative understanding. I illustrated how this account can explain why the virtuous person would not be susceptible to the problems of attention that I listed, and how this provides further support to the idea that understanding is our epistemic goal. Finally, I considered the implications of this for the idea that emotions can tell us about value, and in particular for the question of the conditions in which the virtuous person trusts in the epistemic deliverances of her emotional experiences. I argued that there are such occasions, when emotional experience is reliable and yet the attainment of understanding is precluded by time- and other constraints. The thought at the heart of common-sense thinking about emotion—namely that emotions can disclose value, and can therefore play a role in the justification of evaluative judgement—thus turns out to be true. But the scope of this claim is rather more limited than common-sense, and the perceptual theory of emotion, suggests. We simply do not trust in or rely upon our emotional experiences for evaluative information in *anything like* the way that we trust in or rely upon our perceptual experiences for non-evaluative information. And the virtuous person puts her trust in her emotional experiences even less.

The perceptual model therefore overplays the epistemic credentials that emotional experiences possess. However, the picture that undermines the perceptual model—i.e. the picture which maintains that emotional experience focuses attention on and facilitates critical reflection about emotional appraisals and emotional concerns—helps to illustrate the importance of such experiences for the achievement of our epistemic goal of evaluative understanding. The negative case against the perceptual model of emotion thus gives rise to a positive account, which proposes that emotional experiences have epistemic value in important, interesting, and hitherto neglected ways. Far from undermining the idea that emotions have epistemic value, therefore, criticisms of the perceptual model actually help to illustrate the significant epistemic value that emotional experience can have. The failure of the perceptual model should thus generate optimism, rather than pessimism, about the importance of emotion to our epistemic practices and endeavours.

Bibliography

Alston, W. (1988), 'An Internalist Externalism', *Synthese* 74.

Alston, W. (2005), *Beyond 'Justification': Dimensions Of Epistemic Evaluation*, Ithaca, NY: Cornell University Press.

Annas, J. (1993), *The Morality of Happiness*, New York: Oxford University Press.

Anscombe, G. E. M. (1963), *Intention*, Ithaca, NY: Cornell University Press.

Arpaly, N. (2003), *Unprincipled Virtue*, Oxford: Oxford University Press.

Bach, K. (1994), 'Emotional Disorder and Attention', in Graham and Stephens (eds).

Bagnoli, C. (ed.) (2011), *Morality and the Emotions*, Oxford: Oxford University Press.

Baier, A. (2004), 'Feelings that Matter', in Solomon (ed.).

Barrett, L. (2005), 'Adaptations to Predators and Prey', in Budd (ed.).

Basso, M. R. et al. (1996), 'Mood and Global–Local Visual Processing', *Journal of the International Neuropsychological Society* 2.

Bedford, E. (1957), 'Emotions', *Proceedings of the Aristotelian Society* 57: 281–304.

Ben-Ze'ev, A. (2000), *The Subtlety of Emotions*, Cambridge, MA: MIT Press.

Bernecker, S. and Pritchard, D. (eds) (forthcoming), *The Routledge Companion to Epistemology*, London: Routledge.

Blackburn, S. (1998), *Ruling Passions*, New York: Oxford University Press.

Blacking, J. (ed.) (1977), *The Anthropology of the Body*, London: Academic Press.

Bonjour, L. (2004), 'In Search of Direct Realism', *Philosophy and Phenomenological Research* 69(2): 349–67.

Brady, M. S. (2009), 'The Irrationality of Recalcitrant Emotions', *Philosophical Studies* 145(3): 413–30.

Brady, M. S. (ed.) (2010), *New Waves in Metaethics*, London: Palgrave Macmillan.

Brady, M. S. (2010), 'Virtue, Emotion and Attention', *Metaphilosophy* 41(1–2): 115–31.

Brady, M. S. (2011), 'Emotion, Perception and Reason', in Bagnoli (ed.).

Brewer, W. (2000), *Perception and Reason*, Oxford: Oxford University Press.

Brun, G., Doğuoğlu, U., and Kuenzle, D. (eds) (2008), *Epistemology and Emotions*, Farnham: Ashgate Publishing.

Budd, D. (ed.) (2005), *The Handbook of Evolutionary Psychology*, New York: John Wiley & Sons.

Cannon, W. (1929), *Bodily Changes in Pain, Hunger, Fear and Rage*, New York: Appleton.

Chalmers, D. (2004), 'The Representational Character of Experience', in Leiter (ed.).

Clark, L. and Watson, D. (1994), 'Distinguishing Functional from Dysfunctional Affective Responses', in Ekman and Davidson (eds).

Clore, G. (1994a), 'Why Emotions are Felt', in Ekman and Davidson (eds).

Clore, G. (1994b), 'Why Emotions Require Cognition', in Ekman and Davidson (eds).

Clore, G. and Gaspar, K. (2000), 'Some Affective Influences on Belief', in Frijda, Manstead, and Bem (eds).

Cowan, R. (2011), *Ethical Intuitionism*, University of Glasgow PhD dissertation.

Crane, T. (2011), 'The Problem of Perception', *The Stanford Encyclopedia of Philosophy (Spring 2011 Edition)*, Edward N. Zalta (ed.), <http://plato.stanford.edu/archives/spr2011/entries/perception-problem/>.

Cuneo, T. (2006), 'Signs of Value: Reid on the Evidential Role of Feelings in Moral Judgement', *British Journal for the History of Philosophy* 41(1): 69–91.

D'Arms, J. (2005), 'Two Arguments for Sentimentalism', *Philosophical Issues* 15(1): 1–21.

D'Arms, J. and Jacobson, D. (2000a), 'The Moralistic Fallacy: On the "Appropriateness" of Emotions', *Philosophy and Phenomenological Research* 61(1): 65–90.

D'Arms, J. and Jacobson, D. (2000b), 'Sentiment and Value', *Ethics* 110(4): 722–48.

D'Arms, J. and Jacobson, D. (2003), 'The Significance of Recalcitrant Emotion', in Hatzimoysis (ed.).

D'Arms, J. and Jacobson, D. (2006), 'Anthropocentric Constraints on Human Value', in Shafer-Landau (ed.).

Dalgleish, T. and Power, M. (eds) (1999), *Handbook of Cognition and Emotion*, Chichester: Wiley.

Damasio, A. (1994), *Descartes' Error*, New York: G. B. Putnam's Sons.

Dancy, J. (ed.) (1982), *Perceptual Knowledge*, Oxford: Oxford University Press.

Dancy, J. (ed.) (2000), *Normativity*, Oxford: Blackwell.

Davidson, D. (1980), 'Intending', in *Essays on Actions and Events*, Oxford: Clarendon Press.

de Sousa, R. (1987), *The Rationality of Emotion*, Cambridge, MA: MIT Press.

de Sousa, R. (2010), 'Emotion', *The Stanford Encyclopedia of Philosophy (Spring 2010 Edition)*, Edward N. Zalta (ed.), <http://plato.stanford.edu/archives/spr2010/entries/emotion/>.

Deigh, J. (2010), 'Concepts of Emotions', in Goldie (ed.).

Deonna, J. (2006), 'Emotion, Perception and Perspective', *Dialectica* 60(1): 29–46.

Derryberry, D. and Tucker, D. (1994), 'Motivating the Focus of Attention', in Niedenthal and Kitayama (eds).

Dolan, R. J. (2002), 'Emotion, Cognition, and Behavior', *Science* 298(5596): 1191–4.

Döring, S. (2003), 'Explaining Action by Emotion', *The Philosophical Quarterly* 53 (211): 214–30.

Döring, S. (2007), 'Seeing What to Do: Affective Perception and Rational Motivation', *Dialectica* 61(3): 363–94.

Döring, S. (2008), 'Conflict without Contradiction', in Brun, Doğuoğlu, and Kuenzle (eds).

Dretske, F. (1971), 'Conclusive Reasons', *Australasian Journal of Philosophy* 49(1): 1–22.

Duncan, J. (1999), 'Attention', in Wilson and Keil (eds).

Ekman, P. (1977), 'Biological and cultural contributions to body and facial movement', in Blacking (ed.).

Ekman, P. and Davidson, R. (eds) (1994), *The Nature of Emotion*, Oxford: Oxford University Press.

Elgin, C. (1996), *Considered Judgement*, Princeton: Princeton University Press.

Elgin, C. (2008), 'Emotion and Understanding', in Brun, Doğuoğlu and Kuenzle (eds).

Ellsworth, P. (1994), 'Levels of Thought and Levels of Emotion', in Ekman and Davidson (eds).

Eriksen, C. W. and Hoffman, J. E. (1973), 'The extent of processing of noise elements during selective encoding from visual displays', *Perception and Psychophysics* 14(1): 155–60.

Eriksen, C. W. and St James, J. D. (1986), 'Shifting of attentional focus within and about a visual display', *Perception and Psychophysics* 40(2): 175–83.

Evans, D. (2001), *The Science of Sentiment*, New York: Oxford University Press.

Evans, D. and Cruse, P. (eds) (2004), *Emotion, Evolution, and Rationality*, Oxford: Oxford University Press.

Evans, J. (1990), *Bias in Human Reasoning: Causes and Consequences*, London: Psychology Press.

Faucher, L. and Tappolet, C. (2002), 'Fear and the Focus of Attention', *Consciousness and Emotion* 3(2): 105–44.

Frackowiak, R. et al. (eds) (2003), *Human Brain Function*, 2nd edition, San Diego: Academic Press.

Frederickson, B. L. (1998), 'What good are positive emotions?', *Review of General Psychology* 2(3): 300–19.

Frederickson, B. L. (2001), 'The role of positive emotions in positive psychology: The broaden-and-build theory of positive emotions', *American Psychologist* 56(3): 218–26.

Fredrickson, B. L. and Branigan, C. (2005), 'Positive emotions broaden the scope of attention and thought-action repertoires', *Cognition & Emotion* 19(3): 313–32.

Fricker, M. (2007), *Epistemic Injustice*, Oxford: Oxford University Press.

Frijda, N. (1994), 'Why Emotions are Functional, Most of the Time', in Ekman and Davidson (eds).

Frijda, N., Manstead, A., and Bem, S. (eds) (2000), *Emotions and Beliefs*, Cambridge: Cambridge University Press.

Gable, P. and Harmon-Jones, E. (2010), 'The Blues Broaden, but the Nasty Narrows: Attentional Consequences of Negative Affects Low and High in Motivational Intensity', *Psychological Science* 21(2): 211–15.

Gaspar, K. and Clore, C. L. (2002), 'Attending to the big picture: Mood and global versus local processing of visual information', *Psychological Science* 13(1): 34–40.

Gazzaniga, M. (ed.) (1995), *The Cognitive Neurosciences*, Cambridge, MA: MIT Press.

Gibbard, A. (1990), *Wise Choices, Apt Feelings*, Cambridge, MA: Harvard University Press.

Goldie, P. (2000), *The Emotions*, Oxford: Oxford University Press.

Goldie, P. (2002), 'Emotions, Feelings and Intentionality', *Phenomenology and the Cognitive Sciences* 1(3): 235–54.

Goldie, P. (2004), 'Emotion, Reason, and Virtue', in Evans and Cruse (eds).

Goldie, P. (2008), 'Misleading Emotions', in Brun, Doğuoğlu, and Kuenzle (eds).

Goldie, P. (ed.) (2010), *The Oxford Handbook of Philosophy of Emotion*, Oxford: Oxford University Press.

Graham, G. and Stephens, L. (eds) (1994), *Philosophical Psychopathology*, Cambridge, MA: MIT Press.

Greenspan, P. (1988), *Emotions and Reasons*, London: Routledge.

Griffiths, P. (1998), *What Emotions Are*, Chicago: University of Chicago Press.

Grimm, S. (2001), 'Ernest Sosa, Knowledge, and Understanding', *Philosophical Studies* 106(3): 171–91.

Grimm, S. (2006), 'Is Understanding a Species of Knowledge?', *British Journal for the Philosophy of Science* 57(3): 515–35.

Grimm, S. (forthcoming), 'Understanding', in Bernecker and Pritchard (eds).

Haddock, A. and Macpherson, F. (2008), 'Introduction: Varieties of Disjunctivism', in Haddock and Macpherson (eds).

Haddock, A. and Macpherson, F. (eds) (2008), *Disjunctivism: Perception, Action and Knowledge*, Oxford: Oxford University Press.

Haidt, J. (2001), 'The Emotional Dog and Its Rational Tail: A Social Intuitionist Approach to Moral Judgment', *Psychological Review* 108(4): 814–34.

Haidt, J., Bjorklund, F., and Murphy, S. (2000), 'Moral Dumbfounding: When Intuition Finds No Reason', unpublished manuscript.

Hatzimoysis, A. (ed.) (2003), *Philosophy and the Emotions*, Cambridge: Cambridge University Press.

Hawthorne, J. and Gendler Szabo, T. (eds) (2005), *Oxford Studies in Epistemology*, *Vol. 1*, Oxford: Oxford University Press.

Helm, B. (2001), *Emotional Reason*, Cambridge: Cambridge University Press.

Hills, A. (2010), 'Moral Epistemology', in Brady (ed.).

Hookway, C. (2000), 'Epistemic Norms and Theoretical Deliberation', in Dancy (ed.).

Hookway, C. (2003), 'Affective States and Epistemic Immediacy', *Metaphilosophy* 34 (1–2): 78–96.

Hookway, C. (2006), 'Reasons for Belief, Reasoning, Virtues', *Philosophical Studies* 130(1): 47–70.

Hopkins, R. (2011), 'How to be a Pessimist about Aesthetic Testimony', *Journal of Philosophy* 108(3): 138–57.

Huemer, M. (2001), *Skepticism and the Veil of Perception*, Lanham, MD: Rowman & Littlefield.

Isen, A. M. (2000), 'Positive affect and decision making', in Lewis and Haviland-Jones (eds).

Isen, A. M. and Daubman, K. A. (1984), 'The influence of affect on categorization', *Journal of Personality and Social Psychology* 47(6): 1206–17.

James, W. (1884), 'What is an emotion', *Mind* 9: 188–205.

James, W. (1890), *The Principles of Psychology* (1890/1983), Cambridge, MA: Harvard University Press.

Johnson, A. and Proctor, R. (2004), *Attention: Theory and Practice*, London: Sage.

Johnston, M. (2001), 'The Authority of Affect', *Philosophy and Phenomenological Research* 63(1): 181–214.

Jones, K. (2003), 'Emotion, Weakness of Will, and the Normative Conception of Agency', in Hatzimoysis (ed.).

Kelly, T. (2005), 'The Epistemic Significance of Disagreement', in Hawthorne and Gendler Szabo (eds).

Kenny, A. (1963), *Action, Emotion and the Will*, London: Routledge.

Kimchi, R. and Palmer, S. E. (1982), 'Form and texture in hierarchically constructed patterns', *Journal of Experimental Psychology: Human Perception and Performance* 8(4): 521–35.

Knuuttila, S. (2004), *Emotions in Ancient and Medieval Philosophy*, Oxford: Clarendon Press.

Kvanvig, J. (2003), *The Value of Knowledge and the Pursuit of Understanding*, Cambridge: Cambridge University Press.

Lacewing, M. (2005), 'Emotional Self-Awareness and Ethical Deliberation', *Ratio* 18(1): 65–81.

Lange, K. (1888), *Ueber Gemuthsbewegungen*, Leipzig: Theodor Thomas.

Lazarus, R. (1994), 'Appraisal: The Long and the Short of it', in Ekman and Davidson (eds).

LeDoux, J. (1996), *The Emotional Brain*, New York: Simon & Schuster.

Leiter, B. (ed.) (2004), *The Future for Philosophy*, Oxford: Clarendon Press.

Lewis, M. and Haviland, J. (eds) (2000), *Handbook of Emotions*, 2nd edition, New York: Guildford.

Lyons, W. (1980), *Emotion*, Cambridge: Cambridge University Press.

Macpherson, F. (ed.) (2011), *The Senses*, Oxford: Oxford University Press.

Malebranche, N. (1674/1980), *The Search After Truth*, Columbus, OH: Ohio University Press.

Marks, J. (1982), 'A Theory of Emotions', *Philosophical Studies* 42(2): 227–42.

Martin, M. G. F. (2002), 'The Transparency of Experience', *Mind and Language* 17(4): 376–425.

Matthews, G. and Wells, A. (1994), *Attention and Emotion: A Clinical Perspective*, Hove: Lawrence Earlbaum Associates.

Matthews, G. and Wells, A. (1999), 'The cognitive science of attention and emotion', in Dalgleish and Power (eds).

McBrayer, J. (2009), 'A Limited Defense of Moral Perception', *Philosophical Studies* 149(3): 305–20.

McDowell, J. (1979), 'Virtue and Reason', *The Monist* 62(3): 331–50.

McDowell, J. (1982), 'Criteria, Defeasibility and Knowledge', in Dancy (ed.).

McDowell, J. (1994), *Mind and World*, Cambridge, MA: Harvard University Press.

McDowell, J. (1998a), 'Values and Secondary Qualities', in *Mind, Value, and Reality*, Cambridge, MA: Harvard University Press.

McDowell, J. (1998b), 'Projection and Truth in Ethics', in *Mind, Value, and Reality*, Cambridge, MA: Harvard University Press.

Merleau-Ponty, M. (1945/2008), *Phenomenology of Perception*, trans. Smith, C., London: Routledge.

Mikulincer, M., Kedem, P., and Paz, D. (1990a), 'The impact of trait anxiety and situational stress on the categorization of natural objects', *Anxiety Research* 2(2): 85–101.

Mikulincer, M., Kedem, P., and Paz, D. (1990b), 'Anxiety and categorization. Part 1: The structure and boundaries of mental categories; Part 2: Hierarchical levels of mental categories', *Personality and Individual Differences* 8: 805–21.

Mole, C. (2010), *Attention is Cognitive Unison*, Oxford: Oxford University Press.

Mole, C., Smithies, D., and Wu, W. (eds) (2011), *Attention: Philosophical and Psychological Essays*, Oxford: Oxford University Press.

Morton, A. (2010), 'Epistemic Emotions', in Goldie (ed.).

Niedenthal, P. and Kitayama, S. (ed.) (1994), *The Heart's Eye: Emotional Influences in Perception and Attention*, London: Academic Press.

Nussbaum, M. (1994), *The Therapy of Desire: Theory and Practice in Hellenistic Ethics*, Princeton, NJ: Princeton University Press.

Nussbaum, M. (2001), *Upheavals of Thought*, Cambridge: Cambridge University Press.

Oddie, G. (2005), *Value, Reality, and Desire*, Oxford: Oxford University Press.

O'Hear, A. (ed.) (forthcoming), *Epistemology*, Cambridge: Cambridge University Press.

Öhman, A. (2000), 'Fear and Anxiety: Evolutionary, Cognitive, and Clinical Perspectives', in Lewis and Haviland (eds).

Öhman, A., Flykt, A., and Esteves, F. (2001), 'Emotion drives attention: Detecting the snake in the grass', *Journal of Experimental Psychology* 130(3): 466–78.

Pashler, H. (1998), *The Psychology of Attention*, Cambridge, MA: MIT Press.

Pillsbury, W. B. (1908/1973), *Attention*, New York: Arno Press.

Posner, M. I. (1980), 'Orienting of Attention', *Quarterly Journal of Experimental Psychology* 32(1): 3–25.

Posner, M. I. (1995), 'Attention in cognitive science: An overview', in Gazzaniga (ed.).

Prinz, J. (2004a), *Gut Reactions*, New York: Oxford University Press.

Prinz, J. (2004b), 'Embodied Emotions', in Solomon (ed.).

Pritchard, D. (2006), *What is This Thing Called Knowledge?*, Oxford: Routledge.

Pritchard, D. (forthcoming), 'Knowledge, Understanding and Epistemic Value', in O'Hear (ed.).

Pryor, J. (2000), 'The Skeptic and the Dogmatist', *Noûs* 34: 517–49.

Rawls, J. (1971), *A Theory of Justice*, Cambridge, MA: Harvard University Press.

Reid, T. (1969), *Essays on the Active Powers of the Human Mind*, Brody (ed.), Cambridge, MA: MIT Press.

Roberts, R. (2003), *Emotions: An Essay in Aid of Moral Psychology*, Cambridge: Cambridge University Press.

Robinson, J. (1995), 'Startle', *Journal of Philosophy* 92(2): 53–74.

Rose, R. (1996), *Twelve Angry Men*, London: Methuen Drama.

Salmela, M. (2011), 'Can emotion be modelled on perception?', *Dialectica* 65(1): 1–29.

Scherer, K. (1994), 'Emotions are Functional, Most of the Time', in Ekman and Davidson (eds).

Scherer, K. (1994), 'The Function of Emotions', in Ekman and Davidson (eds).

Schroeder, M. (MS), 'What makes reasons sufficient?'.

Shafer-Landau, R. (ed.) (2006), *Oxford Studies in Metaethics, Vol. 1*, Oxford: Oxford University Press.

Slovic, P. (2007), ' "If I Look at the Mass I Will Never Act". Psychic Numbing and Genocide', *Judgment and Decision Making* 2(2): 79–95.

Snowdon, P. F. (1980), 'Perception, Vision and Causation', *Proceedings of the Aristotelian Society* 81: 175–92.

Solomon, R. (1977), *The Passions*, New York: Anchor.

Solomon, R. (1977), 'The Rationality of the Emotions', *Southwestern Journal of Philosophy* 8(2): 105–14.

Solomon, R. (ed.) (2004), *Thinking about Feeling*, Oxford: Oxford University Press.

Sorabji, R. (2002), *Emotion and Peace of Mind: From Stoic Agitation to Christian Temptation*, Oxford: Oxford University Press.

Stanovich, K. (2004), *The Robot's Rebellion*, Chicago: University of Chicago Press.

Stocker, M. (2010), 'Intellectual and Other Nonstandard Emotions', in Goldie (ed.).

Stocker, M. and Hegeman, E. (1996), *Valuing Emotions*, Cambridge: Cambridge University Press.

Strevens, M. (2008), *Depth: An Account of Scientific Explanation*, Cambridge, MA: Harvard University Press.

Styles, E. A. (1997), *The Psychology of Attention*, New York: Psychology Press.

Tappolet, C. (2000), *Emotions et Valeurs*, Paris: Presses universitaires de France.

Tappolet, C. (forthcoming), 'The Irrationality of Emotions', in Weinstock (ed.).

Titchener, E. B. (1908/1973), *Psychology of Feeling and Attention*, New York: MacMillan/New York: Arno Press.

Vuilleumier, P., Armony, J., and Dolan, R. J. (2003), 'Reciprocal Links between Emotion and Attention', in Frackowiak et al. (eds).

Wedgwood, R. (2001), 'Sensing Values?', *Philosophy and Phenomenological Research* 63: 215–24.

Weinstock, D. (ed.) (forthcoming), *Philosophical Perspectives on Irrationality*, Oxford: Oxford University Press.

Wells A. and Matthews G. (1994), *Attention and Emotion: A Clinical Perspective*, Hillsdale, NJ: Erlbaum.

White, A. R. (1964), *Attention*, Oxford: Basil Blackwell Publishers.

Whiting, D. (2012), 'Are emotions perceptual experiences of value?', *Ratio* 25(1): 93–107.

Wiggins, D. (1987), 'A Sensible Subjectivism?' *Needs, Values, Truth*, Oxford: Blackwell Publishers.

Wilson, R. and Keil, F. (eds) (1999), *The MIT Encyclopedia of Cognitive Sciences*, Cambridge, MA: MIT Press.

Wundt, W. (1907), *Lectures on Human and Animal Psychology*, trans. Creighton, J. B. and Titchener, E. B., New York: Macmillan.

Zagzebski, L. (1996), *Virtues of the Mind*, Cambridge: Cambridge University Press.

Zagzebski, L. (2004), *Divine Motivation Theory*, Cambridge: Cambridge University Press.

Index